Communications
in Computer and Information Science   1571

More information about this series at https://link.springer.com/bookseries/7899

Ulf Brefeld · Jesse Davis · Jan Van Haaren ·
Albrecht Zimmermann (Eds.)

Machine Learning and Data Mining for Sports Analytics

8th International Workshop, MLSA 2021
Virtual Event, September 13, 2021
Revised Selected Papers

 Springer

Editors
Ulf Brefeld
Leuphana University of Lüneburg
Lüneburg, Germany

Jesse Davis ⓘ
Katholieke Universiteit Leuven
Leuven, Belgium

Jan Van Haaren
Katholieke Universiteit Leuven
Leuven, Belgium

Albrecht Zimmermann ⓘ
University of Caen Normandie
Caen, France

ISSN 1865-0929   ISSN 1865-0937 (electronic)
Communications in Computer and Information Science
ISBN 978-3-031-02043-8   ISBN 978-3-031-02044-5 (eBook)
https://doi.org/10.1007/978-3-031-02044-5

This Springer imprint is published by the registered company Springer Nature Switzerland AG
The registered company address is: Gewerbestrasse 11, 6330 Cham, Switzerland

Preface

The Machine Learning and Data Mining for Sports Analytics (MLSA) workshop aims to bring together a diverse set of researchers working on sports analytics in a broad sense. In particular, it hopes to attract interest from researchers working on sports from outside of machine learning and data mining. The 8th edition of the workshop was co-located with the European Conference on Machine Learning and Principles and Practice of Knowledge Discovery, and held virtually on September 13, 2021.

Sports analytics has been a steadily growing and rapidly evolving area over the last decade, both in US professional sports leagues and in European soccer leagues. The recent implementation of strict financial fair-play regulations in European soccer will definitely increase the importance of sports analytics in the coming years. In addition, there is the popularity of sports betting. The developed techniques are being used for decision support in all aspects of professional sports including, but not limited to, the following:

- Match strategy, tactics, and analysis
- Player acquisition, player valuation, and team spending
- Training regimens and focus
- Injury prediction and prevention
- Performance management and prediction
- Match outcome and league table prediction
- Tournament design and scheduling
- Betting odds calculation

The interest in the topic has grown so much that there is now an annual conference on sports analytics at the MIT Sloan School of Management, which has been attended by representatives from over 70 professional sports teams in eminent leagues such as Major League Baseball, the National Basketball Association, the National Football League, the National Hockey League, Major League Soccer, the English Premier League, and the German Bundesliga. Furthermore, sports data providers such as Statsbomb, Stats Perform, and Wyscout have started making performance data publicly available to stimulate researchers who have the skills and vision to make a difference in the sports analytics community. Moreover, the National Football League has been sponsoring a Big Data Bowl where they release data and a concrete question to try to engage the analytics community.

There has also been growing interest in the machine learning and data mining community about this topic, and the 2021 edition of MLSA built on the success of prior editions at ECML PKDD 2013 and ECML PKDD 2015 to ECML PKDD 2020.

In 2021, the workshop received 29 submissions of which 17 were selected after a single-blind reviewing process involving at least three Program Committee members per paper. One of the accepted papers was withdrawn from publication in the proceedings. The 2021 program was arguably an exception compared to past editions since non-soccer submissions—about cricket, baseball, field hockey, handball, basketball, swimming, cycling, and strength exercises—outnumbered soccer ones for a change. Topics included tactical analysis, outcome predictions, data acquisition, performance optimization, and player evaluation. The workshop also included a paper on a non-physical sport, about card coalitions in the venerable Magic: The Gathering.

The workshop featured an invited presentation by Oliver Schulte from Simon Fraser University on "Valuing Actions and Assessing Players: Reinforcement Learning for Sports Analytics".

Further information about the workshop can be found on the workshop's website at https://dtai.cs.kuleuven.be/events/MLSA21/.

October 2021

Ulf Brefeld
Jesse Davis
Jan Van Haaren
Albrecht Zimmermann

Organization

Workshop Co-chairs

Ulf Brefeld	Leuphana University, Germany
Jesse Davis	KU Leuven, Belgium
Jan Van Haaren	SciSports, The Netherlands
Albrecht Zimmermann	Université de Caen Normandie, France

Program Committee

Michael Alcorn	Auburn University, USA
Gennady Andrienko	Fraunhofer IAIS, Germany
Adrià Arbués-Sangüesa	Universitat Pompeu Fabra, Spain
Harish S. Bhat	University of California, USA
Lotte Bransen	SciSports, The Netherlands
Paolo Cintia	University of Pisa, Italy
Arie-Willem de Leeuw	Universiteit Leiden, The Netherlands
Tom Decroos	Facebook, USA
Kurt Driessens	Maastricht University, The Netherlands
Martin Eastwood	pena.lt/y, UK
Clément Gautrais	KU Leuven, Belgium
Kilian Hendrickx	KU Leuven/Siemens Digital Industries Software, Belgium
Leonid Kholkine	University of Antwerp, Belgium
Arno Knobbe	Universiteit Leiden, The Netherlands
Patrick Lambrix	Linköping University, Sweden
Jan Lasek	Systems Research Institute, Poland
Laurentius Meerhoff	Leiden Institute of Advanced Computer Science, The Netherlands
Wannes Meert	KU Leuven, Belgium
Shayegan Omidshafiei	DeepMind, UK
Luca Pappalardo	University of Pisa, Italy
Konstantinos Pelechrinis	University of Pittsburgh, USA
François Rioult	Université de Caen Normandie, France
Pieter Robberechts	KU Leuven, Belgium
Karl Tuyls	University of Liverpool, UK
Maaike Van Roy	KU Leuven, Belgium

Contents

Football

6MapNet: Representing Soccer Players from Tracking Data by a Triplet Network

Hyunsung Kim[1]([✉])([iD]), Jihun Kim[2], Dongwook Chung[1], Jonghyun Lee[1],
Jinsung Yoon[1], and Sang-Ki Ko[1,3]

[1] Fitogether Inc., Seoul, South Korea
hyunsung.kim@fitogether.com
[2] Seoul National University, Seoul, South Korea
[3] Kangwon National University, Chuncheon, South Korea

Abstract. Although the values of individual soccer players have become astronomical, subjective judgments still play a big part in the player analysis. Recently, there have been new attempts to quantitatively grasp players' styles using video-based event stream data. However, they have some limitations in scalability due to high annotation costs and sparsity of event stream data. In this paper, we build a triplet network named 6MapNet that can effectively capture the movement styles of players using in-game GPS data. Without any annotation of soccer-specific actions, we use players' locations and velocities to generate two types of heatmaps. Our subnetworks then map these heatmap pairs into feature vectors whose similarity corresponds to the actual similarity of playing styles. The experimental results show that players can be accurately identified with only a small number of matches by our method.

Keywords: Sports Analytics · Spatiotemporal Tracking Data · Playing Style Representation · Siamese Neural Network · Triplet Loss

1 Introduction

The values of individual players have become astronomical with the growth of the soccer industry. Nevertheless, the absence of objective criteria for understanding players causes a considerable gap between player price and utility. As a result, cheaply scouted players often hit the jackpot, while players signed with a huge transfer fee sometimes fail. Thus, scouts have spent a lot of time and effort watching games of unknown players to find hidden gems without wasting money.

Recently, there have been attempts to quantitatively grasp players' styles using video-based event stream data [5,6,9], but they have some limitations due to the properties of the data. First, since the event data were too sparse to figure out a player's style from a few matches, they used the seasonal aggregations of individual players. This causes difficulty meeting the demand of real-world scouts who do not have an unknown player's full-season data. Moreover, they did not consider that a player could take multiple tactical positions or roles during

U. Brefeld et al. (Eds.): MLSA 2021, CCIS 1571, pp. 3–14, 2022.
https://doi.org/10.1007/978-3-031-02044-5_1

a season, which significantly affects their locational tendency. Above all, the data collection requires much manual work by human annotators. Representing playing styles prove its worth when applied to youth or lower leagues for scouting, while these annotation costs make these studies hard to be widespread.

This paper proposes a triplet network named 6MapNet to find a robust representation of playing styles from in-game GPS data. As the playing style is a subjective concept, there is no label like "These players have similar playing styles." enabling supervised learning. Instead, we construct a semi-supervised learning framework with the label "These inputs have similar playing styles because they are the same player's data taking the same tactical role." Specifically, we use players' locations and velocities to compute their location and direction heatmaps, respectively. Roles are represented and assigned to players per "phase" in matches using the method proposed by Bialkowski et al. [1]. We label the pair of a player's phase data as "similar" only if the player has taken the same role in both phases. Inspired by FaceNet [14], we then build a siamese architecture with triplet loss to make the similarity between the feature vectors implies that between the players' actual playing styles.

We evaluate our method by performing a player identification task proposed by Decroos et al. [5], but with a newly defined likelihood-based similarity named ATL-sim. The experimental results show that our method accurately identifies the anonymized players with only a few matches.

The main contributions of our paper are as follows.

(a) Instead of manually annotated event stream data, automatically collected locations and velocity vectors are used to capture playing style.
(b) Our proposed method is data-efficient in that it can identify a player with only a few matches without using a seasonal aggregation of data.
(c) We take players' roles into account, which is more reasonable in that a player's movements highly depend on the role given for the match.

2   Related Works

2.1   Playing Style Representation in Soccer

With the acquisition of large-scale sports data, several studies have tried to quantitatively characterize [5,6,9,13] or evaluate [3,7,8,11,12] soccer players using those data. Especially, some of them used locations (and directions) of actions to represent each player as a vector. Gyarmati et al. [9] clustered the on-the-ball actions by their start and end locations and made a feature vector for each player by simply counting the events per cluster. Decroos et al. [5] found the principal components of each action type by applying non-negative matrix factorization (NMF) to the action heatmaps. Players' feature vectors were then assembled by concatenating the weights multiplied on the components to reconstruct the original heatmaps. Decroos et al. [6] also proposed a mixture model that fits the distribution of each action type as a combination of finite Von Mises distributions by the locations and directions of actions. Then, they represented each action as the vector of responsibilities for those component distributions.

2.2   Siamese Neural Networks and Triplet Loss

The siamese network is a neural network with multiple subnetworks sharing weights. It learns a representation from pairs of images by decreasing the distance between like pairs and increasing that between unlike ones. It was first proposed by Bromley et al. [2] and embodied by Chopra et al. [4]. Koch et al. [10] showed the power of the siamese network in one-shot image recognition.

Schroff et al. [14] introduced FaceNet, an extended version of the siamese network. They composed triplets from the dataset with two images of the same label and one of another label, respectively. The triplet loss was then minimized by training the triplet network so that the distance between the former pair (named "positive pair") became closer than another (named "negative pair").

In this study, we employ the structure of FaceNet to represent playing styles since it has less strict loss than the original siamese network. That is, the triplet loss remains small as long as the positive pair is closer than the negative pair. As different players (i.e., with distinct labels) can actually have similar playing styles, we think the triplet loss is suitable for our problem.

3   Learning Approach

In this section, we illustrate the process of playing style representation. First, we describe the data preparation step in Sect. 3.1 and the labeling step using the role representation in Sect. 3.2. The location and direction heatmaps are generated in Sect. 3.3 and then augmented in Sect. 3.4 by simple pixel-wise additions. In Sect. 3.5, we introduce a triplet network named 6MapNet that makes the embeddings closer if they are of the same player taking the same role.

3.1   Data Preparation

During soccer matches, wearable GPS devices (OhCoach Cell B developed by Fitogether) are attached to the players' upper backs and track their movements. The devices have successfully recorded the latitudes, longitudes, and speeds 10 Hz from 750 matches of 2019 and 2020 K League 1 and 2, two seasons of the South Korean professional soccer league divisions. (Note that both teams used the devices for some matches, and only one team did for other matches. As such, to avoid confusion, we count twice a match in which both teams are measured.)

After that, we transform the raw locations into the x and y coordinates relative to the pitch. The data from one of the two halves are rotated to maintain the attacking direction. Also, we calculate the 2-dimensional velocities by differentiating the x and y coordinates.

Meanwhile, we divide each match into several *phases* in each of which the players' roles are assumed to be consistent. Considering that most formation changes occur when a new session starts or player composition changes, we split each match by the half time, player substitution, and dismissal times. (Phases with a length of 10 min or less are absorbed into adjacent phases to ensure the minimum duration.) This breaks the whole dataset down into each player's phase-by-phase data, which we call *player-phase entities.*

As a result, 635 matches are divided into 1,989 phases having total of 17,953 player-phase entities generated from 436 players. Each player-phase entity has a time series of locations (s_x, s_y) in meters and velocities (v_x, v_y) in m/s.

3.2   Automated Data Labeling Based on Role Representation

In this section, labels for the triplet network are automatically generated from phase-by-phase role learning and clustering. For the former, we use the role representation proposed by Bialkowski et al. [1]. We define the player-phase entity's role as the most frequent role among the roles assigned frame-by-frame. (Please refer to [1] for more details. Note that Bialkowski et al. ran their algorithm for every *half* of a match, while we do for every *phase.*)

The outcome of [1] is a 2D distribution representing a role per player-phase entity. (Note that distributions of the same role vary slightly by phase.) Since our purpose here is to classify the phase data of each player according to the roles, we perform the player-wise clustering on the mean locations of assigned roles to determine which roles to consider as the same or different. To be specific, we apply K-means clustering per player with between two to four clusters maximizing the silhouette score based on the domain knowledge that a player hardly plays more than four positions. If all the scores are less than 0.6, a single cluster is assigned to the player's entire data. See Fig. 1 as an example.

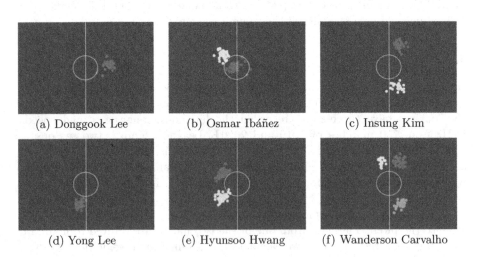

(a) Donggook Lee   (b) Osmar Ibáñez   (c) Insung Kim

(d) Yong Lee   (e) Hyunsoo Hwang   (f) Wanderson Carvalho

Fig. 1. Mean locations of individual players' roles colored per cluster. Even the same player's data get distinct labels if their colors differ from each other. (Color figure online)

We then label player-phase entities as pairs of player IDs and role clusters. Namely, if the roles of the same player's two phases belong to a single cluster, they are labeled as the same identity. On the other hand, if those of the same player belong to different clusters, they are labeled as different identities. We call each of these role-based identities a *player-role entity*.

3.3   Generating Location and Direction Heatmaps

For a labeled time series, two heatmaps are generated by making grids of size 35×50 on the fixed domains and counting data points in each grid cell. Like in Decroos et al. [5], we compute each player-phase entity's location heatmap by making a grid on the soccer pitch. To take into account the running direction, which is not covered by location heatmaps but is still a significant feature, we also compute heatmaps for velocity vectors whose speed is higher than a threshold speed. Like location heatmaps, we overlay a grid on the rectangle

$$\{(v_x, v_y)| -12\,\text{m/s} \le v_x \le 12\,\text{m/s}, -8\,\text{m/s} \le v_y \le 8\,\text{m/s}\},$$

and count the endpoints of the velocity vectors in each grid cell.

The boundary values of the x-axis and y-axis of the direction heatmap (i.e., $\pm 12\,\text{m/s}$ and $\pm 8\,\text{m/s}$, respectively) are determined so that the shape of each grid cell is close to a square. We empirically set the threshold speed as 4 m/s. For lower speed thresholds, data points are concentrated near the origin without any tendency. Also, for higher speed thresholds, the number of data points is not enough for robust analysis. Figure 2 shows an example of a pair of heatmaps.

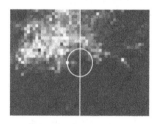 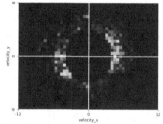

(a) A location heatmap by making a grid on the soccer pitch and counting the locations in each cell.

(b) A direction heatmap by making a grid and counting the endpoints of velocity vectors in each cell.

Fig. 2. The location and direction heatmaps of a player-phase entity.

Before the data augmentation, we split the dataset into training, validation, and test sets. For the fair evaluation in Sect. 4, the test dataset is constructed by sampling ten heatmap pairs (i.e., pair of location and direction heatmaps) for each of the 308 player-role entities with more than 20 phases in the dataset. Similarly, the validation set is constructed by sampling five phases for each of the 332 entities having more than 15 phases in the remaining data.

3.4   Data Augmentation by Accumulating Heatmaps

Before to put heatmaps in 6MapNet, we perform the augmentation to make individual heatmaps have enough durations and to enrich the input data. One of the good properties of players' heatmaps is their "additivity". Namely, we can compute the accumulated heatmaps of the multiple time intervals by simple pixel-wise additions. Formally speaking, let $s_p : \mathcal{T} \to \mathbb{R}^2$ and $v_p : \mathcal{T} \to \mathbb{R}^2$ be the location and velocity of a player p, respectively defined on the time domain $\mathcal{T}$. Also, let $\mathbf{h} : \mathcal{P}\left(\mathbb{R}^2\right) \to \mathbb{Z}_*^{35 \times 50}$ be the heatmap calculated for a set of 2D vectors. Then for $T = \bigcup_{i=1}^m T_i$ with disjoint time-intervals $T_1, \ldots, T_m \subset \mathcal{T}$,

$$\mathbf{h}(s_p(T)) = \sum_{i=1}^m \mathbf{h}(s_p(T_i)), \quad \mathbf{h}(v_p(T)) = \sum_{i=1}^m \mathbf{h}(v_p(T_i)) \qquad (1)$$

Using this additivity, we augment the dataset by accumulating several heatmaps of the same player-role entities. In other words, we "crop" the entire time domain $\mathcal{T}$ of each player-role entity and generate heatmap pairs for the crop.

The augmentation is performed separately for the training, validation, and test datasets so that data in different sets are not mixed. Three heatmaps are sampled from the set of each player-role entity's heatmaps and added to be a single augmented heatmap. We repeat sampling without duplicates to make a large number of augmented heatmaps. Figure 3 illustrates an heatmap augmentation.

Here we choose three as the number of heatmaps from the reasoning below. Too short durations of individual augmented heatmaps are not enough to understand a player's movement tendency. On the other hand, too many heatmaps for one augmentation lead to a high entry barrier for practical use. (i.e., one has to play more matches to have an augmented heatmap.) What we take note of is that three phases of data are collected at once in most cases, since the average duration of a phase is less than 30 min. That is, one can usually make a player's

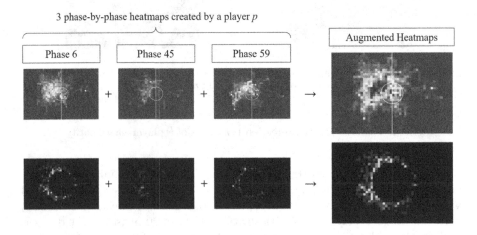

Fig. 3. An example of heatmap augmentation.

3-combination augmented heatmap by measuring a single full-time match. Hence, we deem the 3-combination as optimal since it both ensures enough durations for analysis and hardly requires more matches comparing to the option of no augmentation.

The way of sampling differs between training and validation/test data. For each of the validation and test datasets, three heatmaps are merged through the exhaustive combination. As such, $\binom{5}{3} = 10$ and $\binom{10}{3} = 120$ accumulated heatmap pairs are generated per player-role entity for the validation and test dataset, respectively. On the other hand, since the number of heatmap pairs for each player-role entity varies in the training dataset, the exhaustive combination deepens the class imbalance. To prevent this, we randomly sample 3-combinations by $4 \cdot n_p$ times for each player-role entity p with n_p heatmap pairs and remove the duplicates.

3.5 Building the Sixfold Heatmap Network

In this section, we employ the idea of FaceNet [14] and build a triplet network called *sixfold heatmap network* (6MapNet) which embeds heatmap pairs of similar players to feature vectors close to each other. FaceNet takes a triplet composed of $\mathbf{x}^a$ (anchor), $\mathbf{x}^p$ (positive), and $\mathbf{x}^n$ (negative) as an input, where $\mathbf{x}^a$ and $\mathbf{x}^p$ are images of the same identity and $\mathbf{x}^n$ is that of another. It learns to find an embedding f that satisfies

$$\|f(\mathbf{x}_i^a) - f(\mathbf{x}_i^p)\|_2^2 + \alpha \le \|f(\mathbf{x}_i^a) - f(\mathbf{x}_i^n)\|_2^2 \tag{2}$$

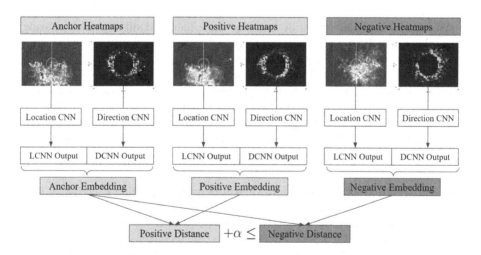

Fig. 4. 6MapNet overview: The anchor and positive heatmap pairs are of the same player-role entity, while the negative is of another entity. The best performance is obtained when α is set to 0.1.

Table 1. The locational and directional branch CNNs of 6MapNet have the same structure as in this table. It includes the batch normalization after Conv and FC layers and the 25% dropout after MaxPool layers and Conv4b.

Layer	Input	Padding	Kernel	Activation	Output
Conv1a	$35 \times 50 \times 1$	1×0	$2 \times 3 \times 4, 1$	ReLU	$36 \times 48 \times 4$
Conv1b	$36 \times 48 \times 4$	1×1	$3 \times 3 \times 4, 1$	ReLU	$36 \times 48 \times 4$
MaxPool1	$36 \times 48 \times 4$	–	$2 \times 2, 2$	–	$18 \times 24 \times 4$
Conv2a	$18 \times 24 \times 4$	1×1	$3 \times 3 \times 16, 1$	ReLU	$18 \times 24 \times 16$
Conv2b	$18 \times 24 \times 16$	1×1	$3 \times 3 \times 16, 1$	ReLU	$18 \times 24 \times 16$
MaxPool2	$18 \times 24 \times 16$	–	$2 \times 2, 2$	–	$9 \times 12 \times 16$
Conv3a	$9 \times 12 \times 16$	1×1	$2 \times 3 \times 32, 1$	ReLU	$10 \times 12 \times 32$
Conv3b	$10 \times 12 \times 32$	1×1	$3 \times 3 \times 32, 1$	ReLU	$10 \times 12 \times 32$
MaxPool3	$10 \times 12 \times 32$	–	$2 \times 2, 2$	–	$5 \times 6 \times 32$
Conv4a	$5 \times 6 \times 32$	1×1	$3 \times 3 \times 64, 1$	ReLU	$5 \times 6 \times 64$
Conv4b	$5 \times 6 \times 64$	1×1	$3 \times 3 \times 64, 1$	ReLU	$5 \times 6 \times 64$
FC1	1920	–	–	ReLU	128
FC2	128	–	–	–	10

by minimizing a triplet loss defined as

$$\mathcal{L} = \sum_i \left[\|f(\mathbf{x}_i^a) - f(\mathbf{x}_i^p)\|_2^2 - \|f(\mathbf{x}_i^a) - f(\mathbf{x}_i^n)\|_2^2 + \alpha \right]_+ \tag{3}$$

We apply this architecture by building three identical subnetworks (sharing weights) named 2MapNet, each of which has two branch convolutional neural networks (CNNs). Each subnetwork takes a heatmap pair $\mathbf{x}_i = (\mathbf{h}(s_i), \mathbf{h}(v_i))$ as an input, and each branch CNN (one for the location heatmap $\mathbf{h}(s_i)$ and the other for the direction heatmap $\mathbf{h}(v_i)$) embeds the corresponding heatmap into $\mathbb{R}^d$. After that, we concatenate the two d-dimensional outputs and normalize the result so that every embedding $f(\mathbf{x}_i) = f(\mathbf{h}(s_i), \mathbf{h}(v_i)) \in \mathbb{R}^{2d}$ has a unit norm. Consequently, the whole architecture of 6MapNet receives six heatmaps

$$(\mathbf{x}_i^a, \mathbf{x}_i^p, \mathbf{x}_i^n) = (\mathbf{h}(s_i^a), \mathbf{h}(v_i^a), \mathbf{h}(s_i^p), \mathbf{h}(v_i^p), \mathbf{h}(s_i^n), \mathbf{h}(v_i^n)),$$

and return a triplet of $2d$-dimensional feature vectors $(f(\mathbf{x}_i^a), f(\mathbf{x}_i^p), f(\mathbf{x}_i^n))$, taking Eq. 3 as a loss to minimize. (See Fig. 4 for the overview of the whole architecture, and Table 1 for the structure of a single branch CNN.)

As in FaceNet, the choice of triplets has a great influence on the performance. Thus, we decided to select a random positive and a hard negative for each anchor. Specifically, we select triplets as follows for every ten or fewer epochs:

(a) Sample five heatmap pairs for each identity to form a candidate set S.
(b) Use every heatmap pair in the dataset as an anchor $\mathbf{x}^a$ and combine it with the corresponding five positive candidates $\mathbf{x}^p \in S^a = \{\mathbf{x}^p \in S | y^p = y^a\}$ (i.e., $\mathbf{x}^p$ with the same label as $\mathbf{x}^a$) to make five positive pairs $(\mathbf{x}^a, \mathbf{x}^p)$.

(c) For each positive pair $(\mathbf{x}^a, \mathbf{x}^p)$, pick one hard negative $\mathbf{x}^n \in S - S^a$ that does not satisfy Eq. 2. If there is no such negative, randomly choose one of the ten negatives with the smallest distance from the anchor.

In particular, the rate of positive pairs with no hard negative in (c), i.e.,

$$\left|\{(\mathbf{x}^a, \mathbf{x}^p) \in P : \|f(\mathbf{x}_i^a) - f(\mathbf{x}_i^p)\|_2^2 + \alpha \le \|f(\mathbf{x}_i^a) - f(\mathbf{x}_i^n)\|_2^2 \ \forall \mathbf{x}^n \in S - S^a\}\right| / |P|$$

(where P is the set of all positive pairs selected in (b)) is used as validation accuracy during the training. If there is no improvement in the validation accuracy, our model finishes the whole learning procedure.

We expect that by making the embedding of the same identity (player-role entity) close together, embeddings of similar identities also become close. Because the first triplet selection at the beginning is entirely random, hard negatives can be either similar to their corresponding anchors in terms of playing style or dissimilar to them. For similar anchor-negative pairs, it is difficult to reduce the triplet loss because their similar input heatmaps remain similar after passing through the model. Thus, the model reduces the loss by alienating the dissimilar negatives from their anchors instead. In this way, similar identities remain relatively close, while dissimilar ones move away from each other.

The above inference is verified by the observation that in most cases, the model achieves the best performance just after training the first selected triplets. This implies that the second triplet selection gives a high proportion of hard negatives with similar playing styles to their anchors, making the loss reduction and performance improvement very difficult. Therefore, the resulting model trained only by several epochs with the first triplet selection is expected to return embeddings whose similarities reflect those between actual playing styles.

4   Experiments

Since no objective answer exists for the similarity between players, there is no de-facto standard for evaluating the performance of our method. Thus, we refer to the player identification task proposed by Decroos et al. [5] that checks how well the model identifies the anonymized players using the data from the other season. Based on the assumption that high similarities between the same identities imply those between identities having similar playing styles, we conclude that the high performance of the player identification task implies the success of our method.

To explain, we anonymize the training data defined in Sect. 3.3 and use the test data to de-anonymize them. Having exactly ten phases in the test dataset, each of 308 players has $\binom{10}{3} = 120$ feature vectors as the result of data augmentation in Sect. 3.4. To take advantage of this plurality, we define and use a likelihood-based similarity instead of L^p norms. We estimate a distribution of training feature vectors per anonymized player-role entity and calculate the log-likelihood that each test feature vector is generated from the distribution. Except for potential outliers, we use the average of m highest values as the similarity among 120 log-likelihoods per player-role entity.

Formally speaking, let $\mathcal{A}$ be the set of player-role entities belonging to both of the training and the test dataset, and $X_{\alpha}^{tr} = \{\mathbf{x}_i^{tr} \in X^{tr} : y_i^{tr} = \alpha\}$ be the set of the training heatmap pairs for $\alpha \in \mathcal{A}$. We estimate a Gaussian probability density $p_{\alpha} : \mathbb{R}^{2d} \to \mathbb{R}_+$ using X_{α}^{tr} and calculate the log-likelihoods

$$l(\alpha; \mathbf{x}^{te}) = \log p_{\alpha}(f(\mathbf{x}^{te}))$$

of test heatmap pairs $\mathbf{x}^{te} \in X_{\beta}^{te}$ of a labeled player-role entity $\beta \in \mathcal{A}$. Then, for the top-m log-likelihoods $l(\alpha; \mathbf{x}_{\beta(1)}^{te}), \ldots, l(\alpha; \mathbf{x}_{\beta(M)}^{te})$, we define the *average top-m log-likelihood similarity* (ATL-sim) of β to α by

$$\text{sim}(\alpha, \beta; m) = \frac{1}{m} \sum_{i=1}^{m} l(\alpha; \mathbf{x}_{\beta(i)}^{te}) = \frac{1}{m} \sum_{i=1}^{m} \log p_{\alpha}(f(\mathbf{x}_{\beta(i)}^{te})). \tag{4}$$

Based on this ATL-sim, we evaluated our method by computing the top-k accuracies and mean reciprocal rank (MRR) for varying m. That is, for each anonymized entity $\alpha^{tr} \in \mathcal{A}$, we check whether our method correctly found k candidates $\beta_1^{te}, \ldots, \beta_k^{te}$ among the test data such that $\alpha^{tr} \in \{\beta_1^{te}, \ldots, \beta_k^{te}\}$.

As an ablation study, we compared the results based on different similarity measures and amounts of identifying (test) data. The following is the description of the conditions, where the label 'p_n-sim' indicates the result based on sim using n phases per entity as the identifying data.

- **p_{10}-L^1**: L^1 distance between feature vectors from accumulated heatmaps.
- **p_{10}-L^2**: L^2 distance between feature vectors from accumulated heatmaps.
- **p_{10}-AL (p_{10}-ATL$_{100}$)**: average log-likelihood without filtering top-m.
- **p_{10}-ATL$_{75}$**: average top-75% log-likelihood (top-90 among $\binom{10}{3} = 120$).
- **p_{10}-ATL$_{50}$**: average top-50% log-likelihood (top-60 among $\binom{10}{3} = 120$).
- **p_6-ATL$_{25}$**: average top-25% log-likelihood (top-5 among $\binom{6}{3} = 20$).
- **p_8-ATL$_{25}$**: average top-25% log-likelihood (top-14 among $\binom{8}{3} = 56$).
- **p_{10}-ATL$_{25}$**: average top-25% log-likelihood (top-30 among $\binom{10}{3} = 120$).
- **p_{10}-ML**: maximum log-likelihood (top-1 among $\binom{10}{3} = 120$).

Table 2 shows the results for the player identification task. The best performance is obtained when average top-25% log-likelihood is used, showing that 46.1% of the players are correctly identified among 308 players using only ten phases of data (about 289 min in total). For most cases (92.5%), our model correctly suggests ten candidates for identifying the anonymized player.

We also obtained several meaningful observations from the table: (a) p_{10}-ATLs outperform p_{10}-L^ps, meaning that log-likelihoods are more suitable similarity measure for models that generate a plurality of feature vectors per player. (b) The accuracy of p_n-ATL improves as n (the number of phases per player-role entity) increases, showing the potential of even better performance as more data is collected. (c) ATL-sim shows the highest performance when m is near 25% of the total number of phases per player-role entity. The superiority of

Table 2. Top-k accuracies and MRRs of the player identification tasks.

Condition	Top-1	Top-3	Top-5	Top-10	MRR
p_{10}-L^1	24.4%	44.5%	58.4%	79.2%	0.402
p_{10}-L^2	24.7%	45.1%	59.7%	80.2%	0.404
p_{10}-AL	35.1%	59.7%	71.4%	84.1%	0.509
p_{10}-ATL$_{75}$	42.5%	66.2%	77.6%	89.3%	0.574
p_{10}-ATL$_{50}$	45.5%	**70.5%**	80.8%	90.6%	0.602
p_6-ATL$_{25}$	34.1%	60.1%	73.7%	84.7%	0.508
p_8-ATL$_{25}$	41.2%	67.2%	77.9%	89.9%	0.574
p_{10}-ATL$_{25}$	**46.1%**	69.8%	**81.8%**	**92.5%**	**0.613**
p_{10}-ML	37.0%	65.9%	77.3%	91.2%	0.547

p_n-ATL$_{25}$ than p_n-AL indicates that removing potential outliers enhances the intra-identity consistency of the remaining feature vectors.

We believe our approach to similar player retrieval is more practical in the scouting industry. For example, scouts often want to find cheaper players to replace the core players leaving the teams. Then, player representation models can extract a target list by retrieving similar players to a benchmark player. However, previous approaches need manual annotations to generate event stream data from a whole season to find robust feature vectors representing playing styles. On the other hand, our method does not need any manual work except for putting a device on each player for a few matches to return reliable outputs. This automaticity and data-efficiency can make our method widely used in real-world soccer, including youth or lower divisions.

5   Conclusion and Future Works

To our knowledge, this is the first study to characterize soccer players' playing styles using tracking data instead of event stream data. Without using any ball-related information, we use each player's locations and velocities to generate two types of heatmaps. We then build a triplet network named 6MapNet that embeds these heatmap pairs to latent vectors whose similarity reflects the actual similarity of playing styles. The experimental results show that 6MapNet with our newly defined similarity measure ATL-sim can accurately identify anonymized players using data from only a few matches.

In the future, we expect that the use of "context" such as sequential information or the movements of teammates and opponents would contribute to the quality of our work. Also, it would justify the choice of model structure to compare ours with some baseline approaches such as principal component analysis or autoencoders. In addition, some practical use cases with real-world examples should be proposed to show the significance of our study. Most of all, we aim to improve the explainability of our model, enabling our work to be understood and practically used by domain participants.

References

1. Bialkowski, A., Lucey, P., Carr, P., Yue, Y., Sridharan, S., Matthews, I.: Large-scale analysis of soccer matches using spatiotemporal tracking data. In: IEEE International Conference on Data Mining (2014)
2. Bromley, J., Guyon, I., LeCun, Y., Sachkinger, E., Shah, R.: Siamese verification using a Siamese time delay neural network. Int. J. Pattern Recognit. Artif. Intell. **7**, 37–744 (1993)
3. Brooks, J., Kerr, M., Guttag, J.: Developing a data-driven player ranking in soccer using predictive model weights. In: ACM SIGKDD International Conference on Knowledge Discovery and Data Mining, pp. 49–55, 13–17 August 2016
4. Chopra, S., Hadsell, R., LeCun, Y.: Learning a similarity metric discriminatively, with application to face verification. In: IEEE Conference on Computer Vision and Pattern Recognition (2005)
5. Decroos, T., Davis, J.: Player vectors: characterizing soccer players' playing style from match event streams. In: Brefeld, U., Fromont, E., Hotho, A., Knobbe, A., Maathuis, M., Robardet, C. (eds.) ECML PKDD 2019, Part III. LNCS (LNAI), vol. 11908, pp. 569–584. Springer, Cham (2020). https://doi.org/10.1007/978-3-030-46133-1_34
6. Decroos, T., Van Roy, M., Davis, J.: SoccerMix: representing soccer actions with mixture models. In: Dong, Y., Ifrim, G., Mladenić, D., Saunders, C., Van Hoecke, S. (eds.) ECML PKDD 2020, Part V. LNCS (LNAI), vol. 12461, pp. 459–474. Springer, Cham (2021). https://doi.org/10.1007/978-3-030-67670-4_28
7. Decroos, T., Van Haaren, J., Bransen, L., Davis, J.: Actions speak louder than goals: Valuing player actions in soccer. In: ACM SIGKDD Conference on Knowledge Discovery and Data Mining (2019)
8. Duch, J., Waitzman, J.S., Nunes Amaral, L.A.: Quantifying the performance of individual players in a team activity. PLoS ONE **5**(6), e10937 (2010)
9. Gyarmati, L., Hefeeda, M.: Analyzing in-game movements of soccer players at scale. In: MIT Sloan Sports Analytics Conference (2016)
10. Koch, G., Zemel, R., Salakhutdinov, R.: Siamese neural networks for one-shot image recognition. In: International Conference on Machine Learning (2015)
11. Luo, Y., Schulte, O., Poupart, P.: Inverse reinforcement learning for team sports: Valuing actions and players. In: International Joint Conference on Artificial Intelligence (2020)
12. Pappalardo, L.: PlayeRank: data-driven performance evaluation and player ranking in soccer via a machine learning approach. ACM Trans. Intell. Syst. Technol. **10**(5), 1–27 (2019)
13. Peña, J.L., Navarro, R.S.: Who can replace Xavi? A passing motif analysis of football players (2015). http://arxiv.org/abs/1506.07768
14. Schroff, F., Kalenichenko, D., Philbin, J.: FaceNet: a unified embedding for face recognition and clustering. In: IEEE Conference on Computer Vision and Pattern Recognition (2015)

A Career in Football: What is Behind an Outstanding Market Value?

Balazs Acs and Laszlo Toka[✉]

MTA-BME Information Systems Research Group, Faculty of Electrical Engineering
and Informatics, Budapest University of Technology and Economics, Budapest,
Hungary
toka@tmit.bme.hu

Abstract. Identifying professional career path patterns is an important
topic in sports analytics. It helps teams and coaches make the best transfers and team compositions. It also helps players find out what skills and
how they need to improve to achieve their career goals. In this paper, we
seek the player characteristics that mostly affect a player's evaluation. To
this end, we first created three-year-long career path segments from the
time series data of 4204 players, then we created clusters from each segment based on the market value change over the examined period. After
the clustering we searched for professional career path patterns where
the market value growth was outstanding. Then we identified the 5 most
important features with dynamic time warping and calculated how these
should change over the years to achieve this career path. Finally we validated our findings with binary classification. We found that it is possible
to explain real life professional career path patterns based on outstanding market value growth with the information collected from the FIFA
video game series data collection. We managed to evaluate the extent
of how these characteristics should change over the years to achieve the
desired career.

Keywords: football · Soccer · professional career path · pattern
search · time-series clustering · dynamic time warping · feature
importance · binary classification

1 Introduction

In the early 2000 s sports analysts had a hard time, because of the limited data
available. Fortunately, with the growing importance of the statistical approach
to achieve competitive advantage, the quantity and quality of sport-related data
has also increased. First baseball, NBA, NHL and NFL enjoyed the benefits of
the analytical approach, but now with the explosive growth of available soccer
data, there are plenty of areas where a solution or tool can be developed, which
may lead to a competitive advantage for both teams and players. There are
many sports analytics models ranging from the effects of situational variables

U. Brefeld et al. (Eds.): MLSA 2021, CCIS 1571, pp. 15–25, 2022.
https://doi.org/10.1007/978-3-031-02044-5_2

on performance [1], through the importance of game context [2], to creating new measurement metrics like EPV [3].

An important topic in the field of football analysis is to determine which players have potential to achieve an extraordinary professional career. This helps both coaches and teams to identify the most promising players and to create a powerful team composition. In addition to all this, players can also benefit from this. They can adapt to the career schemes that are potentially good match to their capabilities. Our goal in this work is to find patterns in football player career paths in terms of outstanding market value growth and to tell which skill features determine success and how those can explain market value.

In Sect. 2 we present our data collection from Sofifa.com [4] and Transfermarkt.com [5]: we highlight the differences in the data from these two sources and the football market inflation observed therein. Next, in Sect. 3 we introduce the steps of modeling: the career path segmentation, clustering and the search for professional career path patterns where the market value growth was outstanding. In Sect. 4 we show the most important skill features of the outstanding players with the help of dynamic time warping and their dynamics during the examined years; afterwards a binary classification with LGBM is presented to validate the role of these features in practice. In Sect. 5 we discuss related work, and finally in Sect. 6 we conclude this work.

2   Player Evaluation Data: Collection and Preparation

Our goal was to collect data diversified by nationality, club, league, or international popularity. We used two sources for this type of data: Sofifa.com and Transfermarkt.com. From Sofifa we were able to collect 15 years of data about players included in the FIFA database. The data from this site plays a big role in this analysis, because it contains 21 different skill scores (e.g., dribbling, shortpassing, finishing), market values, wages and other personal information (e.g., age, weight) for each player. All skill variables are stored in a range from 1 to 99, the higher is the better. It is important to note that the different positions (e.g., ST, GK, CAM) require different skills. For example, for a goalkeeper the gk_handling skill is more important than finishing. Besides the skill and personal features, the market value is a key element.

Collecting the data from Sofifa was not enough because of two reasons. First, between 2007 and 2011, the market value of players is missing from the Sofifa database. As market values are essential in our analysis, we had to collect them from another site, i.e., Transfermarkt.com. Furthermore, within the Sofifa player pricing data there is a significant difference in the year-over-year change of the mean market values compared to the Transfermarkt values, and there is a great fluctuation in the values between 2012 and 2016, raising suspicion about the quality of data.

The range of the collected data is 15 years (from 2007 to 2021) from both sources. In order to deal with the distance between the high-end and low player values, we performed a logarithmic scaling transformation of prices. We normalized all market values by dividing them with the highest value so the value range during the modeling was between 0 and 1. Moreover, we transformed the age feature by subtracting 16, so the feature shows rather the time spent in professional career, being between 0 and 20 in our dataset.

2.1   Market Value Differences Between Transfermarkt and Sofifa

We found a significant difference between the player values we collected from the two sources. First of all we wanted to figure out if the two datasets are from the same population. For this purpose we used the Mann-Whitney U test and Kruskal-Wallis H test. We tested the market values every year, from 2012 to 2021 (before 2012 the Sofifa dataset had missing pricing values). We denote the Transfermarkt dataset as TR and the Sofifa dataset as SO throughout this paper. Except for 2012, the TR and SO datasets were different, we had to reject H0 at 0.05 significance level: we can clearly state that the market values reflected in TR and in SO are different.

Moreover, the mean year-over-year changes are also significantly different: in Fig. 1 it is clear that the price evolution is far from being the same in the two datasets. Since the market values before 2012 were not available in the SO dataset and the fluctuation has been much greater over the years than in TR, we decided to use only the TR prices during the analysis.

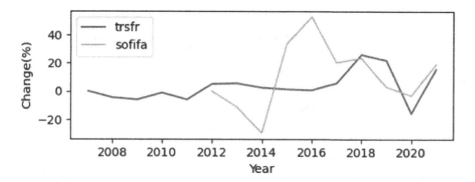

Fig. 1. Transfermarkt vs. Sofifa mean year-over-year market value change

2.2   The 2014–2016 Market Value Boom

In Fig. 1 it is noticeable that something happened between 2014 and 2016. The SO dataset shows a strong market value increment in this period, and the TR values are also increasing during and after this phenomenon. After the decrease from 2012 to 2014, in 2015 there was a 33% growth and from 2015 to 2016 this growth increased to 53% in SO. This exceptionally large jump between 2014 and 2016 is due in part to affluent Arab and Russian investors. In these years United Arab Emirates, Qatar and Saudi Arabia suddenly appeared in the list of the top 20 spenders in the football market across the world. In 2014 Al Arabi (Qatar Stars League) spent over 50 million dollars on the transfer market and with this Al Arabi was the eighth placed club inside the top 10 spenders. In the 2016 transfer season, Arab football teams spent over 200 million dollars on transfers [6].

2.3   Handling the Football Market Value Inflation

We also tackled the issue of price inflation. The inflation in the world of football seems to supersede the regular monetary inflation. For example, 1 British pound in 1990 was worth 2.27 in 2019, but in football 1 pound of 1990 would be worth about 40 now. As a stellar illustration: while in 1989 the whole squad of Manchester United was worth 20 million pounds [7], today the most valuable player of the world is Kylian Mbappé with 144 million pounds. With this observation we calculated the inflation rate of market values over the collected 15 years. We tried different approaches to handle inflation: we adjusted the market values of each year to match the mean, median and the third quartile statistics with those of the latest year values. By doing so our intention was to set the values of each year to their present value as close as possible.

We found that the best statistics was the third quartile (Q3): we set the Q3 in 2021 as the base value, being 1.8M Euros, and linearly scaled each year's values to bring their Q3 to this value. After this transformation every year had 1.8M Euros as Q3: the YOY became uniform, the sudden changes in pricing and even the effects of the 2014–2016 market value boom disappeared.

3   Time Series Analysis of Player Value

In this section we present the steps we made to successfully create our model that identifies if a player had an outstanding market value growth during the examined years of his career. First, we created career path segments for each player based on their professional career, then we created clusters from these segments. Based on the clusters we could find the patterns of the different player career paths. In the end, we find the most important features that affect the outcome of the professional careers of players.

3.1   Career Segmentation

Before the time series clustering, we made some changes in our dataset. For a robust time series analysis we chose players with more than 9 years of data, and removed the rest. Our aim was to create clusters on the dynamics in each 3-year-long career path segment. For example, if a player had 9 years of data, then we were able to create 3 segments with length of 3 years, and we got 3 cluster labels for the career segments of that player. We removed goalkeepers from our dataset, because their most important skills are exceptional. For example, comparing gk_handling or gk_diving to skills in the majority, such as finishing, dribbling, marking and so on, could have been a problem in our evaluation.

Before this filtering step the dataset had 43580 individual players. After the removal, our dataset was reduced by about 90%. In the end we created 3-year-long career path segments for each player with 9, 12 and 15 years of professional career time from a total of 4204 players.

3.2   Player Clustering Based on Value Dynamics

For clustering the 3-year-long segments, we used K-means. To find the best K value we used both the elbow method and silhouette score. With both methods 3 was the optimal number of clusters. Figure 2 shows the 3 clusters we created from the first career path segment of players with 9 years of professional career time. On the X axis we can see the years passed (0, 1 and 2) and Y axis shows the current market value transformed by standard scaler. All the individual segments are indicated with black lines and the red line is the barycenter.

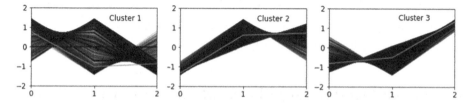

Fig. 2. First segment clusters with K-means (Color figure online)

We labeled the clusters based on the player's path of development in market value: decreasing (1), stagnating (2) and increasing (3). Cluster 3 in Fig. 2 shows strong increasing trend; in cluster 2 the player market value grows in the first year, then it stagnates; in cluster 1 we can see a strong decreasing behavior.

We performed the same clustering on the remaining career segments, and arrived at similar results: in all cases the optimal number of clusters was 3, and the same increasing, stagnating and decreasing trend were grouped in the clusters, the only difference was in the intensity of decline and growth of the market values. Therefore we apply the same labels, i.e., 1, 2 and 3, in every career path segment of each professional career time series (9, 12 and 15 years).

3.3   Pattern Search

With the help of the cluster labels we created we were able to find patterns in the whole career paths. Our aim was to find players with extraordinary market value growth in the examined years, we call them as "selected players" from now on. To this end we looked at the cluster labels of the first 3 segments of each player (as an aging player might end up in worse clusters at the end of their career), and selected the player if the sum of cluster labels was exactly 9, i.e., all increasing segments. By selecting the players with the highest possible sum of cluster labels we wanted to find players whose market value never stagnated or decreased significantly during the examined years. In Fig. 3 we can see the value evolution of two players who were classified as "selected players". X axis shows here the professional career time of the player in years (between 0 and 20), and on the Y axis we can see the normalized market value of the players (the log base 10 form of market value was divided by the highest market value, it is between 0 and 1).

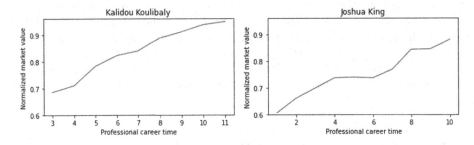

Fig. 3. Players with outstanding market value growth during the examined years

4   Finding Outstanding Players Based on Market Value Change

We want to find out which skill features play the biggest role in becoming an extraordinary player. In addition, we want to know exactly how these variables should evolve over one's career. In this section we present the model we built to determine whether a player is within the selected ones or not with the use of the previously mentioned skill variables.

We created the list of selected players with the pattern search method discussed in the previous section. We found 138 players who have met the conditions, and created the label values accordingly.

The next step was to find the most important features. We searched for the largest distances between the selected and other players features: we used dynamic time warping (dtw) for this purpose. First we calculated the distance of features between the selected players and we got 18 906 distance records for each feature. Next, we did the same on the rest of the players. In order to reduce the computation time, we only used every 10th player for the latter. In the end we got 165 242 distance records for each feature from the other players. Finally we compared the distances with the scores given by dtw. Figure 4 shows the final feature distances between the selected and other players. Each skill variable had a distance score between 25 and 13. X axis shows the feature ID and Y axis shows the distance scores.

For the most important features we decided to select the skills with a distance score above 20, because a larger gap was observed between the distances above and under 20. The highest feature distance score under 20 was 18 and most of the remaining features were in the interval of 15 and 17. Therefore the 5 most important features are: Marking (24.296), which is the ability of a player to prevent the opposing player from obtaining the ball; Standing_tackle (23.871), the ability to perform a tackle to capture the ball; FK_accuracy (20.282), measures the free kick accuracy and the chance of scoring a goal from it; Finishing (20.264), which determines the ability of a player to score from an opportunity; and Long_shots (20.180), the accuracy of shots from long distances. After we found the top 5 features, we wanted to know exactly how they changed for the selected and other players during the period under review. We calculated the mean change of every skill and compared them. In Fig. 5 we can see the results. Each dot represents the mean change of the skills over the 9 years. The red number shows the mean difference of the skill development between the selected players (blue) and other players (orange). The ranking is almost the same with so much difference that the finish came in second place in terms of difference. For example to become a selected player, the player must boost the Marking skill by +7.62 compared to the other players, or improve Finishing by +6.45 over 9 years.

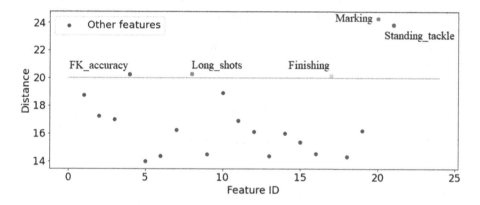

Fig. 4. DTW distances

To check our findings in practice, we created a binary classification. In this classification our predictors were the top 5 features we selected and we wanted to predict if a player is selected or not. We used an LGBM classifier for this task and we measured our model with AUC. We used a train-test split in order to train our model and validate the findings on the test set. The model AUC score with the top 5 features was about 0.71. If we added the remaining features the score improved to about 0.75, but we can state that the 5 selected features played the biggest role during the classification. This relatively low score is highly due to the lack of available data. Sofifa only stores player data from 2007 and we

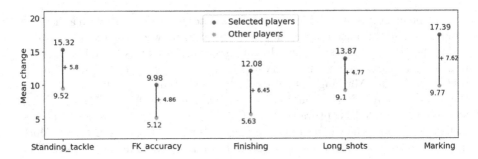

Fig. 5. Difference between the mean improvement of the top 5 features of the selected and the other players (Color figure online)

could only use the characteristics of the 4204 players (138 selected) whose data were available for a time interval with the required length.

To check if we can achieve different results by augmenting the dataset, we created career segments with an overlapping method. Instead of creating the segments from 1–3, 4–6 and 7–9 years of professional career, we created them from 1–3, 2–4, 3–5 years and so on. With this method the number of observations has increased significantly. In total 12166 player career segments were examined: 3148 selected and 9018 other players. Therefore the ratio of 1:400 (selected:other) changed to 1:3.

In addition we considered to change our approach of clustering. Previously we created 3 clusters based on the elbow method and silhouette score. In Fig. 2, it is observable that the barycenters are correct but some players might have been misclassified. To make sure every item is correctly clustered we created 5 clusters; in Fig. 6 we can see almost the same patterns as before and we labeled them as usual. Clusters 1 and 2 are decreasing (1), Cluster 3 is stagnating (2) and finally, Clusters 4 and 5 are increasing (3) trends.

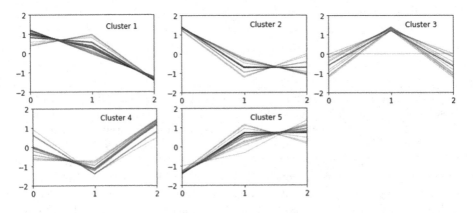

Fig. 6. Modified clusters

After the clustering we did the same steps as before. Surprisingly the dynamic time warping results were exactly the same. The same 5 features had outstanding impact on careers, as we showed in Fig. 5. After a train-test split and binary classification with LGBM, the AUC score was about 0.70 which is almost the same as the results from the previous model. This exercise validates the robustness of the model, and we can clearly state that even if we increase the number of observations the results will not change drastically.

5   Related Work

Many related works have appeared in this topic. Here we discuss what are the key differences compared to our work, and what conclusions can be drawn.

Bettina Schroepf and Martin Lames searched for career patterns in German football youth national teams [8]. They managed to find 8 typical career types. It has been found that the careers of youth players last up to 1 or 2 years in Germany and only a few players can achieve long-lasting career. It is interesting how big is the churn rate by young players in major European football nations, so it is already a privilege here for someone to be among the pros. In our paper we have broaden the search and tried to find career paths of adult players around the globe. A recent study revealed that in Portugal the length of a career as a football player is decreased, but the years of youth career increased: it follows that the career path started earlier in the last 3 decades [9]. Remaining in Portugal, Monteiro et al. identified that the best result the players performed was in the age of 27 and they ended their career at around 33 [10]. Other researchers revealed that the peak performance by female football players is around the age of 25 [11] or between 25 and 27 [12] in case of male players. In our study we preserved the players between the age of 16 and 34 and the majority of the examined players were between the age of 22 and 27.

Identifying the career potential of athletes is a very difficult task. Coaches play a big role in this aspect, because they have the closest relationship with the players. However they also encounter difficulties. In the article of Cripps, A. J. et al., the authors found that coaches can predict the career outcome more accurately for late maturing athletes, but they are less accurate for early maturing players [13]. It is important to keep in mind that the way of maturation can easily affect the career path both positively and negatively.

It is also interesting, how it is possible to draw a parallel between psychology and performance in terms of success. Schmid, M. J. et al., found patterns in rowing by connecting these variables. They measured the proactivity, ambition and commitment of the athletes for the past year and 30 months later. As a result, if a highly motivated rower had poor performance in the past year, it was more likely that he/she performed at a very high level in the future. Athletes with low moral and motivation were more likely to drop out or perform weaker [14]. Good motivation is a key to perform better. Highly achievement oriented players have a better chance to accomplish an outstanding career [15]. We only used skill/performance variables but based on these statements, there is potential in the introduction of certain psychological features into our model.

Vroonen, R. et al. [16] predicted the potential score (available on Sofifa.com) of professional football players. They selected a player and searched for similar players from the same age. Based on the evolution of the latter, they predicted if he/she had great potential score in the future. In contrast, in our paper we recognized continuous market value growth patterns and we have shown which skill development is required to achieve this goal. We did not predict the potential scores of Sofifa, rather we paralleled the available information from Sofifa with the development of real market prices and we successfully explained the real life career path patterns we were looking for with them.

6 Conclusion

In this paper we presented an approach to identify patterns in football player career paths based on extraordinary market value changes and skill features that are responsible for excellence. The time segmenting and time series clustering method we applied was successful and we managed to find the patterns we were looking for. Next we found the 5 most important features and the exact dynamics of how these variables should evolve to enter the high class of football players. The need to develop Marking (+7.62) and Finishing (+6.45) skills has been outstanding over the years, but Standing_tackle (+5.8), Free-kick_accuracy (+4.68) and Long_shots (+4.77) were also strongly needed to achieve an outstanding career path. Finally we validated the results in practice with binary classification, the AUC score of the model with the 5 selected features was 0.71 and with the other skill features was 0.75. We proved that despite the fact that at first we worked with little data, the model is robust, because with increased amount of data we got the same score results. As the increased sample size could not affect the results, there is a need for additional features to enhance the model. In the future there is a potential to improve these findings by involving psychological or situational variables.

Teams, coaches and players can have a wide range of benefits from this study. Teams and coaches can use the lessons learned for strategical decisions, for example how to train youth players in order to sell them early with high return. This could bring a profitable decisions and additional source of income, vital for today's competitive environment in the top leagues. It is also a good indicator for coaches to identify future high class players. In the future we want to broaden the scope of the model so we can apply the findings on career goals other than high valuation, like playing in Champions League finals, being a member of the national team, transferring to a higher division or ending up contracted to a desired club.

Acknowledgment. Project no. 128233 has been implemented with the support provided by the Ministry of Innovation and Technology of Hungary from the National Research, Development and Innovation Fund, financed under the FK_18 funding scheme.

References

1. Gómez, M.A., Lago-Peñas, C., Pollard, R.: Situational variables. In: McGarry, T., O'Donoghue, P., Sampaio, J. (eds.) Routledge Handbook of Sports Performance Analysis, pp. 277–287. Routledge, London (2013). https://doi.org/10.4324/9780203806913
2. Power, P., Ruiz, H., Wei, X., Lucey, P.: Not all passes are created equal: objectively measuring the risk and reward of passes in soccer from tracking data. In: Proceedings of the 23rd ACM SIGKDD International Conference on Knowledge Discovery and Data Mining, pp. 1605–1613. Association for Computing Machinery, Halifax, NS, Canada (2017)
3. Fernández, J., Bornn, L., Cervone, D.: Decomposing the immeasurable sport: a deep learning expected possession value framework for soccer. In: MIT Sloan Sports Analytics Conference 2019, Boston (2019)
4. Sofifa. https://sofifa.com/. Accessed 21 June 2021
5. Transfermarkt. https://www.transfermarkt.com/. Accessed 21 June 2021
6. Raisi, O.A.: The Economics of Middle East's Football Transfers. https://www.sportsjournal.ae/the-economics-of-middle-easts-football-transfers/. Accessed 21 June 2021
7. Christou, L.: The true extent of spiralling inflation in football's transfer market. https://www.verdict.co.uk/football-transfer-market-inflation/. Accessed 21 June 2021
8. Schroepf, B., Lames, M.: Career patterns in German football youth national teams - a longitudinal study. Int. J. Sports Sci. Coach. **13**(3), 405–414 (2018)
9. Carapinheira, A., et al.: Career termination of Portuguese elite football players: comparison between the last three decades. Sports **6**(4), 155 (2018)
10. Monteiro, R., et al.: Identification of key career indicators in Portuguese football players. Int. J. Sports Sci. Coach. **15**(4), 533–541 (2020)
11. Barreira, J.: Age of peak performance of Elite Women's soccer players. Int. J. Sports Sci. **6**(3), 121–124 (2016)
12. Dendir, S.: When do soccer players peak? A note. J. Sports Anal. **2**(2), 89–105 (2016)
13. Cripps, A.J., Hopper, L.S., Joyce, C.: Can coaches predict long-term career attainment outcomes in adolescent athletes? Int. J. Sports Sci. Coach. **14**(3), 324–328 (2019)
14. Schmid, M.J., Conzelmann, A., Zuber, C.: Patterns of achievement-motivated behavior and performance as predictors for future success in rowing: a person-oriented study. Int. J. Sports Sci. Coach. **16**(1), 101–109 (2021)
15. Zuber, C., Zibung, M., Conzelmann, A.: Motivational patterns as an instrument for predicting success in promising young football players. Int. J. Sports Sci. **33**(2), 160–168 (2015)
16. Vroonen, R., et al.: Predicting the potential of professional soccer players. In: Davis, J., Kaytou, M., Zimmermann, A. (eds.) ECML PKDD 2017, vol. 1971, pp. 1–10. Springer, Skopje (2017)

Inferring the Strategy of Offensive and Defensive Play in Soccer with Inverse Reinforcement Learning

Pegah Rahimian[1] and Laszlo Toka[1,2(✉)]

[1] Budapest University of Technology and Economics, Budapest, Hungary
[2] MTA-BME Information Systems Research Group, Budapest, Hungary
{pegah.rahimian,toka}@tmit.bme.hu

Abstract. Analyzing and understanding strategies applied by top soccer teams has always been in the focus of coaches, scouts, players, and other sports professionals. Although the game strategies can be quite complex, we focus on the offensive or defensive approaches that need to be adopted by the coach before or throughout the match. In order to build interpretable parameterizations of soccer decision making, we propose a batch gradient inverse reinforcement learning for modeling the teams' reward function in terms of offense or defense. Our conducted experiments on soccer logs made by Wyscout company on German Bundesliga reveal two important facts: the highest-ranked teams are planning strategically for offense and defense before the match with the largest weights on pre-match features; the lowest-ranked teams apply short-term planning with larger weights on in-match features.

Keywords: Soccer Analytics · Inverse Reinforcement Learning · Deep Learning · Decision Making

1 Introduction

Although soccer is a relatively simple sport compared to other sports in terms of rules and basic game play, deciding about strategies to be applied with the aim of wining can be quite complex. Among the vast options of the applied strategies, playing offensive or defensive is one of the most important decisions that needs to be taken by the coach before, or throughout the matches. There are several factors that might affect this decision. Several studies proposed conceivable factors and robust methods for deriving the optimal strategies to be applied for a team (e.g., [6–8,22]).

Apart from deriving the optimal strategy, understanding the logic behind the decisions made by high-ranked clubs in the leagues, helps other clubs to learn those decisions and possibly imitate those. In this work, we propose a novel soccer strategy analysis method, taking advantage of inverse reinforcement learning (IRL). IRL is the field of learning an expert's objectives, values, or rewards

U. Brefeld et al. (Eds.): MLSA 2021, CCIS 1571, pp. 26–38, 2022.
https://doi.org/10.1007/978-3-031-02044-5_3

by observing its behavior. The motivation behind the choice of this algorithm is that we can observe the behavior of a team in some specific matches, and learn which states of the environment the team is trying to achieve and what the concrete goals might be. On the other hand, soccer is a sparse rewarding game. Thus, designing a manual reward assignment method for each action of the players might not be an easy task. IRL helps to infer the intention behind the smart offensive or defensive strategies throughout the matches by recovering the reward function. In summary, we seek to answer the following questions: "why does a team decide to play offensive or defensive?", "what are the most important features for each team to decide about this strategy?", "how to distinguish offensive teams from defensive ones?". The contribution of our work is multi-fold:

- We propose an end-to-end framework that receives raw actions, and infers the intention behind those via IRL by converting soccer match action logs to a possession model in an environment, which we assume to be Markovian;
- We propose a model to coaches and sports professionals to understand the policy of the top clubs, and possibly imitate those by developing robust deep recurrent neural networks for cloning the offensive and defensive behavior of the soccer clubs from their match logs;
- We design a novel reward function and corresponding features for maximizing teams' winning probabilities, and we recover those from soccer match logs;
- We make our code available online[1].

This paper is organized as follows. We present the current literature on sports analytics in Sect. 2. Section 3 provides some preliminaries of GIRL, an IRL method we apply. We explain our IRL framework for soccer analytics in Sect. 4. Section 5 describes the experimental IRL framework and extensive numerical computations for getting interesting inference results. Finally, we conclude our work in Sect. 6.

2   Related Work

Soccer players mostly take actions according to the rewards that they expect to gain from their behavior. This reward is usually dictated by the coach to the players. Although, several works tried to suggest generic action valuation methods, focusing on passes and shots (e.g., [4,5,9,17], etc.), and some others cover all types of actions (e.g., [2,12,13], etc.), recovering the assigned reward of offensive and defensive actions, which is specific for each soccer team, is ignored in the literature of sports analytics. The works by Gambarelli et al. [8], and Hirotsu et al. [10] derived the optimal strategy of playing offensive or defensive via game-theory. In this paper, we focus on inferring the intention behind those strategies for different teams rather than deriving the optimal strategy for them.

Recently, deep learning models proved to be promising in soccer analytics. In this domain, Fernandez and Bornn [4] present a convolutional neural network

---

[1] https://github.com/Peggy4444/soccer_IRL.

architecture that is capable of estimating full probability surfaces of potential passes in soccer. Liu et al. took advantage of Q-function in reinforcement learning for action valuation in ice-hockey [13] and soccer [12]. With regards to the application of IRL in team sports, Luo et al. [14] combined Q-function with IRL to provide a player ranking system, and Muelling et al. [16] used IRL for extracting strategic elements from table tennis data. However, a particular application of gradient IRL to recover the previously assigned reward of the performed offensive and defensive actions is missing in the literature. In this work, we use a truly batch Gradient IRL method, which eliminates the necessity of environment dynamics and online interaction of the players with the environment. Our method extracts intention behind strategies solely from soccer logs, thus, conforms to real soccer matches and is applicable for coaches and sports professionals.

3   Preliminaries of Gradient Inverse Reinforcement Learning

In this section, we provide basic notations and formulations of IRL, used throughout this paper.

3.1   Markov Decision Processes Without Reward

A Markov Decision Process without Reward $(MDP\backslash R)$ [19] is denoted by the tuple (S, A, P), where S is the state space, A is the action space, and $P : S \to A \to S$ is the transition function. In this environment, the expert's behavior is described by a stochastic policy $\pi : S \to A$. In this work, we consider that policies are differentiable and belong to a parametric space $\prod_\Theta = \{\pi_\theta : \theta \in \Theta\}$, where θ is the policy parameter.

3.2   Inverse Reinforcement Learning

The goal of IRL is to infer a reward function R given an optimal policy $\pi^* : S \to A$ for the $MDP\backslash R$. Typically, we observe samples (s, a) of states and actions recorded from full history of expert's trajectories $\tau = (s_0, a_0, ..., s_{T-1}, a_{T-1}, s_T)$, which are following policy π^*. In order to recover the rewards gained by each action of the expert, we define a parametric linear reward function as the weighted combination of features in (1).

$$R_\omega(s, a) = \sum_{i=1}^{q} \omega_i f_i(s, a) = \omega^T \mathbf{f}(s, a), \tag{1}$$

where $\mathbf{f}$ is the vector of reward features, ω is the vector of weights, and q is the number of our selected reward features. Moreover, ω^E can be defined as the weight vector of the rewards, which we assume to be optimized by expert E.

Furthermore, the feature expectation of policy π can be described as:

$$\psi^{\pi} = E\left[\sum_{t=0}^{\infty} \gamma^t \mathbf{f}(S_t, A_t)\right], \tag{2}$$

where γ is discount factor (set to 0.99 in this work), $A_t \sim \pi(.|S_t)$, and $\pi_\theta \in \Pi_\Theta$, that $(\psi(\theta) = \psi^{\pi_\theta})$. Finally, the expected value under policy π_θ of our reward feature vector $\mathbf{f}$ can be formulated as:

$$J(\theta, \omega) = E\left[\sum_{t=0}^{\infty} \gamma^t R_\omega(S_t, A_t)\right] = \omega^T \psi(\theta). \tag{3}$$

3.3 Gradient Inverse Reinforcement Learning

Solving an IRL problem through Policy Gradient (PG) is a straightforward solution when the policy is parameterized and can be estimated and consequently represented through its parameter θ. Several algorithms using this method are proposed by different studies, e.g., [15,18,20].

In general, policy gradient under linear reward function can be defined as the gradient of the expected value of the expert's policy as in (4).

$$\nabla_\theta J(\theta, \omega) = E_{\tau \sim \pi_\theta}\left[\left(\sum_{l=0}^{t} \nabla_\theta \log \pi_\theta(A_l|S_l)\right)\left(\sum_{t=0}^{\infty} R_\omega(S_t, A_t)\right)\right], \tag{4}$$

and according to (3),

$$\nabla_\theta J(\theta, \omega) = \nabla_\theta \psi(\theta)\omega, \tag{5}$$

where $\nabla_\theta \psi(\theta)$ is a Jacobian matrix. Assuming that the expert optimized the policy under some unknown R^E, its policy gradient should be zero in R^E. In other words, if the expert's policy π_{θ^E} optimizes its reward function R_{ω^E}, then the policy parameter θ_E will be a stationary point of the expected value $J(\theta, \omega^E)$. Thus, one way to recover the weight ω^E is to get it from the null space of the Jacobian $\nabla_\theta \psi(\theta)$. A good approach is discussed in the method called Gradient Inverse Reinforcement Learning (GIRL) [18]. GIRL is a method of recovering reward function that minimizes the gradient of a parameterized representation of the expert's policy. At the first step, we assume that the expert's policy π^E is known, and GIRL tries to recover the weight ω^E, associated with its reward function R^E. Pirotta et al. [18] discuss that estimating the Jacobian matrix $\nabla_\theta \psi(\theta)$ from expert trajectories might result in a full rank matrix. Thus, it might prevent finding the corresponding null space. As a solution to this problem, GIRL proposes recovering ω by searching for the direction of minimum growth by minimizing the $L^2 - norm$ of gradient, as in (6):

$$\min_\omega \left\|\nabla_\theta \psi(\theta^E)\omega\right\|_2^2 \tag{6}$$

4 IRL Framework for Reward Recovery in Soccer

In this section, we propose an end-to-end framework, which gets the raw expert team's trajectories from the soccer logs, estimates expert team's policy by training robust convolutional recurrent neural networks and understands the intuition behind playing offensive or defensive actions by recovering the expert team's reward function through GIRL.

4.1 Behavioral Cloning

The estimation of the Jacobian matrix $\nabla_\theta \psi(\theta)$, i.e., policy gradient, can be performed with several methods, such as REINFORCE algorithm [21], or G(PO)MDP [1]. Furthermore, an approximation of the expert's policy parameter θ^E can be estimated through Behavioral Cloning (BC) in the expert's trajectories. One reasonable approach to estimate this parameter is to use Maximum-Likelihood estimation. In this work, we proceed with developing robust deep neural networks, which are able to estimate the expert's policy from its trajectories. Consequently, feeding any kind of state with the corresponding features from expert's trajectory, this network should accurately estimate the occurrence probability of action space: $\pi(a|s)$. Thus, the expert's policy will be accurately learned by the networks.

IRL Experts, Actions, and Trajectories in Soccer. We aim to construct a Markovian possession environment from soccer logs. To this end, data preparation is a core task to achieve a reliable IRL model.

In our soccer analysis task, we assume that the coach and players of each team are always trying to maximize their winning probabilities. Thus, the performed policy of playing offensive or defensive, which is dictated by the coach and obeyed by the players, is optimal in their own opinion. This assumption totally matches the optimality assumption of IRL, in which the expert policy from its demonstrations must be optimal in their own opinion. In this setting, we consider each team competing in the leagues as an IRL expert. Therefore, we have a set of expert teams $\mathbf{E} = (E_1, E_2, ..., E_m)$, and set of unknown reward functions $\mathbf{R} = (R_{\omega_1}, R_{\omega_2}, ..., R_{\omega_m})$ for each of them.

Moreover, each expert team demonstrates a set of trajectories. In a game, in which two teams are competing with each other, we always set one team as the IRL expert, and the other team as the opponent. Both teams demonstrate a set of ball possessions, i.e., action sequences. In this work, we assume that the possession is transferred if and only if the team is not in the possession of the ball over two consecutive events. Thus, the unsuccessful touches of the opponent in fewer than 3 consecutive actions are not considered as a possession loss.

In the offensive vs defensive analysis, we define each trajectory τ_t as one possession of the match. Then we separate the possessions according to their possessor of being the expert team or the opponent. Now the expert team has four options as an action: perform offensive action by terminating an own possession with a "shot", or perform defensive actions for terminating the opponent's possession with "tackle", "clearance", or "interception". Consequently, each expert team demonstrates the set of trajectories as $D_i = (\tau_1, \tau_2, ..., \tau_t)$, which terminate with the four above-mentioned offensive or defensive actions.

State Representation: In order to address the sequential nature of actions in the soccer logs, we define the state as one possession. We describe a game state by generating the most relevant state features and labels to them. In order to demonstrate and prepare states for machine learning, we built a set of hand-crafted spatial state features. For each time-step, we demonstrate the state as a 7-dimensional feature vector X (see Table 1), and one-hot representation of the action A for all the actions within each possession, excluding the ending action. Thus, the varying possession length is the number of actions inside a possession, excluding the ending one. Then, the state is a 2-dimensional array, with the first dimension of possession length (varying for each possession), and the second dimension of features (of the fixed length of 7). Therefore, a mth state, i.e., m^{th} possession, with length of n actions is represented as:

$$S_m = [[X_0, A_0], [X_1, A_1], ..., [X_{n-1}, A_{n-1}]]$$

.

Table 1. State features list

State feature name	Description
Angle to goal	the angle between the goal posts seen from the shot location
Distance to goal	Euclidean distance from shot location to center of the goal line
Time remaining	time remained from action occurrence to the end of match half
Home/Away	is the action performed by home or away team?
Action result	successful or unsuccessful
Body ID	is the action performed by head or body or foot?
Goal difference	actual difference between the expert team and opponent goals

Network Architecture. As mentioned before, each soccer team is considered as an expert denoted by E_i. As the first step, we are interested in recovering the behavioral policy of each expert team from the set of trajectories demonstrated by them. To this end, we formulate the problem as follows: each team plays 34 matches in the league in 34 rounds, competing with 17 other opponent teams. Thus, we need to run IRL 18 times for 18 independent expert teams. In order to recover the behavioral policy for each of them, we collected 2 different datasets. The first dataset consists of all possessions of the expert team through one season of the league. The second dataset is the concatenation of all possessions of the other 17 opponent teams competing with the expert team in that league. Then, we trained a CNN-LSTM network [3], using CNN for spatial feature extraction of input possessions, and an LSTM layer with 100 memory units to support sequence prediction and to interpret features across time steps. Since the input possessions have a three-dimensional spatial structure, CNN is capable of picking invariant features for different actions inside a possession. Then, these learned consolidated spatial features serve as input to the LSTM layer. Finally, the dense output layers are used with sigmoid and softmax activation functions to perform our binary and multi-classification task. The sigmoid activation function classifies the offensive possessions to the two ending actions of "Shot" and "Not Shot", and softmax activation function classifies the defensive possessions (i.e., the offensive possessions from opponent which are terminated by expert team through a defensive action) to the four ending actions of "Interception", "Tackle", "Clearance", and "Others".

Note that the feature vector X is of fixed length for each action, but it varies for all actions in the state (because possession length or the number of actions varies). This is one of the main challenges in our work as most machine learning methods require fixed-length feature vectors. In order to address this challenge, we use truncating and padding. We mapped each action in possession to a 9 length real-valued vector. Also, we limit the total number of actions in a possession to 10, truncating long possessions and we pad the short possessions with zero values. The architecture for cloning behavioral policy of the expert team is depicted in Fig. 1.

- The offensive network is trained with all expert team possessions, and estimates the probability of the expert team's possession resulting in a shot. Intuitively, this network recovers the offensive part of the expert team's policy by estimating the probability of expert's possessions ending up in a shot.
- The defensive network is trained with all opponent's team possessions in the same matches with the expert team, and estimates the probability of the opponent team's possession ending in one of the defensive actions, (i.e., clearance, tackle, intercept) made by the expert team. The aim of this network is to recover the defensive part of the expert team policy.

4.2 Rewards Features and Weights Recovery

We aim to employ GIRL algorithm to infer the intention behind soccer teams for playing offensive or defensive tactics through the matches with different opponents. More specifically, we seek to find valid answers for the following questions: "Why does a team decide to play offensive or defensive? How do they reward the offensive vs defensive actions throughout the match?". To achieve this goal, first, we need to define reward functions according to (1). In our soccer analysis, the features representing the reward are the combination of pre-game information (e.g., own ranking, opponent ranking, home advantage) and in-game information at each moment of the match (e.g., goal difference, time remaining, and player's intention to play offensive or defensive - correlating with the player's market value according to the money-ball analysis in [11]). Table 2 lists the corresponding reward features and their correlations with the number of offensive actions in the Bundesliga dataset. Thus, we formulate the reward function according to (7).

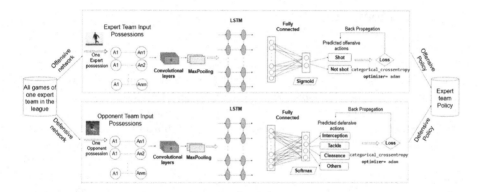

Fig. 1. Offensive and Defensive networks for the expert team behavioral cloning

$$R_\omega = \underbrace{\omega_1 f_1}_{\text{Expert rank}} + \underbrace{\omega_2 f_2}_{\text{Opponent rank}} + \underbrace{\omega_3 f_3}_{\text{H/A}} + \underbrace{\omega_4 f_4}_{\text{GD}} + \underbrace{\omega_5 f_5}_{\text{TR}} + \underbrace{\omega_6 f_6}_{\text{PI}} \qquad (7)$$

Now we can employ GIRL algorithm to recover weights ($\omega_i s$), according to (4), (5), (6), to understand what each team cares about the most, i.e., which set of features. After recovering the weights, we will be able to compute the assigned reward to each action through the matches by the personal opinion of the coach and players.

Table 2. Reward features list

Notation	Reward feature name	Type	Description	Correlation to offensive actions
f_1: Expert rank	Expert team ranking	pre-game	Inverse of the expert team place in the league table at the date of the match; fixed in a match; varying through a season	0.63
f_2: Opponent rank	Opponent team ranking	pre-game	Inverse of the opponent team place in the league table at the date of the match; fixed in a match; varying through a season	-0.21
f_3: H/A	Home/Away	pre-game	Expert team is home team or away team?; fixed in a match; varying through a season	0.33
f_4: GD	Goal Difference	in-game	Goal difference of expert team and opponent at each time-step; varying in a match; varying through a season	-0.12
f_5: TR	Time Remaining	in-game	Time remaining to the end of the game at each time-step; varying in a match; varying through a season	0.39
f_6: PI	Player Intention ∼ market value [11]	in-game	Offensive or defensive intention of the player performing the action at each timestep; varying in a match; varying through a season	0.41

5   Experiments and Results

Dataset: In order to conduct the experiments of our proposed approach, we use a match event dataset[2] provided by Wyscout. The Wyscout dataset covers 1,941 matches, 3,251,294 events, and 4,299 players from an entire season of seven competitions (La Liga, Serie A, Bundesliga, Premier League, Ligue 1, FIFA World Cup 2018, UEFA Euro Cup 2016). Our results prove the sufficiency of this dataset size for our experiments. Moreover, players' market value and dynamic teams ranking in the leagues are collected from `transfermarkt.com`, and `worldfootball.net`. In order to facilitate the reproducibility of the analysis, we converted the format of event stream data to SPADL representation[3]. In this section we show the result of our experiment on the 2017–2018 season of German Bundesliga competition, which consists of 306 matches, 142 teams, and 519407 events. The teams in the collection of matches are the following: Bayern München, Bayer Leverkusen, Augsburg, Eintracht Frankfurt, Borussia M'gladbach, Köln, Werder Bremen, Hoffenheim, Hannover 96, Stuttgart, Mainz 05, Schalke 04, Wolfsburg, Hertha BSC, Freiburg, Hamburger SV, RB Leipzig, and Borussia Dortmund.

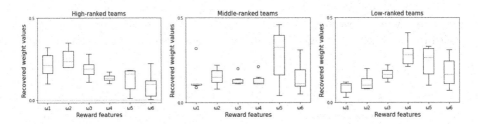

Fig. 2. Range of reward weights recovered by GIRL. The algorithm finds large pregame weights for high-ranked teams, whereas large in-game weights for low-ranked teams in 2017–2018 season of German Bundesliga.

Behavioral Cloning Results: For each iteration of the GIRL algorithm, one team in this collection is assigned as the IRL expert team, and the rest of the teams are the opponents. Thus, the prepared dataset for each result consists of 34 matches of an expert team from 34 rounds of 2017–2018 season of German Bundesliga, in which the expert team participated. As the first step, we estimated the Jacobian $\nabla_\theta \psi(\theta)$ by training the offensive and defensive networks separately for each expert team. Learning all weights from the expert's team trajectories in the Bundesliga dataset took about 90 s (5 s for each expert team on average) on a server with a Tesla K80 GPU. The input data size to each network was approx. 3300 possessions for each of the expert team and opponent teams. Consequently, each network constructed 56,890 trainable parameters on average. Validation split of 30% of consecutive possessions is used to evaluate BC

---

[2] https://figshare.com/collections/Soccer_match_event_dataset/4415000/5.
[3] https://github.com/ML-KULeuven/socceraction.

models during training, and cross-entropy loss on train and validation datasets is used to evaluate the model, achieving the accuracy of 79% and loss of 0.4 (cross entropy) on average through all expert teams for predicting the actions.

Reward Weights Recovery Results: Table 3 presents the results of reward weight estimation for each expert team in Bundesliga. The value of each recovered weight is an indicator of the importance of that feature for that expert team. For instance, the "ω_1: own ranking" feature is the most important feature for FC Schalke team. Hoffenheim mostly cares about "ω_2: opponent ranking" feature in its reward assignment. After recovering the weight of the rewards by GIRL, one can estimate the assigned reward using (7) for each team. We classified the teams into 3 categories according to their final ranking in the league: high-ranked, middle-ranked, and low-ranked teams. By analyzing the range of weights recovered by GIRL, we found it surprising that high-ranked teams mostly pay attention to the pre-game features (own ranking, opponent ranking, home advantage) with large weights: $(\omega_1, \omega_2, \omega_3)$. Thus, it seems that the coaches in these teams are planning strategically to play offensive or defensive. On the other hand, low-ranked teams apply short-term planning with large weights $(\omega_4, \omega_5, \omega_6)$ on in-match features: (goal difference, time remaining, and

Table 3. Reward weights recovered for expert teams

Rank	Expert team	pre-game features			in-game features		
		ω_1	ω_2	ω_3	ω_4	ω_5	ω_6
1	Bayern München	0.20	−0.22	0.28	0.12	0.18	0.00
2	FC Schalke 04	0.32	−0.27	0.20	0.10	−0.01	0.09
3	1899 Hoffenheim	0.10	−0.35	0.22	0.17	0.04	0.12
4	Borussia Dortmund	0.29	−0.31	0.11	0.12	−0.17	0.00
5	Bayer Leverkusen	0.15	−0.20	0.15	0.14	0.18	0.22
6	RB Leipzig	0.22	−0.20	0.18	0.15	−0.15	0.1
7	VfB Stuttgart	0.32	−0.15	0.12	0.15	0.04	0.22
8	Eintracht Frankfurt	0.10	−0.22	0.14	0.12	0.33	0.09
9	Mönchengladbach	0.11	−0.20	0.11	0.11	0.42	0.05
10	Hertha BSC	0.11	−0.08	0.11	0.21	−0.11	0.31
11	Werder Bremen	0.11	−0.15	0.20	0.11	−0.32	0.11
12	FC Augsburg	0.09	−0.11	0.12	0.11	0.46	0.11
13	Hannover 96	0.05	−0.08	0.19	0.41	0.10	0.11
14	1. FSV Mainz 05	0.11	−0.20	0.22	0.25	−0.15	0.01
15	SC Freiburg	0.03	−0.15	0.14	0.32	−0.32	0.22
16	VfL Wolfsburg	0.09	−0.08	0.18	0.21	0.33	0.11
17	Hamburger SV	0.12	−0.11	0.12	0.31	−0.31	0.25
18	1. FC Köln	0.11	−0.09	0.15	0.22	−0.22	0.31

player intention). Moreover, middle-ranked teams show small variance except for ω_5: time remaining. Figure 2 is the evidence of these claims.

Evaluation: Using the 2018–2019 season of Bundesliga dataset, Fig. 3 shows a comparison of the mean recovered reward for offensive and defensive actions by our proposed approach, versus the actual offensive/defensive rating collected from whoscored.com. It is the evidence of the robustness of our reward recovery approach as it recovered larger positive reward of offensive actions for the offen-

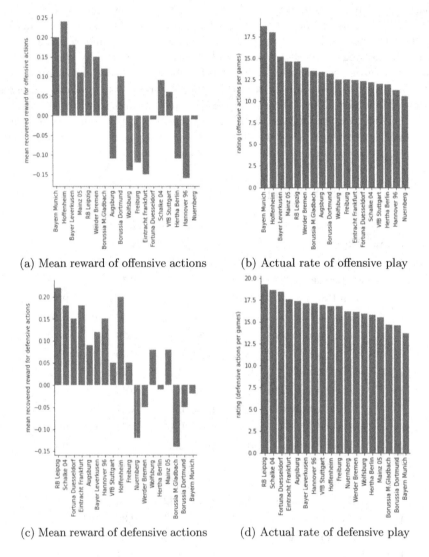

(a) Mean reward of offensive actions

(b) Actual rate of offensive play

(c) Mean reward of defensive actions

(d) Actual rate of defensive play

Fig. 3. Comparison of the mean recovered reward with the actual rating of offensive and defensive play

sive teams (e.g., Bayern, Hoffenheim, etc.) in Figs. 3a and b, and larger positive reward of defensive actions for the defensive teams (e.g., Leipzig, Schalke, etc.) in Figs. 3c and d.

6   Conclusion

In the current literature of sports analytics, the following two domains are intensively studied by researchers: 1) action valuation methods, 2) deriving optimal strategies. However, the study of inferring the reward assigned to offensive and defensive actions by the coaches and players, which are team-specific, is missing in the literature. In this work we proposed a model for inferring the intention behind playing offensive or defensive tactics according to some intuitive features. Our experimental results showed that the high-ranked teams mostly plan based on pre-match information, and play strategically. The low-ranked teams plan on short-term based on information available throughout the game. Finally, we showed how the recovered reward of *offensive* and *defensive* actions in German Bundesliga teams are conforming with their final ranking in the league with respect to their *offensive* and *defensive* plays. Our framework will help coaches and sports professionals to infer the intention of soccer actions from highest-rank clubs, and possibly imitate those. Moreover, the recovered rewards for each action can be used for any action and player evaluation tasks. To the best of our knowledge, our work constitutes the first usage of truly batch gradient inverse reinforcement learning to infer the intention behind offensive or defensive plays in soccer. As future work, we aim to use the recovered rewards for deriving the optimal strategy to be applied by each team via reinforcement learning.

Acknowledgment. Project no. 128233 has been implemented with the support provided by the Ministry of Innovation and Technology of Hungary from the National Research, Development and Innovation Fund, financed under the FK_18 funding scheme.

References

1. Baxter, J., Bartlett, P.L.: Infinite-horizon policy-gradient estimation. J. Artif. Intell. Res. **15**, 319–350 (2001)
2. Decroos, T., Bransen, L., Van Haaren, J., Davis, J.: Actions speak louder than goals: valuing player actions in soccer. In: The 25th ACM SIGKDD Conference on Knowledge Discovery and Data Mining (KDD 2019) (2019)
3. Donahue, J., et al.: Long-term recurrent convolutional networks for visual recognition and description. CoRR abs/1411.4389 (2014)
4. Fernández, J., Bornn, L.: SoccerMap: a deep learning architecture for visually-interpretable analysis in soccer. In: Dong, Y., Ifrim, G., Mladenić, D., Saunders, C., Van Hoecke, S. (eds.) ECML PKDD 2020, Part V. LNCS (LNAI), vol. 12461, pp. 491–506. Springer, Cham (2021). https://doi.org/10.1007/978-3-030-67670-4_30
5. Fernandez, J., Bornn, L., Cervone, D.: Decomposing the immeasurable sport: a deep learning expected possession value framework for soccer. In: In Proceedings of the 13th MIT Sloan Sports Analytics Conference (2019)

6. Fernandez-Navarro, J.: Analysis of styles of play in soccer and their effectiveness. Ph.D. thesis, Universidad de Granada (2018)
7. Fernandez-Navarro, J., Fraduab, L., Zubillagac, A., Forda, P.R., McRobert, A.P.: Attacking and defensive styles of play in soccer: analysis of Spanish and English elite teams. J. Sports Sci. **34**, 1–10 (2016)
8. Gambarelli, D., Gambarelli, G., Goossens, D.: Offensive or defensive play in soccer: a game-theoretical approach. J. Quant. Anal. Sports **15**(4), 261–269 (2019)
9. Gyarmati, L., Stanojevic, R.: QPass: a merit-based evaluation of soccer passes (2016)
10. Hirotsu, N., Wright, M.: Modeling tactical changes of formation in association football as a zero-sum game. J. Quant. Anal. Sports **2**(2), 1–15 (2006)
11. Inna, Z., Daniil, S.: Moneyball in offensive vs defensive actions in soccer. Eur. Econ. Labor Soc. Cond. eJournal (2020)
12. Liu, G., Luo, Y., Schulte, O., Kharrat, T.: Deep soccer analytics: learning an action-value function for evaluating soccer players. Data Min. Knowl. Discov. **34**(5), 1531–1559 (2020). https://doi.org/10.1007/s10618-020-00705-9
13. Liu, G., Schulte, O.: Deep reinforcement learning in ice hockey for context-aware player evaluation. In: Proceedings of the Twenty-Seventh International Joint Conference on Artificial Intelligence (IJCAI-18) (2018)
14. Luo, Y., Schulte, O., Poupart, P.: Inverse reinforcement learning for team sports: valuing actions and players. In: Bessiere, C. (ed.) Proceedings of the Twenty-Ninth International Joint Conference on Artificial Intelligence, IJCAI-20, pp. 3356–3363 (2020)
15. Metelli, A.M., Pirotta, M., Restelli, M.: Compatible reward inverse reinforcement learning. In: The Thirty-first Annual Conference on Neural Information Processing Systems (2017)
16. Muelling, K., Boularias, A., Mohler, B., Schoelkopf, B., Peters, J.: Inverse reinforcement learning for strategy extraction. In: ECML PKDD 2013 Workshop on Machine Learning and Data Mining for Sports Analytics (MLSA 2013) (2013)
17. Peralta Alguacil, F., Fernandez, J., Piñones Arce, P., Sumpter, D.: Seeing in to the future: using self-propelled particle models to aid player decision-making in soccer. In: Proceedings of the 14th MIT Sloan Sports Analytics Conference (2020)
18. Pirotta, M., Restelli, M.: Inverse reinforcement learning through policy gradient minimization. In: AAAI (2016)
19. Puterman, M.L.: Markov Decision Processes: Discrete Stochastic Dynamic Programming. Wiley, Hoboken (1994)
20. Tateo, D., Pirotta, M., Restelli, M., Bonarini, A.: Gradient-based minimization for multi-expert inverse reinforcement learning. In: 2017 IEEE Symposium Series on Computational Intelligence (SSCI), pp. 1–8 (2017)
21. Williams, R.J.: Simple statistical gradient-following algorithms for connectionist reinforcement learning. Mach. Learn. **8**, 229–256 (1992)
22. Zaytseva, I., Shaposhnikov, D.: Moneyball in offensive vs defensive actions in soccer. Eur. Econ. Labor Soc. Cond. eJournal (2020)

Predicting Player Transfers in the Small World of Football

Roland Kovacs and Laszlo Toka(⌷)

MTA-BME Information Systems Research Group, Faculty of Electrical Engineering
and Informatics, Budapest University of Technology and Economics,
Budapest, Hungary
toka@tmit.bme.hu

Abstract. Player transfers form the squad of the football clubs and
play an essential role in the success of the teams. A carefully selected
player squad is a prerequisite for successful performance. Consequently,
the main topic of the football world during summers is the transfer
rumors. The aim of our research is to predict future player transfers
using graph theory. In this paper, first, we examine the networks formed
in the football world and whether if these networks have small-world
property. To do this, we set up an acquaintance graph among professional footballers based on if they have ever been teammates. We make
a similar graph for the managers, in which we consider two coaches connected if they have coached the same club. Moreover, we also analyze
the network that has developed among the teams in the past 14 years,
in which links illustrate player transfers. Using the graphs' metrics and
the information about these transfers, we make a data mining model
for predicting the future transfer of players. The model can be used to
predict who will transfer into a selected league. Different leagues show
different features as the most important ones when it comes to buying
a player, but in every case that we studied, the features extracted from
the graphs are among the most essential ones. These features improved
the performance of the player transfer prediction model, giving sensible
possibilities about the transfers that will happen. Network science has
become widespread in recent years, allowing us to explore more and more
networks. By examining complex networks, we can obtain information
that would not otherwise be possible and that can have a massive effect
on predictions. We show that by using this information we can create
meaningful features that can improve the performance of the predictive
models.

Keywords: sports analytics · European football · soccer ·
small-world · network · machine learning · player transfer

1 Introduction

This article consists of two parts, first we perform network analysis using graph
theory and then we use data science to predict football players' transfers using
the information extracted from the networks that we build in the first part.

U. Brefeld et al. (Eds.): MLSA 2021, CCIS 1571, pp. 39–50, 2022.
https://doi.org/10.1007/978-3-031-02044-5_4

Networks appear in our everyday lives and affect numerous aspects like the spread of information, or the distribution of vaccines during a pandemic. Our brain is essentially a network of connected neurons and our society likewise forms a network with various acquaintances.

Today we know plenty about complex networks and scale-free networks, thanks to numerous research results in this field [1–4]. These networks are usually small-world networks, for which the main characteristic is that the average shortest path between the vertices is small. This means that we can get from any vertex to another without having to go through a lot of other vertices. One of the best-known pieces of research on this topic is named after Milgram who proved that social networks are small-world networks, and Albert Barabasi proved the same about the Internet [1,2]. In this paper, we analyze the networks formed in the world of football. We are looking for an answer to the question: do the graphs developed in that world have small-world properties? To do this we first examine the graph formed by the players' relationship of familiarity. We consider two players to be familiar if they have ever been teammates. Using a similar method, we create a graph among the managers in which they have a link if they have managed the same club. Not only relationships between people can be worth exploring, thus we also involve teams in our research and build a network based on the player transfers that emerged between those. With these networks we can analyze such complex problems that cannot be done in any other way since we can understand not only the single elements but also their relationships and interactions.

In football, player transfers play an essential role as those form the squad of the teams. The hottest topic of summers in the world of football is transfer rumors and guesses which team will purchase a given player. Football clubs want to strengthen their squads every year, and if they succeed, they could have great success next season. The opposite is also true, if the club fails to strengthen the squad, they may soon be at a disadvantage against the rival teams. Using the information of the graphs, we create a model that predicts future player transfers. The goal is not only to be able to predict transfers using past transfer data, but also to make more accurate forecast using information extracted from complex networks.

The paper is organized as follows. In Sect. 2 we present the results of the relevant research from network science and sports analytics. In Sect. 3 we present the basic properties of our constructed networks, with great emphasis on scale-free networks and the small-world property. Then, in Sect. 4, we specify the steps we took to develop the player transfer prediction model and describe the results of our research. Finally, we summarize the most important conclusions in Sect. 5.

2   Literature Review

One of the biggest breakthroughs in the world of network science was brought by Pal Erdos and Alfred Renyi who discovered random networks [5]. The above-mentioned scientists both wanted to examine complex graphs, but at that time it was not that obvious how to model networks. They thought most of the networks that occur in real life are unpredictable, asymmetric in structure, and rather appear random. Due to this assumption, the formation of graphs was characterized by the principle of randomness, which means that the best way to build a graph is to add the edges completely randomly between the nodes. Accordingly, each vertex has the same probability to collect edges, so most of the nodes have approximately the same degree. This means that if we want to draw a histogram of the degrees, we get a curve with a Poisson distribution. This was proven by Erdős's student, Béla Bollobás in 1982 [4]. The degree distribution, in this case, follows a bell curve, it has a maximum point, and the other vertices do not deviate much from this. We do not find vertices with very extreme degrees that differ from the average to a large extent. This suggests that, if we look at a social network, all people have nearly the same number of acquaintances. Or if we look at the World Wide Web and measure the connectivity of websites, pretty much each page points to the same number of other pages. Although most networks today are known to be non-random networks, their discovery has greatly contributed to the development of network science.

As stated above, numerous networks have been proven to be small-world networks. These networks have unique characteristics. According to Granovetter's studies, small-world networks have higher clustering coefficients thanks to the many complete subgraphs [3,6]. Clustering coefficient is a metric in network science, which measures the probability if two neighbors of a vertex are also adjacent to each other. Real-world networks usually have a clustering coefficient between 0.1 and 0.5 [7]. Another vital feature of small-world networks is that the length of the average distance grows only logarithmically with the number of vertices [1]. Consequently, the average distance is relatively small. According to Amaral and his co-authors, the diameter, which is the largest shortest distance between nodes, is also small in the small-world networks [3]. Additionally, the degree distribution of such networks follows a power-law distribution. This means most of the nodes have a small degree while only a few have greater degrees. These nodes are responsible for the weak connections and we usually call those hubs. Such scale-free networks are all small-world networks [3] and inherently differ from random networks.

Research has already been done in the world of sports related to the analysis of networks. Yuji Yamamoto and Keiko Yokoyama examined the networks that emerged in a football game, representing the players and the passes between them. They concluded that the degree distribution follows a power law and that the exponent values are very similar to real world networks. They also managed to identify the key players who play a big role in the team's performance [8]. Javier López Pena and Hugo Touchette also used information about passes to create networks and to describe football strategy [9], just like Raffaele Trequattrini et al. did, who analyzed an UEFA Champions League match [10]. They visualized the line-up of the teams and determined the importance of the players. Pablo Medina et al. used social network analysis to determine match results. They not only developed and analyzed networks but also studied their relevance to the results [11]. Paolo Cintia et al. measured team performance with networks as well. They not only used passes to determine the edges between players, but many other actions as well, like tackles, fouls, clearances, etc. They observed that the network indicators correlate with the success of the teams, and then used it to predict the outcome of the matches [12]. Filipe Manuel Clemente et al. suggested that defenders and midfielders have the most connectivity in the team [13]. Also Clemente et al. got similar results when they analyzed the Switzerland national football team in the 2014 FIFA World Cup [14]. E. Arriaza-Ardiles et al. used graph theory and complex networks to understand the play structure of the team. They used clustering and centrality metrics to describe the offensive play [15]. Opposed to the listed works that are all analyzing in-game relationships, our intention is to create a graph theoretical model on the club level in order to forecast player transfers between clubs.

3   Network Research Approach and Findings

In this section we present the graphs we created for modeling the relationship among players, coaches and clubs, respectively.

3.1   Players' Graph

Table 1. The basic metrics of the player graphs.

Metrics	Premier League	Top 5	European	World
Nodes	6,407	22,509	242,827	92,969
Edges	271,083	1,070,595	1,964,482	5,299,404
Average degree	84.62	95.13	91.74	114.00
Max degree	486	570	583	801
Min degree	23	20	19	19

We created four different graphs with more and more leagues involved. In this way, we could examine how the network metrics have changed with the increasing number of nodes. We started the analysis with one of the most competitive leagues in the world, the English Premier League. For this graph, we used the information available on the official website of the league [17]. We studied the teams from the 1992/93 season to the 2020/21 one, so this part of our research covered the entire history of the Premier League. We created three more graphs: we named the first one as Top 5 as it includes the best 5 European football leagues; the second graph, named as European, contains 24 first division leagues from Europe; the third graph, named as World, contains 58 leagues from all over the world. Both first, second, third and in some cases even fourth divisions are included. These latter 3 graphs are based on FIFA computer game data, which is published every year with updated squads [18]. We used information about players since the 2007 release. We created familiarity graphs, in which the players became the nodes and two players considered to be adjacent if they were teammates for at least a season. After defining the edge list, the developed graphs have the following metrics, summarized in Table 1.

First, we examined the degree distribution of the graphs, which can be decisive in answering our question. Small-world networks have power function distribution, which means that most players have only a few connections, but some players have a lot. Indeed, a power function is followed by the distribution of the degrees in the four graphs we created as Fig. 1 shows.

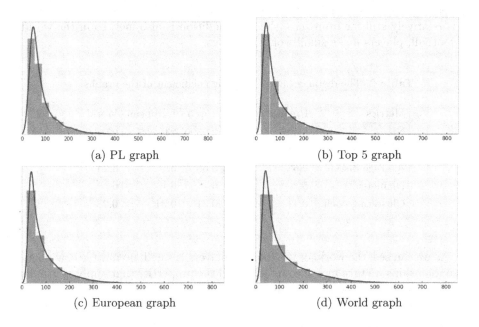

(a) PL graph

(b) Top 5 graph

(c) European graph

(d) World graph

Fig. 1. Degree distribution of the graphs follow power law

The average shortest distance and the diameter are both relatively small in small-world networks. Quite precisely, these numbers are roughly equal to the logarithm of the number of nodes. The average distance is 2.63, while the diameter is 5 of the Premier League graph. As 6,407 base 10 logarithm is 3.8, the average distance is even smaller than what is required for a small-world graph. This means that in the Premier League, the distance between players is very short, averaging less than 3 players and even between the farthest players, the distance is only 5. As shown in Table 2, these metrics are also small for the other graphs and increase at a slower rate than the logarithm of the number of vertices. It is utterly amazing that in the examined leagues, which cover the entire world, players are just over three steps apart on average. What is more, it only takes a maximum of six steps to connect any two players, even if they play in the farthest parts of the world.

The third characteristic which we examined is the clustering coefficient metric. It seems logical that this should be comparatively big, since teammates form a complete subgraph within the graph. The whole network is made up of such subgraphs connected by players who have turned up in several teams. When examining the clustering coefficient, we are curious about the extent to which there are triangles in the graph, so this property is also commonly referred to as triadic closure [16]. We will use these two words as synonyms hereafter. This metric for the Premier League players' graph is 0.41 which is closer to the upper limit of the standard value described earlier. Table 2 suggests that with the increasing number of vertices the clustering coefficient becomes smaller. But as it is relatively still far from zero, the last condition is also met, so in the world of football, players make small-world networks.

Table 2. The distances and clustering coefficient of the graphs.

Metrics	Premier League	Top 5	European	World
Nodes	6,407	22,509	242,827	92,969
Log of nodes	3.81	4.35	4.63	4.97
Average distance	2.63	3.00	3.17	3.24
Diameter	5	6	6	6
Clustering coeff	0.41	0.31	0.31	0.25

As we can see, the world of the football players is small, no matter how many championships we take into account, since all the properties that apply to graphs with small-world properties are fulfilled in them.

3.2   Managers' Graph

We did similar studies on the coaches of the Premier League. The used data is also collected since the 1992 season, available on the official Premier League website. Since two managers cannot lead the same team at once, we have defined the acquaintances in this network as two coaches knowing each other if they have managed the same team during their careers. Thus, we obtained a graph of 236 vertices and 1,843 edges, where the average degree is 15.62. This graph can be seen in Fig. 2.

First, we examined the degree distribution, which shows a power function distribution in this case too. It is well observed that the degrees are much lower than among the players, which is understandable since there were far fewer coaches than active players. The smallest degree is 1 and the largest is 81, which is Sam Allerdyce's degree, who managed 7 different teams and holds the records with the most clubs coached in the history of Premier League.

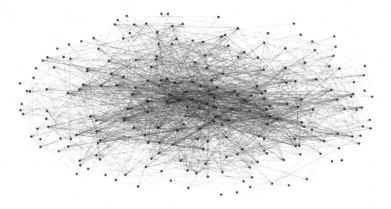

Fig. 2. The layout of the managers' graph.

Next, we examined the shortest path and diameter. Since the graph consisted of several components, we had to delete the smallest components to determine the average shortest path, as it can be determined only on one component. Two components had to be removed with 3 vertices each. The average shortest path of the resulting graph is less than it is among players, 2.53, and the diameter is only 5. The former number is less than the logarithm of 1,837, which is 3.2, so the network also meets this criterion.

Finally, we examined the clustering coefficient metric, which also meets the requirements, as it is 0.55, that is particularly high. This means that a manager's two neighbors probably coached the same club.

The results show that not only do players make up a small world in the Premier League but coaches do as well.

3.3   Teams' Graph

We have seen both players and coaches form a small world. We could also see from the example of the players that this is true not only to one league but to the whole world. But what about the teams? They are also in constant contact with each other, as they have a chance to purchase or borrow players from each other twice a year. For the study of the graph of player transfers, we used data available on Transfermarkt.com from 2007 to 2020, which includes all transfers between teams. Transfermarkt is the most well-known site that deals specifically with player evaluation.

In this case, the vertices of the graph are not players but teams, and two teams are adjacent if there was any transfer between them during the examined period. Thus, we obtained a network of 7,612 vertices with 49,805 edges. The average degree is 13.09, the highest is 330, and the lowest is 1.

The degree distribution follows a power curve. It is definitely true that most teams have only a low degree and there are only a few teams that have a high one. However, these teams are also extremely far from the average. The average shortest path is 3.6, which is less than 3.88, the logarithm of the number of nodes. Diameter is 7, which means that for some clubs it can take up to 7 steps to get to another, but on average 3–4 steps are enough.

The triadic closure is the smallest among the networks examined so far with the value of 0.18, but it is still sufficient to be a small-world network. It shows well that since now the nodes do not have teammates who are also adjacent to each other this value decreases. The relatively high value is likely given by the leagues, as within those, transfers are more common than usual.

In summary, this network is also a small-world network as the necessary conditions have been met. It also seems to be true in the world of football clubs that the world is small.

4   Predicting Player Transfers

To build the transfers' graph, we used historical information about the transfers. With this information advantageous correlation could be found, that can help the prediction of future transfers. Therefore we built a model for this purpose. We limited the data set only to transfers, as loan transactions are different in nature. Thus, starting from 2007, we had a total of 17 431 transfers which could be used to train the model. The goal of this model is to predict who will be transferred into a selected league, as the data is too spare to predict the same for clubs. During modeling we focused on the Top 5 leagues, but the same method can be applied to any other leagues as well.

The model was created based on the following features: the transferred player's age, market value, nationality, position, the league he was playing before the transfer, the FIFA computer game's player statistics, and information extracted from the graphs.

As the players' market value has been increasing steadily since 2007, we used a correctional scaling by dividing every value with the given season's 75th percentile value. In 2019, a player with the same parameters costed four times as much as in 2007, which would have led to a deterioration in the performance of the model. First we decided to do the correction with the mean of the seasons, but just a few high values can easily distort it, so it would not give us a clear picture about the market of the players. Then, we tried the median of the players' market value and noticed the distribution of it is unequal. Most of the players have a lower market value compared to the high profile players who play in the top leagues. Therefore, we decided to use the 75th percentile of the market values that is a decent indicator for a footballer playing in on of the top leagues. The result of the scaling is presented in Fig. 3.

The FIFA statistics include various abilities that rank players on a scale of 1 to 100. The higher this number, the better the given ability of the player is. There are abilities like dribbling, finishing, short passes, preferred foot, international reputation and many more. These abilities can be grouped into six main abilities, that FIFA also uses for the online game modes. Using these grouped main abilities also, like Defending, Passing, Shooting, Pace, Dribbling, and Physique

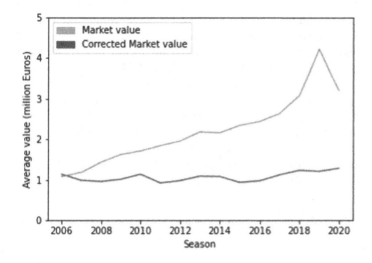

Fig. 3. Market value correctional scaling.

slightly improved our model. We also used features extracted from the graphs to get information not only about the transfers, but also about their relationships. We used the players' graph to get information about the players' acquaintance. For this purpose, we built graphs for every year to avoid the scenario when a player gets an acquaintance with a player with whom he played later. For example, if a transfer happened in 2015, we used the graph that has the data from 2007 to 2014 to avoid a player's score being influenced by a later teammate . We extracted the degree number divided by the number of seasons the player has been playing; the eigenvector, which is a centrality metric to measure the node's importance in the graph; and the number of links each player has with the top 5 leagues. The number of years between two transfers of the same player has also been calculated, in order to get how many years the given player spent in a particular team.

We encoded the categorical variables with CatBoost Encoder to avoid creating hundreds of columns, which would have been caused by the Country and the League variables. To fill the empty values Iterative Imputer has been used, which uses modeling to predict the missing values in a column, as it resulted in the best performance. After standardizing the dataset and testing different models, XGBoost was found to be the most accurate one. We used cross validation to train the model, and grid search to find the best parameters. We chose the set of hyperparameters with the highest recall metric, that has a high accuracy as well, as we wanted to predict as many actual transfers as possible. The best set of parameters are 5000 estimators, 0.7 subsample, 6 maximum depth, and 0.1 learning rate.

As the data set contains many leagues, the number of transfers into the selected league is dwarfed relative to the entire data set. This degrades the quality of the model, so we used the SMOTE (Synthetic Minority Oversampling

Technique) to reproduce the favorable data if there were too few positive cases in the selected league and it led to performance degradation. The SMOTE technique uses oversampling with the k-nearest algorithm to smooth the data set. After trying several models, oversampling with SVM (Support Vector Machine) worked the best. Using this method the recall metric increased greatly, but creating too many records resulted in over-fitting, so only a few percent has been added to the positive cases.

After finding the best parameters of the model, we used it on the FIFA 21 computer game's data, that includes almost 20,000 players. We ran the model for the Top 5 European leagues, and compared the most important features according to the XGBoost model. These are listed in Table 3.

Table 3. The most important features of the Top 5 leagues.

Premier League	La Liga	Ligue 1	Serie A	Bundesliga
League	Country	League	Serie A	League
MarketValue	League	Ligue 1	League	Market Value
Eigenvector	Market Value	Country	Country	Age
Country	Foot	IntReputation	MarketValue	Reactions
Age	Eigenvector	Age	Degree	IntReputation
IntReputation	GK kicking	Premier League	Foot	Country
Foot	Defending	GK diving	La Liga	Short passing
GK kicking	Passing	Eigenvector	Eigenvector	GK diving
Physical	IntReputation	Market Value	Age	Defending
Shooting	Age	La Liga	Sliding Tackle	Dribbling

In some leagues the most meaningful variables are the graph variables, most notably the number of links with the league for which the transfer prediction is made, like the Ligue 1 and Serie A. These leagues are particularly characterized by transfers predominantly within the league. We denote each of these features by the name of the respective league. The eigenvector also turns up among the most vital features as one of the graph variables. The country, market value, current league, and age also play great part in the prediction. The international reputation feature is only missing from the Serie A's top 10, while the preferred foot is missing from the Ligue 1 and Bundesliga. The main attributes from FIFA also appear. In the Premier League the most essential ones are the shooting and the physical attribute, while in the La Liga the defending and passing.

The accuracy of the models varies between 93–95 depending on the selected league. The F1 score also differs among the leagues. The highest one is the Ligue 1 with 86, and the lowest one is for the La Liga with 46. There are numerous false positive predictions, as in the result there are 1500–3000 players predicted to transfer into the selected league. This is mainly because we do not take into account some vital features, like performance features or when the players' contracts expire. Involving these features could further improve our model. Also worth mentioning that due to the loss of revenue caused by the corona virus pandemic, clubs spend much less this season, and purchase much fewer players, then in those years on which the model was trained.

The La Liga and the Bundesliga have the fewest number of transfers in the training set, and the model works the worst for these two leagues. However, for the Premier League and for the Serie A, it predicted 25 out of 47, and 24 out of 64 transfers well, respectively, that have recently happened (in 2021). For the Ligue 1, 15 of 38 transfers were predicted correctly. Running the models without the graph metrics resulted in worse result, except for the Bundesliga. Without those features the model produces significantly more false positives and the accuracy is 2 percent higher, when those metrics are included.

Table 4 shows some of the transfers predicted correctly by the model for the Top 5 leagues.

Table 4. Some of the correctly predicted transfers

Premier League	La Liga	Serie A	Bundesliga	Ligue 1
B. White	R. De Paul	M. Darmian	J. Gvardiol	J. Lucas
E. Buendía	M. Depay	F. Tomori	K. Boateng	D. Da Silva
A. Townsend	S. Agüero	M. Maignan	R. Hack	L. Balerdi
J. Grealish	D. Alaba	E. Hysaj	M. Uth	L. Badé
B. Soumaré	E. Lamela	R. Patrício	G. Haraguchi	A. Bassi

Overall, the model works well for the purpose of showing who could be considered if a team wants to buy a player for the above mentioned three leagues based on the results so far. The information extracted from the graphs improved the performance of the model, as the accuracy is increased by reducing the false positive predictions.

5   Conclusions

In our research, we have demonstrated that the networks that emerge in the world of football, just like many naturally occurring networks, are small-world networks. Both players, managers, and teams with their transfers form small worlds. Using the information of these graphs, information of historical transfers, and information of FIFA computer games we predicted future player transfers. The model can be used to predict movements into the selected league, but to predict the same for clubs the available data is too sparse. The information extracted from the graphs have a great importance in the predictive models and improve their performance. The most vital features of the transfers were also presented of the top 5 leagues.

Acknowledgment. Project no. 128233 has been implemented with the support provided by the Ministry of Innovation and Technology of Hungary from the National Research, Development and Innovation Fund, financed under the FK_18 funding scheme.

References

1. Newman, M., Barabasi, A.-L., Watts, D.J. (eds.): The Structure and Dynamics of Networks. Princeton University Press, Princeton (2006)
2. Milgram, S.: The small-world problem. Psychol. Today **1**, 60 (1967)
3. Amaral, L.A.N, Scala, A., Barthelemy, M., Stanley, H.E.: Classes of small-world network (2000)
4. Barabasi, A.-L.: Linked: How Everything is Connected to Everything Else and What It Means for Business. Science and Everyday Life. Plume Books, New York (2003)
5. Erdos, P., Renyi, A.: On the evolution of random graphs. Publ. Math. Inst. Hung. Acad. **5**, 17–61 (1960)
6. Granovetter, M.S.: The strength of weak ties. Am. J. Sociol. **78**, 1360–1380 (1973)
7. Javier, M.H., Piet, V.M.: Classification of graph metrics (2011)
8. Yamamoto, Y., Yokoyama, K.: Common and unique network dynamics in football games. PLoS ONE **6**(12), e29638 (2011)
9. Pena, J.L., Touchette, H.: A network theory analysis of football strategies, in Sports Physics. Clanet, C (ed.) Proceedings of the 2012 Euromech Physics of Sports Conference, pp. 517–528. (2012)
10. Trequattrini, R., Lombardi, R., Battista, M.: Network analysis and football team performance: a first application (2015)
11. Medina, P., et al.: Is a social network approach relevant to football results? Chaos, Solitons Fractals **142**, 110369 (2021)
12. Cintia, P., Rinzivillo, S., Pappalardo, L.: A network-based approach to evaluate the performance of football teams. In: Workshop on Machine Learning and Data Mining for Sports Analytics, pp. 46–54, Porto, Portugal (2015)
13. Clemente, F.M., Couceiro, M.S., Martins, F.M.L., Mendes, R.S.: Using network metrics to investigate football team players' connections: a pilot study. Motriz, Rio Claro **20**(3), 262–271 (2014)
14. Clemente, F.M., Martins, F.M.L., Kalamaras, D., Oliveira, J., Oliveira, P., Mendes, R.S.: The social network of Switzerland football team on FIFA World Cup 2014. In: Acta Kinesiologica, vol. 9, pp. 25–30 (2015)
15. Arriaza-Ardilesa, E., Martín-González, J.M., Zunigac, M.D., Sánchez-Floresd, J., de Saae, Y., García-Mansoe, J.M.: Applying graphs and complex networks to football metric interpretation. Hum. Mov. Sci. **57**, 236–243 (2018)
16. David, E., Jon, K.: Networks, Crowds, and Markets: Reasoning about a Highly Connected World, pp. 48–50. Cambridge University Press, Cambridge (2010)
17. Premier League official website. https://www.premierleague.com/players. Last Accessed 20 Aug 2021
18. FIFA players. https://www.premierleague.com/players. Accessed 20 Aug 2021

Similarity of Football Players Using Passing Sequences

Alberto Barbosa[1]([✉]), Pedro Ribeiro[1], and Inês Dutra[2]

[1] INESC-TEC and DCC/FCUP, University of Porto, Porto, Portugal
alberto.barbosa@fc.up.pt
[2] CINTESIS and DCC/FCUP, University of Porto, Porto, Portugal

Abstract. Association football has been the subject of many research studies. In this work we present a study on player similarity using passing sequences extracted from games from the top-5 European football leagues during the 2017/2018 season. We present two different approaches: first, we only count the motifs a player is involved in; then we also take into consideration the specific position a player occupies in each motif. We also present a new way to objectively judge the quality of the generated models in football analytics. Our results show that the study of passing sequences can be used to study player similarity with relative success.

1 Introduction

Association football is one of the most popular team sports in the world. Traditionally, studying many aspects of the game has been relying on the empiric experience of coaches and scouts. However, some aspects of the game have been the subject of research in many different fields of science, given the growing availability of data related to football matches. Player injury forecasting [14], team behaviour visualisation [9,18], talent discovery [5,13,15] and transfer market analysis [3,7,8] are some of the features of the football industry that have been continuously receiving attention from different fields of computer science.

This work has two major contributions: the study of passing networks using network motifs and the study of player similarity, using different ways to measure the quality of the results and models obtained.

2 Related Work

Research on association football has been growing in popularity and many aspects of the game have been receiving recent attention, like visualising and analysing team formations and their dynamics [17] or predicting match results [1]. Given the subject this paper, we will mainly focus on research that delved into studying motif based patterns in passing networks.

A passing network can be seen as a graph where the nodes represent the players and there is an edge going from player A to player B if player A successfully passed the ball to player B. Milo et al. defined network motifs as "patterns of interconnections occurring in complex networks at numbers that are significantly higher than those in randomised networks" [10]. Later, Gyarmati et al [4] defined flow motifs. Considering a passing sequence, a flow motif is a subsequence of the passes where labels represent distinct players without identity. In the context of this paper, all motifs are flow motifs. We will next make a short description previous research on this topic.

Bekkers and Dabadghao [2] applied network motif methodology to football passing networks in data comprising 4 seasons of 6 major football leagues. They were able to identify unique play styles for both teams and players.

Håland et al. [6] studied the Norwegian elite league of football, concluding that passing can be modelled using networks and sequences of passes can be mapped into flow motifs. Their most relevant finding was that although more compact motif types (with fewer different players involved) had a lower likelihood of leading to shots, no connection between the ranking of a team and their distribution of flow motifs was clear.

Peña et al. [12] also applied flow motifs to football passing networks and clustered players according to their participation in different flow motifs, trying to identify unique play styles. The outlier in their analysis was the former FC Barcelona midfielder Xavi Hernández, which formed a singleton cluster due to his unique passing style and its influence in Barcelona's play style.

Gyarmati et al. [4] propose a quantitative method to evaluate the styles of football teams through their passing structures, through the study of network motifs, concluding that FC Barcelona's tiki-taka does not consist of uncountable random passes but has a finely constructed structure instead.

Wiig et al. [16] identify some players as key passers and/or passing recipients using network analysis on passing networks of teams in Norway. Some interesting conclusions of their work consist on showing that offensive players tend to have a high closeness centrality measurements and high PageRank values for pass recipients, whereas defenders tend to have high PageRank values for passers.

3   Data Description

The data used in this work was retrieved from a public data set containing spatio-temporal events in association football [11]. The data set contains events from the 2017/2018 season of the top tier leagues in Spain, England, Italy, Germany and France. In addition to that, data of the World Cup 2018 and of the European Cup 2016 is also provided. However, our analysis embraces the club competitions only, due to higher number of matches and events they provide, having the potential to yield more trustful and data reliable conclusions than small competitions with less data to extract knowledge from.

We pre-processed the raw data events to transform them into sequences of passes between the players involved and to cut the players that did not partic-ipate in, at least, 80% of the games that season. The later decision was made because, since we only have one season of match and event information, we pre-ferred to work with players that had more consistent data regarding their passing

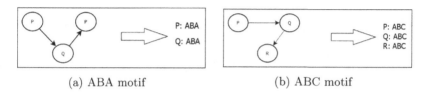

(a) ABA motif   (b) ABC motif

Fig. 1. Processing passing sequences into motifs. In (a), we have a sequence of passes from player P to player Q and then to P again. This is processed as both players participating in an ABA motif. In (b) we have a different sequence of passes involving three different players: P passes to Q which then passes to R, all of them participating in an ABC motif. When we have bigger sequences of passes, these are divided into motifs of size k and processed in a similar way.

and play styles and also it was important to our evaluation model to work with players that had played throughout the season consistently.

4   Methodology and Results

Our methodology and results will be described along each other as we discuss each of the two different approaches we followed in solving the problem of assessing player similarity in association football.

Our initial approach was to count the frequency of different size 3 and size 4 network motifs for each of the players involved. Such motifs were extracted from the passing sequences as in Fig. 1. These motif sizes offer a good initial compromise between having enough data to analyse (larger passing sequences are less frequent) and having a relatively small number of different motifs that will constitute the features that we incorporate in our proposed distance metric, depicted in Eq. 1. As said, we compute the distance between players A and B by considering M, the set of all motifs of size 3 and 4. P_m represents the normalised number (between 0 and 1) of motifs that player P was involved in. When normalising P_m we divide the number of times a player was involved in a motif of type m by the total number of times a player has been involved in all motifs in M.

$$D(A, B) = \sqrt{\sum_{m \in M} (A_m - B_m)^2} \qquad (1)$$

After counting the number of times a player was involved in a specific passing pattern, we computed the distance from him to every other player, as in Eq. 1, to every other in order to see which players were the most similar to each other.

We evaluate our results in two different ways: visually and objectively. For a visual evaluation, we draw radar plots that mirror the participation of the player in all different motifs considered and visually compare their similarity. We also check the most similar players and use our domain knowledge to interpret the results. Since we analysed over 560 players, it would be impossible to present the radar plots of all the players and we choose a sample of 4 players to showcase

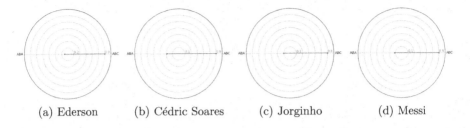

(a) Ederson   (b) Cédric Soares   (c) Jorginho   (d) Messi

Fig. 2. Radar plots of the four example players considering only size 3 motifs.

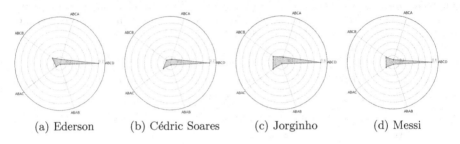

(a) Ederson   (b) Cédric Soares   (c) Jorginho   (d) Messi

Fig. 3. Radar plots of the four example players considering only size 4 motifs

the empirical analysis we performed, namely the goalkeeper Ederson (Manchester City), the defender Cédric Soares (Southampton), the midfielder Jorginho (Napoli) and the forward Lionel Messi (Barcelona).

We felt that a visual comparison of radar plots was not enough since we wanted a more objective way to score and compare different approaches. Our evaluation model was achieved by dividing our data set in two halves (first and second half of the season). With those two new data sets, we performed the same task of counting the motifs each player was involved in and we calculated the distance between all players. The evaluation score is given by the number of players that have themselves in the top-10 of similarity in different halves. This model is based on the intuition that the same player in the same season should have a similar behaviour when it comes to passing and play styles.

For each experimental setting, we performed two different tests: first we tested our approach with data from each league individually and then with data from the top-5 leagues in Europe simultaneously. This was done to test the ability of our model to deal with more data and noise, since the task of identifying similar players gets harder as we increase the amount of players to compare.

In Figures 2 and 3 a visual analysis of the radar plots of some players showed us that it was very hard to clearly obtain a fingerprint of the play style of the player merely through it. With size 3 motifs, we can barely notice any difference between different players, and the main observation that we can extract is that the fraction of ABC patterns seem to be higher in every player, which seems reasonable (it is much more likely that 2 consecutive passes go through 3 different players that two players passing between each other). Also, a difference in the

Table 1. Top-5 similar players to our 4 example players according to their participation in size 3 passing sequences. We compared the passing patterns of each player in the 1st half of the season to the patterns of the entire set of players (of all leagues) in the 2nd half of the season.

	1st	2nd	3rd	4th	5th
Ederson	Douglas Costa	J. Alonso	K. Koulibaly	Campaña	I. Diop
Cédric Soares	Y. Sabaly	D. Suárez	K. Naughton	M. Olsson	Cédric Soares
Jorginho	E. Zukanovic	E. Pulgar	S. Missiroli	I. Bebou	Jorginho
Messi	M. Kruse	D. Yedlin	F. Guilbert	P. Faragò	C. Traoré

Table 2. Top-5 similar players to our 4 example players according to their participation in size 4 passing sequences. We compared the passing patterns of each player in the 1st half of the season to the patterns of the entire set of players (of all leagues) in the 2nd half of the season.

	1st	2nd	3rd	4th	5th
Ederson	Allan	Hradecky	B. Dibassy	C.Schindler	Maxi Gómez
Cédric Soares	I. Gueye	K. Naughton	G. Bonaventura	S. Ascacíbar	á. Correa
Jorginho	Zielinski	J. Lascelles	M. Veljkovic	M. Politano	K. de Bruyne
Messi	E. Pulgar	L. Suárez	S. Papastathopoulos	B. Oczipka	Malcom

Table 3. Accuracy values obtained when analysing the flow motifs of sizes 3 and 4 without considering the specific position of each player in each motif.

	England	France	Germany	Italy	Spain	All
Size 3	14,61%	17,20%	10.60%	13.20%	21,02%	2.86%
Size 4	36.59%	28.74%	26.38%	28.20%	28.50%	8.57%

fraction of ABA and ABC passing patterns can be noticed in some players (for example between the ABA frequency in Ederson radar plot against the ABA frequency in Cédric Soares).

The size 4 motif plots give us more visual information regarding the play style of each player, with richer and more varied topological patterns. For instance, we can notice that defensive players like Ederson and Cedric Soares tend to have a higher percentage of participation in ABCD plays than more offensive players like Jorginho and Messi. This can be due to fact that more dynamic and offensive players tend to participate in more types of plays and tend to appear in more than one passing role in small sequences of passes. Even so, we can hardly notice really significant differences between different players that play very different roles in a game of football.

To complement the visual analysis of the results, we studied a sample of the 5 most similar players reported by the algorithm according to their participation in size 3 and size 4 motifs, as presented in Tables 1 and 2, respectively. The majority of players that are reported as being the most similar to the players

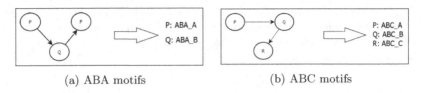

(a) ABA motifs   (b) ABC motifs

Fig. 4. Processing passing sequences into motifs considering the specific position each player represents in the motif. In (a), we have a sequence of passes from player P to player Q and then to player P again. This is processed as player P participating in an ABA_A motif (position A in ABA motif) and as player Q participating in an ABA_B motif (position A in ABA motif). In (b) we have a different sequence of passes between three players and the corresponding position motifs. As before, bigger passing sequences are divided into motifs of size k.

in our study sample have really different play styles (for example, in Table 1 Douglas Costa (a winger) is reported to be the most similar player to Ederson (a goalkeeper)). Even though, there seems to exist an improvement when we take into consideration size 4 motifs instead of only size 3 motifs, as in Table 2. The fact that Hradecky, a goalkeeper, is reported as one of the most similar players to Ederson, also a goalkeeper, and the fact that Messi and L. Suárez, both forwards in FC Barcelona, are also being reported as similar seems to indicate some sort of improvement when using size 4 motifs instead of size 3 motifs, as the radar plots showed.

Our objective evaluation model also mirrors the intuition that the empirical analysis based on the radar plotting of the results. The average accuracy of this initial approach when running only with a single league was roughly 15, 32% for size 3 motifs and of 28, 68% for size 4 motifs and the accuracy obtained when considering all top-5 European Leagues simultaneously was of 2.86% for size 3 motifs and 8, 57% for size 4 motifs, as shown in detail in Table 3. These results show that our initial approach, as the visual analysis seemed to show, had serious problems in capturing a player's unique play style.

Given the poor practical results in our initial approach, we decided to enhance it by looking not only to the motifs each player is involved in, but also which specific position in the motif they occupy, or the orbit of each player, as shown in Fig. 4. This would provide more variability and more features to help separate players from each other but would also help in identifying, for example, if a player is more of a play starter or a play finisher or if a player tends to be involved in more than one role in the same passing sequence. A new visual analysis of the results of applying this new approach seems to show more significant fingerprints of each player, as seen in Figs. 5 and 6.

A much higher quantity of information can be extracted from these radar plots. When considering size 3 motifs, Ederson, a goalkeeper, tends to be in the starting part of the plays he participates in: he has a much higher participation in ABC_A (ABC_A means that the player occupies position A in the ABC motif) and ABC_B than in other motifs. This is confirmed again when considering size

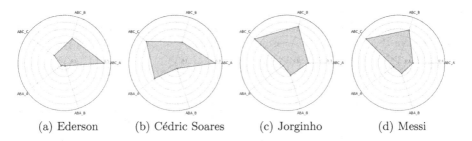

(a) Ederson   (b) Cédric Soares   (c) Jorginho   (d) Messi

Fig. 5. Radar plots of the four example players considering size 3 motifs and specific player roles (or orbit) in each motif

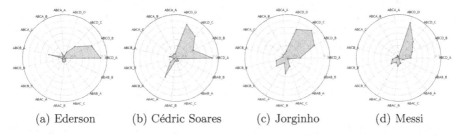

(a) Ederson   (b) Cédric Soares   (c) Jorginho   (d) Messi

Fig. 6. Radar plots of the four example players considering size 4 motifs and specific player roles (or orbit) in each motif

4 motifs, with the high values of $ABCD\_A$ and $ABCD\_B$. On the other hand, Messi, a forward, seems to exhibit a very different behaviour on the pitch. He participates much more in the ending side of the plays, due to his play style and position. This is confirmed by his higher percentage of ABC_C and ABC_B in size 3 motifs and $ABCD\_C$ and $ABCD\_D$ in size 4 motifs.

Other aspects of each of these players can be deduced from the radar plots characterising them. For instance, the fact that Cédric Soares, a full back, seems to appear more often either at the start of the plays or at the end of the plays, but less frequently in the middle of those plays. This can be justified with the fact that a full back in modern day football such as Cédric Soares has to be capable of being at the start of the plays due to the defensive nature of the role he has on the pitch, but also has to be capable of appearing in more offensive areas, usually to cross the ball to the teammates in the opponent's box.

This empirical analysis of the radar plots of each player seems to point that looking not only at the motifs each player participates in, but also looking at which position they occupy in each motif they participate in, causes the passing and playing style of each player to emerge in the visualisation of the results.

The most similar players, according to this approach, to each player in our study group are reported in Table 4 and Table 5. Empirically, the players reported as similar to the ones in our study group really seem to make more sense than the ones obtained with the previous approach. We can see, for example, that when considering either size 3 or size 4 motifs, Ederson is only similar

Table 4. Top-5 similar players to our 4 example players according to their participation and specific position in size 3 passing sequences. We compared the passing patterns of each player in the 1st half of the season to the patterns of the entire set of players (of all leagues) in the 2nd half of the season.

	1st	2nd	3rd	4th	5th
Ederson	Alisson	M. ter Stegen	S. Ulreich	S. Ruffier	H. Lloris
Cédric Soares	L. Venuti	C. Traoré	R. Bertrand	Jordi Alba	A. Masina
Jorginho	D. Demme	R. van La Parra	D. Liénard	Koke	Fabián
Messi	G. Bonaventura	S. Missiroli	Bernardo Silva	A. Mooy	T. Hazard

Table 5. Top-5 similar players to our 4 example players according to their participation and specific position in size 4 passing sequences. We compared the passing patterns of each player in the 1st half of the season to the patterns of the entire set of players (of all leagues) in the 2nd half of the season.

	1st	2nd	3rd	4th	5th
Ederson	Pepe Reina	D. de Gea	S. Ulreich	Ederson	Alisson
Cédric Soares	D. Suárez	M. Olsson	Y. Sabaly	L. Dubois	J. Korb
Jorginho	D. Liénard	N. Hoefler	X. Shaqiri	M. Antenucci	A. Knockaert
Messi	A. Sánchez	Koke	Kalou	E. Hazard	B. Cristante

Table 6. Accuracy values obtained when analysing the flow motifs of sizes 3 and 4 considering the specific position of each player in each motif.

	England	France	Germany	Italy	Spain	All
Size 3	38,62%	55,75%	42,59%	40,98%	49,07%	13,6%
Size 4	39,84%	52,30%	38,89%	44,36%	49,53%	17,59%

to goalkeepers (even to himself). Alisson is the partner of Ederson in defending the goal for the Brazilian national team and it is widely known that they have similar play styles. This is clearly mirrored in the results, given the fact that Alisson is reported to be similar to Ederson when considering both size 3 or size 4 motifs. Moreover, some other player similarities seem to be really accurate from an empirical point of view: Jorginho and Demme, Messi and Bernardo Silva or Hazard, Cédric and L. Dubois or L. Venuti, among others.

We wanted to see if the accuracy of the evaluation model supported our empirical analysis of the results. As seen in detail in Table 6, the accuracy when considering each league individually was 45,44% for size 3 motifs and 44,98% for size 4 motifs. The accuracy considering the top-5 Leagues was of 13,60% for size 3 motifs and of 17,59% for size 4 motifs.

These results show a clear improvement in the accuracy of the model when we take into consideration not only the motifs each players participates in, but also the specific position each player occupies in that passing sequence.

Nonetheless, there seem to be limitations in this approach. When considering all five leagues simultaneously, we can see that the current method still struggles with properly identifying the same player in different parts of the season.

Among other possible explanations to this decrease in performance, we believe that since we only worked with data from a single season, meaning that when dividing the data in half in order to build our evaluation model we only had data from 16 to 18 games at most to build a fingerprint of a player in two distinct halves of the season, the model is really sensitive to small fluctuations that may occur in the performance of the player in those games.

5   Conclusions

In this work we presented a study on the similarity of association football players according to their passing behaviours during the course of one season in 5 different European football leagues.

Studying similarity measures for football players can be very useful for football teams, since they can help the scout department discover new players with potential to join the team they work form.

When taking into consideration only the frequency of participation of the player in different passing motifs, the results showed that little information was actually being extracted from that data, especially when only considering size 3 motifs.

With the addition of the specific position a player occupies in each motif he participates in, we could see a great improvement in player characterisation and similarity both empirically and objectively.

However, even though the results show a great improvement and seem to yield good practical results, some limitations are evident. The fact that the addition of more players to the data set really decreases performance seems to indicate that the algorithm has some difficulties in identifying the uniqueness in player's play style when the amount of data is increased. This could be due to the fact that the amount of data available is not enough to the algorithm to behave better with noisier data set or it could be the fact that more aspects of the game have to be taken into account in order to uniquely identify the play style of a player.

6   Future Work

The results achieved in this work show real promise and, as such, some future work can be done to complement and enhance this approach.

The introduction of the spatio-temporal dimension of the passing data into the model can help in calculating player similarity.

The availability of tracking data of the players can help understand player movement when he does not have the ball. During most of the game, a player does not have the ball in his control, so a huge part of the role of a player in football match is being discarded.

Study team behaviour and similarity using a similar methodology may be possible and useful to improve the knowledge a team has of their opponent, which can help in designing a unique strategy to beat an opponent.

Acknowledgements. This research was funded by FCT and INESC-TEC under the grant SFRH/BD/136525/2018, Ref CRM:0067161.

References

1. Baboota, R., Kaur, H.: Predictive analysis and modelling football results using machine learning approach for English premier league. Int. J. Forecast. **35**, 741–755 (2019)
2. Bekkers, J., Dabadghao, S.: Flow motifs in soccer: what can passing behavior tell us? J. Sports Anal. **5**(4), 299–311 (2019)
3. Fűrész, D.I., Rappai, G.: Information leakage in the football transfer market. Eur. Sport Manage. Q. 1–21 (2020)
4. Gyarmati, L., Kwak, H., Rodriguez, P.: Searching for a unique style in soccer. arXiv preprint arXiv:1409.0308 (2014)
5. Haave, H.S., Høiland, H.: Evaluating association football player performances using Markov models (2017)
6. Håland, E.M., Wiig, A.S., Hvattum, L.M., Stålhane, M.: Evaluating the effectiveness of different network flow motifs in association football. J. Quant. Anal. Sports **16**, 311–323 (2020)
7. Kroken, C., Hashi, G.: Market efficiency in the European football transfer market (2017)
8. Matesanz, D., Holzmayer, F., Torgler, B., Schmidt, S.L., Ortega, G.J.: Transfer market activities and sportive performance in European first football leagues: a dynamic network approach. PLoS ONE **13**, e0209362 (2018)
9. McLean, S., Salmon, P., Gorman, A.D., Wickham, J., Berber, E., Solomon, C.: The effect of playing formation on the passing network characteristics of a professional football team. Human Mov. **2018**, 14–22 (2018)
10. Milo, R., Shen-Orr, S., Itzkovitz, S., Kashtan, N., Chklovskii, D., Alon, U.: Network motifs: simple building blocks of complex networks. Science **298**(5594), 824–827 (2002)
11. Pappalardo, L., et al.: A public data set of spatio-temporal match events in soccer competitions. Sci. Data **6**(1), 1–15 (2019)
12. Peña, J.L., Navarro, R.S.: Who can replace Xavi? a passing motif analysis of football players. arXiv preprint arXiv:1506.07768 (2015)
13. Reinders, H.: Talent identification in girls soccer: a process-oriented approach using small-sided games (2018)
14. Rossi, A., Pappalardo, L., Cintia, P., Iaia, F.M., Fernández, J., Medina, D.: Effective injury forecasting in soccer with GPS training data and machine learning. PLoS ONE **13**, e0201264 (2018)
15. Tovar, J., Clavijo, A., Cardenas, J.: A strategy to predict association football players' passing skills. Universidad de Los Andes Department of Economics Research Paper Series (2017)
16. Wiig, A.S., Håland, E.M., Stålhane, M., Hvattum, L.M.: Analyzing passing networks in association football based on the difficulty, risk, and potential of passes. Int. J. Comput. Sci. Sport **18**, 44–68 (2019)

17. Wu, Y., et al.: ForVizor: visualizing spatio-temporal team formations in soccer. IEEE Trans. Visual. Comput. Graph. **25**, 65–75 (2019)
18. Yu, Q., Gai, Y., Gong, B., Gómez, M.Á., Cui, Y.: Using passing network measures to determine the performance difference between foreign and domestic outfielder players in Chinese football super league. Int. J. Sports Sci. Coach. **15**, 398–404 (2020)

The Interpretable Representation of Football Player Roles Based on Passing/Receiving Patterns

Arsalan Sattari[(✉)], Ulf Johansson, Erik Wilderoth, Jasmin Jakupovic, and Peter Larsson-Green

Jönköping University, Gjuterigatan 5, 551 11 Jönköping, Sweden
arsalan.sattari@ju.se

Abstract. In this study, we define a new way of representing football player roles based on passing and receiving interactions. We develop a definition of player roles consisting of a linear combination of 12 common and interpretable passing/receiving patterns. Linear combinations are derived from the decomposition of players' pitch passing and receiving networks using non-negative matrix factorization (NMF). Our model shows that 43% of the 1491 players studied in this paper had a maximum weight of less than 50% in each of the 12 common passing/receiving patterns. This suggests that a substantial percentage of players do not follow the specific passing/receiving patterns typically associated with their conventional role. The model also reveals the underlying differences in passing/receiving patterns amongst players who hold the same conventional role. It shows the intricacies of player patterns optimally when tasked with analyzing the most complex conventional roles such as midfielders, wingers, and forwards. Lastly, we show that the combinations of the 12 common passing/receiving patterns can be used as a footprint to find players with similar passing/receiving styles. For instance, our model found that Shaqiri and Fabinho had the highest similarity in passing/receiving styles to Oxlade-Chamberlain and Henderson. This is consistent with Liverpool FC's transfers of Shaqiri and Fabinho to replace Oxlade-Chamberlain and Henderson's positions respectively in the summer of 2018.

Keywords: Football analytics · Passing networks · Player roles

1 Introduction

Predicting the future tactical compatibility of a football player to a potential team is a highly difficult task as there are a multitude of factors to take into consideration. One common way of determining a player's tactical compatibility is to analyze their individual performance metrics in a conventional role (e.g. defender, midfielder, forward) [4]. Performance metrics and current conventional roles typically characterize a player as a singular entity. However, they do not take into

© The Author(s), under exclusive license to Springer Nature Switzerland AG 2022
U. Brefeld et al. (Eds.): MLSA 2021, CCIS 1571, pp. 62–76, 2022.
https://doi.org/10.1007/978-3-031-02044-5_6

consideration how the role can be further defined by a player's interactions - including passes and receptions - with other players. Football players constantly interact with each other in passing and receiving the ball and making off-ball runs. They often deviate from their main roles to achieve optimal coverage and disrupt the defensive order of their opponents. Therefore, their tasks are not limited to where their role specifies where they should be on the pitch. A more thorough characterization of player roles needs to take into consideration the dynamic interactions - specifically, passes and receptions - between players on the football pitch. This can contribute to a more complete picture of a player when a player is assessed for their future tactical compatibility with a potential team.

Defining player roles through dynamic interactions in a quantitative manner is a complicated task. Studies focusing specifically on player role definition are not prevalent. A seminal paper by Aalbers and Van Haaren [1] aimed to broaden the conventional definitions of player roles in creating a more expansive set of 21 roles for football players, which was not based solely on positioning. The authors incorporated offensive and defensive duties, technical ability, player intelligence, strength, agility and endurance into their definition of roles. They then trained a supervised machine learning model to predict player roles (based on the 21 roles) using players' basic statistics and performance metrics across many games.

Although studies on player roles based on interactions between players are not numerous, scientists have investigated the broader subject of team behaviours and developed models of further investigation [4]. The following literature review will give a summary of the research completed on investigating and understanding team behaviour and how to capture the complexity of a team's dynamics. We draw from these insights as a starting point from which to generate ideas on a new definition of player roles based on dynamic interactions, specifically, 12 common pitch passing/receiving patterns.

2   Literature Review

2.1   Automatic Formation Detection

Automatic formation detection is a technique, which finds the average position of players relative to each other. Pappalardo et al. [15] proposed a method to identify eight different football roles based on their positioning. These roles were identified by clustering the position of events (e.g. passes) which players were involved in. Bialkowski et al. [3] also used a clustering technique to assign 10 roles to players based on spatiotemporal tracking data. Narizuka and Yamazaki [14] and Shaw and Glickman [18] also used hierarchical clustering techniques on spatiotemporal tracking data to find unique sets of formation for football teams. Although the methods which investigate team formation give information about the average positioning of players with respect to each other, they do not take into account the patterns found in interactions between players.

2.2 Team Passing/Team Pitch Passing Network Analysis

Team passing network analysis is an approach with which we can investigate player roles by investigating how a player is connected to the rest of the team. A team passing network has two components: nodes and links. The nodes represent players and links represent the passes exchanged between them. Each link is assigned a weight, which corresponds to the number of passes between the two nodes that it connects. Buldú et al. [5] showed how different team passing network metrics, such as clustering coefficient and centrality distribution, can capture the complexity of a team's passing patterns. Buldú et al. [5] also provided evidence of how Pep Guardiola's FC Barcelona has unique team passing network characteristics not seen in other teams.

It is proposed by Herrera-Diestra et al. [11] that team pitch passing networks can also capture the uniqueness of a football team's tactics. The difference between a team passing network and a team pitch passing network is that in team pitch passing networks, nodes represent regions in the football pitch instead of players. It is also been shown that team pitch passing networks can be an indicator of performance and the tactical evolution of a team [6,8]. Our study builds upon these concepts by looking at patterns in *player* pitch passing networks, which we will explain further in Sects. 3 and 5.

2.3 Passing Flow Motives

Automatic formation detection and passing network analyses investigate general team behaviour but they do not specifically address players' roles in the sequence of passing. Bekkers and Dabadghao [2], Gyarmati et al. [10] and Peña and Navarro [17] proposed analyses of a team's passing flow motif in order to study this problem. Bekkers and Dabadghao [2] discussed the frequency and variation in individual players' involvement in specific passing flow motifs as an indicator of a player's playing style. Gyarmati et al. [10] analysed the passing flow motifs of teams involved in the 2012–2013 season of the top five European football leagues. This study found that FC Barcelona has a unique pattern of passing flow motifs, which is a result of their tiki-taka style of play. Mattsson and Takes [13] showed that top-performing teams in the top five European football leagues (in the 2017–2018 season) also exhibit a higher level of complexity in their passing sequences. Although passing flow motives shed light on the involvement of players in the sequences of passing, they do not take into account players' locations on the football pitch, which is something we take into consideration in our study.

3 Model/Approach

We look at a new way of defining player roles, which takes into consideration the dynamic interactions - specifically, common passing/receiving patterns - between players. Defining player roles through common passing/receiving patterns can not only lead to a more in-depth representation of a player but also assist in determining a potential player's tactical compatibility with a team. That is to say, if we assume the way a player has been trained and interacts with their previous team is similar to the style of play of a potential new team, then the player can potentially adapt more readily to the new team, which can lead to overall greater team compatibility.

In this study, we aim to explore players' roles by extracting the patterns in players' pitch passing/receiving networks in order to find each individual's unique combination of passing/receiving patterns. To do so, each player's pitch passing/receiving network is decomposed by using a dimensionality reduction technique known as non-negative matrix factorization (NMF) [9]. This results in a linear combination of 12 common passing/receiving patterns for each player.

In this study, we argue that a player's role in a team is not limited to one conventional role but is rather, a combination of 12 different passing/receiving patterns. Moreover, it is shown that that the combination of the 12 different passing/receiving patterns can be used as a footprint to find players with similar passing/receiving styles.

4 Dataset

The dataset used in this study is play-by-play match event data of the top five European football leagues released by Wyscout [16]. This dataset contains all of the 2017–2018 season match data of the top five European leagues (i.e. English first division, French first division, Italian first division, German first division and Spanish first division). It provides information on a total of 98 teams, 3073 players, and 1826 matches. Each match has around 1700 events. Passes are the most common events in every match and form about 50% of the events. Each pass in the dataset is specified by the location it originates from, the location it is delivered to, the player who executed the pass, and the player who received the pass.

5 Methodology

5.1 Player Pitch Passing/Receiving Networks

In this paper, we explore players' roles by analysing the patterns in players' pitch passing/receiving networks with the aim of finding each player's unique combination of 12 common passing/receiving patterns. A player pitch passing/receiving network is a weighted, directed graph. This type of network consists of: a) nodes and b) weighted, directed edges. Each node represents a separate region on the football pitch. Nodes are connected by directed edges. These edges represent passes that are sent from one node to another. The direction of an edge is defined by the direction of a pass from the region it is sent from to the region it is received at. Each edge is assigned a weight (w), which is defined by the number of passes/receptions occurring along that particular edge.

To build a player pitch passing/receiving network, a football pitch is divided into regions. In this study, the football pitch is partitioned into a 8 by 6 mesh. This means that the length of the pitch is divided into 8 subdivisions and the width of the pitch into 6 subdivisions. Therefore, the football pitch is divided into a total of 48 regions. Each region is represented by a node located in the middle of the region. We chose an 8 by 6 mesh to work with as this size achieves optimal results. A smaller mesh (e.g. 4 by 6) causes loss of information since a larger area is represented by each node. A larger mesh (e.g. 8 by 10) needs a higher amount of passes than our dataset can provide in order to capture common passing/receiving patterns.

Each player on a team is assigned a pitch passing and receiving network. The first type of network corresponds to passes that the player makes. The second one corresponds to the passes that the player receives. It should be noted that the direction of attack in both types of networks is always from left to right and that halftime changes of side have been accounted for in the data used to create the networks. To provide an example of a player's pitch passing/receiving networks, Fig. 1 shows Messi of Barcelona FC's networks during the entire season of La Liga 2017–2018. The network on the left ("Passes") shows the passes that Messi executed. The network on the right ("Receptions") shows the passes Messi received. For visualization purposes, the size of each node in the pitch passing/receiving network examples is correlated to the total number of passes/receptions that were performed or received in that node. The thickness of the edges is correlated to the weight of - or the number of passes/receptions performed along - that edge. These pitch passing and receiving networks give a general idea of where Messi was most active in both passing and receiving.

Passes   Receptions

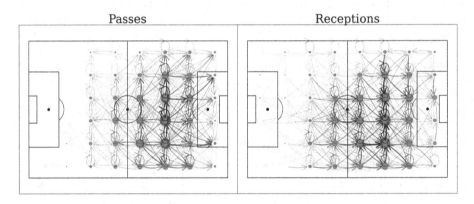

Fig. 1. The pitch passing/receiving networks for Messi during the entire 2017–2018 season of La Liga. The size of each node in the passing/receiving networks is correlated to the total number of passes/receptions that were performed or received in that node. The thickness of each edge is correlated to the number of passes/receptions performed along that edge.

However, mere observation of these graphs can only give a basic understanding of player passing/receiving patterns. The next step is to implement a method to automatically extract the underlying patterns in these networks in order to quantify the data and compare different players' patterns. In the next section, we will discuss how this is done using non-negative matrix factorization.

5.2   Non-negative Matrix Factorization (NMF)

Non-negative matrix factorization (NMF) is a technique, which computationally decomposes a non-negative matrix, X, into a non-negative matrix, W, and a non-negative matrix, H, according to the following equation:

$$X_{nm} = \sum_k W_{nk} \times H_{km}, \tag{1}$$

where, k, is the number of components, n, is the number of samples and m is the number of features in each sample. In other words, the ith row of the matrix X is decomposed as below:

$$\begin{pmatrix} X_{i1} \\ \cdot \\ \cdot \\ \cdot \\ X_{im} \end{pmatrix} = W_{i1} \times \begin{pmatrix} H_{11} \\ \cdot \\ \cdot \\ \cdot \\ H_{1m} \end{pmatrix} + \quad \dots \quad + \quad W_{ik} \times \begin{pmatrix} H_{k1} \\ \cdot \\ \cdot \\ \cdot \\ H_{km} \end{pmatrix}. \tag{2}$$

Therefore, if we assume that i^{th} row of the matrix X represents an object i, it can be shown that $Object_i$ can be decomposed as a linear combination of k parts.

$$Object_i = W_{i1} \times Part_1 + \quad \dots \quad + \quad W_{ik} \times Part_k. \tag{3}$$

Specifically, each object is represented by a vector of weights multiplied by each part as shown here:

$$Object_i \equiv [W_{i1}, \quad \dots \quad , W_{ik}] \tag{4}$$

To give an example, if objects in the equation refer to facial images, then the objects will be decomposed into component parts such as images of different types of lips, eyes, jawbones, etc. If objects refer to textbooks, they can be decomposed into different topics such as science, sports, politics, etc. [12]. For further information about optimization and the technicality of NMF, the reader is referred to Cichocki and Phan [7] and Févotte and Idier [9].

It should be noted that principal component analysis (PCA) is another matrix factorization technique where rows of matrix H are orthogonal and represent the direction of the largest variance [12]. However, rows of H in PCA can contain negative values as well, which make them difficult to interpret visually. Hence, we chose the NMF technique for our model.

5.3   Implementation

This study uses the NMF technique to break down a player's pitch passing/receiving networks in order to find each individual's unique linear combination of 12 common passing/receiving patterns. Objects in Eq. 3 in the previous section refer to the pitch passing/receiving networks of a player. In order to decompose pitch passing/receiving networks, the networks first need to be turned into vectorized objects.

In order to vectorize the networks, one only needs to include the weight of all the possible links in the network. The location of nodes are not included since they are fixed and shared between all these networks. Wherein each network has 48 nodes in this study, there therefore can be 2304 (48 × 48) possible directed links between the nodes. These links can be described as the following set:

$$Links \quad = \quad \{l_1, ..., l_{2304}\}. \tag{5}$$

Each player is assigned two networks: one for passing and one for receiving. Therefore, each player's pitch passing/receiving network can be shown by a vector consisting of 4608 elements. Each element gives the weight of a corresponding link in these networks shown below:

$$Player = [w_{l_1}^{pass}, ..., w_{l_{2304}}^{pass}, w_{l_1}^{reception}, ..., w_{l_{2304}}^{reception}]. \tag{6}$$

The next step is to construct matrix X by concatenating the vectors of all the players. In this study, the original dataset we used contained the data of 3073 players. However, only 2565 players had an opportunity to play during the entire season. From those 2565 players, we extracted data from players with only more than a total of 600 passes plus receptions during the entire season. Players with less than a total of 600 passes and receptions do not have enough passes/receptions for their pitch passing/receiving networks to show any specific patterns. Exclusion of these players also enhances the result of the matrix factorization. Therefore, only 1491 players remained. (We would arrive at a similar number of players if we were to take the assumption that each of the 98 teams in the dataset has 15 players - composed of 11 main players plus four main substitutes - who play regularly, which gives a total of 1470 players.) Figure 2 provides a visual illustration of the total passes plus receptions completed by the players in the dataset. It is shown that over 1000 players had less than 600 passes plus receptions during the entire season.

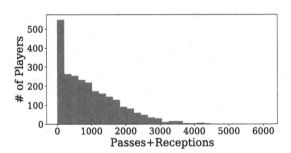

Fig. 2. Histogram of total passes plus receptions completed by players during the 2017–2018 season in the top five European leagues.

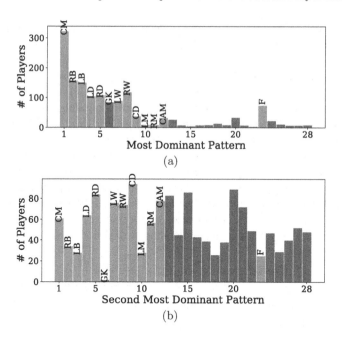

Fig. 3. Histograms of (a) the most dominant and (b) the second most dominant player patterns of the initial 28 passing/receiving patterns found in this study. The red columns in each histogram show the 12 common passing/receiving patterns selected in this study. Pattern names are located at the top of each column.

Subsequently, the decomposition of matrix X is done using the scikit-learn Python package with Kullback-Leibler beta loss and the multiplicative weight update solver [9]. Matrix X is decomposed into 28 components ($k = 28$). This means that 28 passing/receiving patterns (H) have been found. 12 of these 28 patterns have been chosen as the common passing/receiving patterns of players that we focus on in this study (Fig. 4). The largest weight ($max(W_{i1}, ..., W_{i28})$) for 87% of players in this study corresponds to one of these 12 common passing/receiving patterns. Figure 3 shows the most dominant and second most dominant passing/receiving patterns. CM (central midfield), RB (right back), LB (left back), LD (left defense), RD (right defense), LW (left wing), RW (right wing), CD (central defence), CAM (central attacking midfield), and F (forward), which we will explain further in the next section, were selected as they appeared as the strongest patterns found amongst players. The pattern represented by the number 20 was not included as it is a close variant of the F passing/receiving pattern. Although LM (left midfield) and RM (right midfield) are not amongst the most dominant passing/receiving patterns, they have been included in the 12 common passing/receiving patterns as they appear as the most dominant pattern amongst top midfielders such as Modric and Iniesta. In addition, unlike the passing/receiving patterns shown by blue columns in Fig. 3, they are not close variants of the 10 common passing/receiving patterns that we selected and mentioned above.

The GK (goal keeper) pattern is excluded from the 12 common passing/receiving patterns since the role of a goal keeper in passing and receiving does not add any value to our model. According to Fig. 3b, the GK pattern has almost no contribution to the second most dominant passing/receiving patterns.

Now that these 12 common patterns are extracted, Eq. 1 can be solved again by replacing H with all of these 12 common patterns. However, this time we do not update H at every iteration of the optimization process. This way, the weight of the contribution of these common patterns can be calculated in matrix W.

In order to calculate the individual style of play for each player, each player's weight vector has to be normalized according to the following equation to cancel out the imbalances in the differences of total number of passes/receptions between players. The jth normalized element of player i's vector is:

$$Normalize(W_{ij}) = W_{ij} \times \frac{\sum_{n=4698} H_{jn}}{\sum_{n=4608} X_{in}}. \tag{7}$$

$Normalize(W_{ij})$ refers to the percentage of player i's total passes/receptions, which comes from pattern j.

6 Results

Figure 4 shows the 12 common passing/receiving patterns that our model found. Each of the 12 patterns has two pitch networks: the network on the left-hand side shows a passing network and the network on the right shows a receiving network. For the sake of clarity, each network represents only the top 100 edges with the most passes/receptions within each network. Each common passing/receiving pattern is associated with the patterns of a conventional role; hence, they are named after that particular role.

The central midfield (CM) pattern is a common pattern amongst midfielders. It is characterized by a uniform distribution of passes and receptions around the center of the pitch and involves many short-length passes and receptions between neighbouring nodes. The right back (RB) and left back (LB) patterns are common patterns amongst fullbacks. As is shown in Fig. 4, the RB and LB patterns mirror each other. Passes and receptions in these patterns are concentrated along the sidelines of the pitch. These patterns show short-length, horizontal and backwards passes to the center of the pitch. They also show the reception of short and long passes along the pitch sidelines. The left defense (LD) and right defense (RD) patterns are common amongst defenders. The passes and receptions are concentrated on the left or right side of the pitch. The patterns involve many short passes to the center and towards the corresponding sidelines of the pitch. The left wing (LW) and right wing (RW) patterns are typically seen in wingers. These patterns involve a high amount of short passes and receptions between the two pitch sidelines and behind the 18-yard box. The central defence (CD) pattern is common amongst central defense midfielders and central defenders

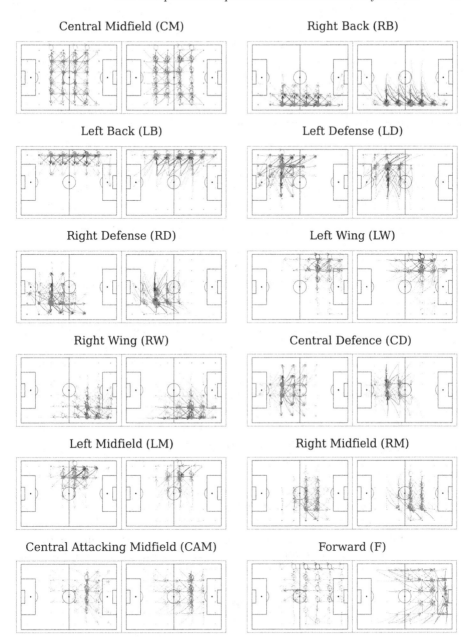

Fig. 4. The 12 common passing/receiving patterns identified in this study by matrix H. In each pattern, the network on the left is associated with passes while the network on the right is associated with receptions.

who act as a pivot in the center of the pitch. The pattern is characterized by many short and long passes from the center of the player's own half of the pitch towards both sidelines of the pitch in a variety of angles. The player also receives passes in the same manner. The left midfield (LM) and right midfield (RM) patterns are characterized by short passes concentrated on the left or right-hand side of the opponent's half. These patterns are not limited to midfielders and include players who are more active in the midfield areas. The central attacking midfield (CAM) pattern appears most frequently in playmakers (also known as "number 10s"). This pattern is characterized by numerous receptions behind the opponent's box and forward passes. Lastly, the forward (F) pattern is seen most often amongst strikers and forwards. This pattern involves short passes all across the opponent's half and numerous receptions behind and inside the opponent's 18-yard box.

Table 1 shows the common passing/receiving patterns of 29 different players. Each player is represented by a combination of 12 common passing/receiving patterns. These players were selected as examples since they are amongst the most well known in their conventional roles. In looking at each player's combination of 12 patterns, one can interpret the individual passing/receiving style of a player. These combinations show that the players' styles have a correlation to their conventional roles. However, conventional roles do not give the full picture of a player's passing/receiving patterns. 43% of the 1491 players studied in this paper had a maximum weight of less than 50% in each of the 12 common passing/receiving patterns. This suggests that a substantial percentage of players do not follow the specific pattern typically associated with their conventional role. One example of this is the defender Koulibaly whose patterns are comprised of 41% LD, 14% CD, 30% of LM, and 13% CM. The 43% total of his LM and CM patterns is a result of his contribution to playmaking in the midfield.

We chose to include the conventional role category in Table 1 in order to highlight the differences our model finds between players within the same conventional role. One significant finding from this table comes from the LM and RM patterns. LM and RM characterize patterns of passing/receiving focused predominantly on the left or right-hand side of the pitch. Yet, some full backs such as Delph and Walker have around 20% of these patterns, which is due to their frequent movements from the sidelines into the midfield. These type of full backs are known as "inverted full backs". At the same time, there are full backs, such as Meunier, who have 0% of these patterns. This shows that our model can distinguish between different types of patterns amongst players who hold the same conventional role.

In looking at the 12 common passing/receiving patterns, one can see occurrences of each pattern in players who hold different conventional roles. For example, the CAM pattern is seen frequently in midfielders, wingers, and forwards. The higher the percentage of this pattern that a player has, the higher the probability that the player is involved in making plays behind the 18-yard box. As a winger, Messi's CAM pattern stands at 37%. Mertens, as a forward, also has a

Table 1. This table shows the common passing/receiving patterns of 29 different players. Each player is represented by a combination of 12 common passing/receiving patterns. The maximum weight associated with each player is shown in bold.

Conventional Role	Player	Common Passing/Receiving Patterns (%)											
		CM	RB	LB	LD	RD	LW	RW	CD	LM	RM	CAM	F
Full Back	T. Meunier	1	**91**	0	0	0	1	4	0	0	0	1	2
	K. Walker	2	**73**	0	0	5	0	4	0	0	16	0	0
	J. Alba	5	0	**76**	8	0	7	0	0	5	0	0	0
	F. Delph	6	0	**61**	6	0	3	0	0	21	0	2	0
Midfielder	S. Busquets	**60**	0	0	2	0	0	0	19	1	9	9	0
	K. D. Bruyne	**29**	12	4	0	0	13	21	0	3	10	8	0
	A. Iniesta	22	0	6	2	0	23	0	1	**29**	0	17	0
	L. Modric	**39**	5	0	0	10	0	16	2	0	22	7	0
	Jorginho	**70**	0	0	0	0	0	0	0	19	5	6	0
	N. Kante	**72**	0	1	0	1	0	3	2	2	8	12	0
	G. Wijnaldum	**56**	1	3	2	0	4	2	1	10	7	11	3
Defender	G. Pique	6	7	0	2	**68**	0	1	7	0	9	0	1
	K. Koulibaly	13	0	0	**41**	0	1	0	14	30	0	0	1
Winger	J. Sancho	9	0	29	0	0	**52**	1	0	2	0	3	3
	Neymar	14	0	13	0	0	**39**	1	0	9	3	22	0
	E. Hazard	12	0	5	0	0	**29**	17	0	1	5	27	3
	C. Ronaldo	3	3	8	0	0	**34**	20	0	2	4	9	17
	L. Insigne	3	0	36	1	0	**49**	0	0	5	0	3	3
	M. Salah	0	12	0	0	0	1	**63**	0	0	5	11	7
	L. Messi	10	4	0	0	0	3	23	0	1	21	**37**	2
	M. Ozil	17	3	4	0	0	**20**	17	0	7	12	19	0
	P. Dybala	25	7	2	0	0	3	**29**	0	0	10	20	4
Forward	R. Firmino	12	3	5	0	0	20	**22**	0	2	6	16	14
	L. Suarez	4	1	4	0	0	**31**	11	0	1	1	21	25
	R. Lewandowski	15	0	2	0	0	15	16	0	1	1	16	**33**
	H. Kane	7	0	2	0	1	18	14	0	1	2	**29**	26
	D. Mertens	8	0	2	0	0	23	6	0	1	5	**37**	18
	T. Werner	2	9	14	0	0	20	**27**	0	0	0	3	24
	A. Griezmann	**29**	4	5	0	0	15	17	0	0	2	21	7

37% CAM pattern. The CM pattern appears in all of the players' patterns. It is highest in midfielders but some players such as Dybala (winger) and Griezmann (forward) have over 25% of this pattern.

Table 2. List of players most similar to A. Oxlade-Chamberlain, J. Henderson and L. Messi based on Euclidean distance. The similar players are listed by order of greatest similarity to each respective player.

Player	Common Passing/Receiving Patterns (%)											
	M	RB	LB	LD	RD	LW	RW	CD	LM	RM	CAM	F
A. Oxlade-Chamberlain	22	12	4	0	1	9	26	0	0	16	9	0
X. Shaqiri	24	16	1	0	0	2	29	0	0	12	13	3
J. Mata	20	15	3	0	0	14	30	0	1	10	4	3
K. De Bruyne	29	12	4	0	0	13	21	0	3	10	8	0
J. Henderson	79	1	0	0	1	0	1	4	0	14	0	0
J. Weigl	77	0	0	0	2	0	0	9	0	11	0	0
T. Ndombele	74	0	1	0	1	0	3	2	1	15	3	0
Fabinho	74	0	0	4	1	0	2	6	3	9	2	0
L. Messi	10	4	0	0	0	3	23	0	1	21	37	2
E. Lamela	7	6	3	0	0	7	25	0	0	19	32	2
C. Eriksen	29	2	3	0	0	7	16	0	1	15	27	0
Rodrigo	17	2	4	0	0	9	21	0	1	5	26	16
P. Dybala	25	7	2	0	0	3	29	0	0	10	20	4
R. Saponara	31	0	0	0	0	11	18	0	0	10	29	0
M. Özil	17	3	4	0	0	20	17	0	7	12	19	0

Our model shows the intricacies of player patterns best when tasked with analyzing the most complex conventional roles such as midfielders, wingers, and forwards (in comparison to less complex roles such as defenders and full backs). For instance, the midfielder De Bruyne is a combination of 29% CM, 12% RB, 4% LB, 13 % LW, 21% RW, 3% LM, 10% RM, and 8% CAM.

One can use these representations of player passing/receiving patterns to find players with similar passing/receiving patterns. Table 2 provides examples of players most similar to Messi, Oxlade-Chamberlain, and Henderson (based on Euclidean distance) in our dataset. Players such as Lamela, Eriksen, Dybala, and "Ozil are highly similar to Messi. These players are all known as playmakers as well.

One can also see similarities between the results presented in Table 2 and two actual transfers that occurred in the summer of 2018. Shaqiri and Fabinho were transferred to Liverpool FC from Stoke City FC and AS Monaco FC respectively. Shaqiri was transferred to replace Oxlade-Chamberlain who was suffering from a knee injury. Liverpool FC's main central defensive midfielder in the 2017–2018 season was Henderson. Henderson was replaced by Fabinho to give him the opportunity to play higher up on the pitch. As shown in Table 2, our model found that Shaqiri was the player most similar to Oxlade-Chamberlain and Fabinho was the third most similar player to Henderson.

7 Conclusion

In this study, we defined a new model of representing football player roles based on passing and receiving interactions. We developed a definition of player roles, which consist of a linear combination of common and interpretable passing/receiving patterns. Using non-negative matrix factorization (NMF), we decomposed players' pitch passing and receiving networks into a linear combination of 12 common passing/receiving patterns for each player. Our results showed that 43% of the 1491 players studied in this paper had a maximum weight of less than 50% in each of the 12 common passing/receiving patterns. We interpret this to mean that a significant number of players do not follow the specific passing/receiving patterns typically associated with their conventional role. The model also showed considerable differences in passing/receiving patterns amongst players playing the same conventional role. It has also been discussed that the model shows the most effective results in studying players with more complex conventional roles such as midfielders, wingers, and forwards. One can use the model to compare players and find similar players. For example, our model found that Shaqiri and Fabinho had the highest similarity in passing/receiving styles to Oxlade-Chamberlain and Henderson. This is consistent with Liverpool FC's transfers of Shaqiri and Fabinho to replace Oxlade-Chamberlain and Henderson's positions respectively in the summer of 2018.

It is worth mentioning that due to lack of data, the definition of player roles in this study is only based on passing and receiving and does not incorporate the off-ball movements and defensive roles of a player. Also, our model does not address the tactical compatibility of a player when transferring from one conventional role to a different conventional role.

In future research, we will incorporate off-ball movements and defensive interactions in our model in order to generate a more comprehensive representation of football player roles. The research may also explore the potential correlations between team formations and player roles.

Acknowledgment. This work was supported by the Swedish Knowledge Foundation (DATAKIND 20190194).

References

1. Aalbers, B., Van Haaren, J.: Distinguishing between roles of football players in play-by-play match event data. In: Brefeld, U., Davis, J., Van Haaren, J., Zimmermann, A. (eds.) MLSA 2018. LNCS (LNAI), vol. 11330, pp. 31–41. Springer, Cham (2019). https://doi.org/10.1007/978-3-030-17274-9_3
2. Bekkers, J., Dabadghao, S.: Flow motifs in soccer: what can passing behavior tell us? J. Sports Anal. **5**(4), 299–311 (2019)
3. Bialkowski, A., Lucey, P., Carr, P., Yue, Y., Sridharan, S., Matthews, I.: Identifying team style in soccer using formations learned from spatiotemporal tracking data. In: 2014 IEEE International Conference on Data Mining Workshop, pp. 9–14. IEEE (2014)

4. Bransen, L., Robberechts, P., Davis, J., Decroos, T., Van Haaren, J.: How does context affect player performance in football? (2020)
5. Buldú, J., Busquets, J., Echegoyen, I., et al.: Defining a historic football team: using network science to analyze Guardiola's FC Barcelona. Sci. Rep. **9**(1), 1–14 (2019)
6. Buldú, J.M., Busquets, J., Martínez, J.H., Herrera-Diestra, J.L., Echegoyen, I., Galeano, J., Luque, J.: Using network science to analyse football passing networks: Dynamics, space, time, and the multilayer nature of the game. Front. Psychol. **9**, 1900 (2018)
7. Cichocki, A., Phan, A.H.: Fast local algorithms for large scale nonnegative matrix and tensor factorizations. IEICE Trans. Fundam. Electron. Commun. Comput. Sci. **92**(3), 708–721 (2009)
8. Cintia, P., Rinzivillo, S., Pappalardo, L.: A network-based approach to evaluate the performance of football teams. In: Machine Learning and Data Mining for Sports Analytics Workshop, Porto, Portugal (2015)
9. Févotte, C., Idier, J.: Algorithms for nonnegative matrix factorization with the β-divergence. Neural Comput. **23**(9), 2421–2456 (2011)
10. Gyarmati, L., Kwak, H., Rodriguez, P.: Searching for a unique style in soccer. arXiv preprint arXiv:1409.0308 (2014)
11. Herrera-Diestra, J., Echegoyen, I., Martínez, J., Garrido, D., Busquets, J., Io, F.S., Buldú, J.: Pitch networks reveal organizational and spatial patterns of Guardiola's FC Barcelona. Chaos, Solitons Fractals **138**, 109934 (2020)
12. Lee, D.D., Seung, H.S.: Learning the parts of objects by non-negative matrix factorization. Nature **401**(6755), 788–791 (1999)
13. Mattsson, C.E.S., Takes, F.W.: Trajectories through temporal networks. Appl. Netw. Sci. **6**(1), 1–31 (2021). https://doi.org/10.1007/s41109-021-00374-7
14. Narizuka, T., Yamazaki, Y.: Clustering algorithm for formations in football games. Sci. Rep. **9**(1), 1–8 (2019)
15. Pappalardo, L., Cintia, P., Ferragina, P., Massucco, E., Pedreschi, D., Giannotti, F.: Playerank: data-driven performance evaluation and player ranking in soccer via a machine learning approach. ACM Trans. Intell. Syst. Technol. (TIST) **10**(5), 1–27 (2019)
16. Pappalardo, L., et al.: A public data set of spatio-temporal match events in soccer competitions. Sci. Data **6**(1), 1–15 (2019)
17. Peña, J.L., Navarro, R.S.: Who can replace Xavi? A passing motif analysis of football players. arXiv preprint arXiv:1506.07768 (2015)
18. Shaw, L., Glickman, M.: Dynamic analysis of team strategy in professional football. Barça Sports Anal. Summit, 1–13 (2019)

Other Team Sports

Learning Strength and Weakness Rules of Cricket Players Using Association Rule Mining

Swarup Ranjan Behera$^{(\boxtimes)}$ and V. Vijaya Saradhi

Indian Institute of Technology Guwahati, Guwahati, Assam, India
{b.swarup,saradhi}@iitg.ac.in

Abstract. Association rule mining is an important data mining technique that finds association rules by mining frequent attributes. This work aims to construct association rules that determine cricket players' strengths and weaknesses. We propose an approach to learn the association of strengths or weaknesses exhibited by batters (or bowlers) with the type of delivery they have faced (or bowled). In essence, the bowling (or batting) features that may be associated with the batter's (or bowler's) strengths or weaknesses are investigated. Each delivery is represented as a set of bowling and batting features, similar to the set of items representing a transaction in association rule mining. Apriori algorithm of association rule mining is used to obtain the strength association rules and weakness association rules. Cricket text commentary data are obtained from the EspnCricInfo website and utilized for finding player's strength and weakness rules. Rules for more than 250 players are constructed by analyzing text commentaries over one million deliveries for 13 years (2006–2019). The data, codes, and results are shared at https://bit.ly/3rj6k6c.

Keywords: Sports text mining · Cricket analytics · Association rule mining

1 Introduction

With the rapid increase in technology consumption, the amount of data generated and published has grown exponentially over the past few years. As a result, newer avenues have opened up where data mining techniques can prove indispensable to make sense of a large amount of data. We identify sports text commentary analysis as a field with enormous potential, leading to a better understanding of the game dynamics and characterization of various elements. We focus on the game of cricket to extract information from online archives of text commentary.

Cricket as a sport is renowned for recordkeeping. Cricket statistics have been widely analyzed for years. However, information carried by statistics is limited. It only captures the gameplay at the macroscopic scale and fails to capture the

U. Brefeld et al. (Eds.): MLSA 2021, CCIS 1571, pp. 79–92, 2022.
https://doi.org/10.1007/978-3-031-02044-5_7

details. For instance, although statistics provide a perspective on how fluent batters are (in terms of averages, runs, etc.), they fail to give an insight into how the batters played or performed. However, cricket text commentary is rich in description and contains a lot of information about the minute details of the gameplay. It captures the commentators' opinion about how the batter played, how the bowler bowled, and other auxiliary information.

In this work, we discuss the application of Association Rule Mining (ARM) in constructing rules that account for individual player's strengths and weaknesses from the cricket text commentaries. Specifically, we build rules that explain the strengths of a batter (or bowler) and rules that explain the weaknesses of a batter (or bowler). In addition, we make the following research contributions.

- We have collected a large and first-of-its-kind dataset of over one million deliveries, covering all international cricket Test matches for 13 years.
- We propose several domain-specific features to represent each delivery with fine-grained details.
- We provide the computationally feasible definition of strength and weakness rule and propose to use ARM to obtain these rules.

The paper is organized as follows. In Sect. 2, we introduce the game of cricket. In Sect. 3, we present the literature related to ARM. The methodology is briefed in Sect. 4. In Sect. 5, we describe the cricket text commentary data and associated challenges. Unigram and bigram modeling is presented in Sect. 6. Features extraction is discussed in Sect. 7. Strength and weakness rules construction is presented in Sect. 8. The work is finally concluded in Sect. 9.

2   Cricket

Cricket is a bat-and-ball game played between two teams of eleven players each in a field at the center of which is a rectangular strip called the *pitch*. A standard cricket field with the playing area or pitch is presented in Fig. 1. Cricket field is divided into - *infield* inside the 30 yard circle and *outfield* from circle to boundary.

In cricket, a player can be a (i) *batter* who hits the ball to score runs, (ii) *bowler* who bowls the ball towards the batter, (iii) *fielder* who stops the ball hit by the batter in the field, and (iv) *wicket-keeper* who stands behind the wicket to collect the ball bowled by the bowler.

Each match is divided into innings. In every innings, one team bats and the opposite team fields (or bowls), which is decided by a coin toss. The bowler bowls on a 22-yard pitch, a hard surface made of clay and has two wickets (3 wooden stumps) on either side. Batter bats on one side of the wicket, and the bowler bowls from the other side of the wicket. A ball can be delivered onto the batter in different ways to get the batter out. Fast bowlers aim to rely on their speed or use the seam of a ball so that it swings or curves in flight. Spinners bowl slowly but with a rapid rotation to change the ball's trajectory on striking the pitch. Each ball also has attributes like length (how far down the pitch the ball is

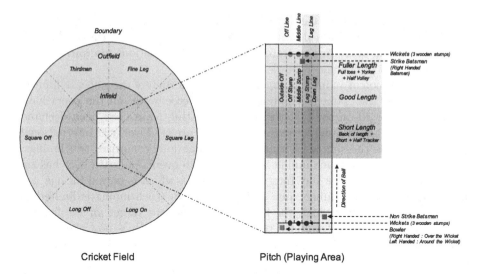

Fig. 1. A standard cricket field, showing the rectangular cricket pitch (white) at center, infield (medium green) inside the 30 yard circle, outfield (light green) from circle to boundary, and shot areas (thirdman, square off, long off, long on, square leg, and fine leg) for right handed batter/batsman. (Color figure online)

pitched), line (how far to the left or right of the wicket the bowler bowls the ball), type (nature of the delivery), speed (speed of the ball after it is released), and movement (movement of the ball w.r.t. the batter). These batting and bowling attributes are listed in Table 1.

At any moment, two batters of a team are present on the pitch. One is called the striker batter who hits the ball, and another is the non-striker batter on the opposite side of the striker (or bowler's end). Each batter continues batting until she is out, which happens when the batter hits the ball, but it is caught by a fielder without bouncing (caught) or when the bowler strikes the wickets (bowled) or when the ball would have struck the wicket but was rather blocked by batter's body except the hand holding the bat (leg before wicket or LBW) and a few other scenarios. A batter can score one/two/three/four runs by running between wickets, i.e., both the striker and the non-striker must reach their respective opposite ends the requisite number of times. A batter may also score four runs (ball hits the ground before hitting/passing the boundary) or six runs (ball passes or hits the boundary without bouncing), without running, by striking the ball to the boundary. Batters react to a bowler in a variety of ways. They could defend the ball (block the ball) from hitting the wickets, attack (play aggressive shots) it for a boundary scoring four or six runs, or get beaten (play poor shot) by the bowler. The batter can play different shots to hit the ball to different regions of the field (shot areas). The cricket field can be divided into six regions such as *thirdman, square off, long off, long on, square leg,* and *fine leg.*

A batter (or a bowler) can be left-handed or right-handed. In Fig. 1, line of delivery and shot areas are shown for right-handed batters. For the left-handed batters, these notations are mirrored. Similarly, the notations are mirrored for left-handed and right-handed bowlers as well.

The completion of an innings depends upon the format of the game. In limited over formats of the game, an inning gets completed when all the overs have been bowled, or 10 out of 11 batters of the batting team have been declared out (all-out). The two limited formats of cricket are (i) Twenty20 International (T20I), which is the shortest format of the game and comprises two innings, one innings per team (each inning is limited to 20 overs, and each over has six deliveries/balls), (ii) One Day International (ODI), which is played for one day and comprises of two innings, one innings per team (each inning is limited to 50 overs). In the first innings, the batting team sets the target for the fielding team, and in the second innings, the fielding team (which is now the batting team) tries to achieve the target. The team which scores the most runs wins the match.

Another format of the game, which is not limited by overs, is Test cricket. It is the longest and purest form of the game because it tests teams' technique and temperament over a more extended time. Test match is played for a maximum of five days (each day has three sessions of two hours each) and comprises four innings, two innings per team. Usually, teams will alternate after each innings. A team's innings ends when (i) team is all-out, (ii) team's captain declares the innings, (iii) team batting fourth scores the required number of runs to win, or (iv) time for the match expires. Let Team-A bat in the first innings and Team-B field. Next, Team-B bat in the second innings. If, after the second innings, Team-A leads by at least 200 runs, the captain of Team-A may order (enforcing the follow-on) Team-B to bat in the next innings. In this case, the usual order of the third and fourth innings is reversed. Now, Team-A will bat in the fourth innings. The team which scores the most runs in its two innings wins the match.

3   Literature Review

Association Rule Mining (ARM) is a data mining technique in which the extracted knowledge is in the form of association rules that describe a relationship between different attributes. Agrawal et al. [1] introduced ARM to discover interesting co-occurrence between products in supermarket data (market basket analysis). ARM extracts frequent sets of items that are purchased together and generates association rules of the form $A \rightarrow B$, where A and B are disjoint sets of items, and B is likely to be purchased whenever A is purchased. ARM is widely used in many domains, such as health care [2], financial transactions [3], and retail [4], etc.

ARM is applied in the sports domain as well [5–7]. In cricket, Raj et al. [8] used ARM to find the association between the factors in cricket matches such as toss outcome and playing conditions with the outcome of the game. UmaMaheswari et al. [9] proposed to model an automated framework to identify

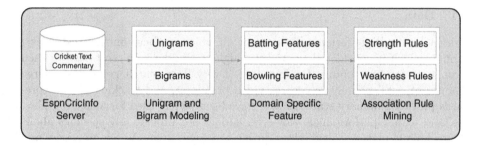

Fig. 2. Overview of our approach.

find correlations among play patterns in cricket. ARM has not been applied to the sports text commentary data for detecting player-specific rules in the literature.

In our previous works, we have used the unstructured data, namely cricket text commentary, to visualize (i) cricket player's strengths and weaknesses [10, 12] and (ii) the temporal changes in player's strengths and weaknesses [11,12].

4 Methodology

An association rule has the form $A \rightarrow B$, where A and B are disjoint sets of items, and the B set is likely to happen whenever the A set occurs. This paper analyzes the association of strength/weakness exhibited by a batter with the type of delivery she has faced. In essence, the paper investigates the bowling features that may be associated with the batter's strength/weakness.

There is no universally agreed-upon definition of strength and weakness as different players exhibit strength or weakness at varying instances of deliveries. When a batter or bowler exhibits a particular behavior repeatedly, it amounts to her strength or weakness. For example, a batter yielding wicket to deliveries pitched outside the off-stump consistently amounts to her weakness. *Strength* is when a batter or a bowler exhibits perfection for a particular delivery. Similarly, *weakness* is when a batter or a bowler exhibits imperfection for a particular delivery.

Please refer to Fig. 2 for an overview of our approach. We collect text commentary data from the web and perform extensive processing to extract useful information from this text. We propose several domain-specific discrete-valued features to represent each delivery and represent each player's batting (or bowling) features in this feature space. Finally, we identify the relationship between batting and bowling features of each player using ARM and construct the strength and weakness rules.

5 Data and Challenges

This section first describes the data and then highlights several challenges encountered when analyzing this data.

5.1 Data

Cricket has multiple formats of the game, of which we focus on the *Test cricket* format, which is considered as cricket's highest standard. In *Test cricket*, each team bats for two innings for five days. Every Test match generates a large amount of data, namely scorecard, video broadcast, and tracking data. Scorecards provide summary statistics and have been widely used for analyzing players' and teams' performance. However, it does not provide any specifics about the technique player has exhibited during the game's play. Video broadcast and tracking data have a detailed description of the play. However, these are not publicly available and are also expensive to process. In addition to the above forms of data, cricket matches generate text commentary pertaining to every match ball. This data is publicly available and is inexpensive to analyze. This data describes the ball-by-ball proceedings of the game with minute details. *Text commentary* corresponding to every delivery/ball of every match are acquired from the ESPNCricInfo[1] archive.

Consider an example of text commentary:

> 3.2, Finn to Sehwag, Four run, 136 kph, short of a length, but a little wide, enough for Sehwag to stand tall and punch it with open face, past Pietersen at point.

This commentary describes the second delivery in the fourth over of the game. Bowler Finn has bowled this delivery to the batter Sehwag. The outcome of the ball is four runs. The speed of the delivery is 136 kph (kilometer per hour). The rest of the text is unstructured and describes how the ball is delivered and how the batter played it. For instance, this commentary describes several features of bowling, such as length (short of a length) and line (a little wide). Similarly, it describes batting features such as response (punch it) pointing to the batter's strength.

Consider another example of text commentary given below where the technical word *outside edge* points to the batter's imperfection or weakness against *good length* and *angling in* delivery.

> 106.1, Anderson to Smith, 1 run, 144 kph, England have drawn a false shot from Smith! well done. good length, angling in, straightens away, catches the outside edge but does not carry to Cook at slip.

We can analyze a large number of deliveries played by a batter. If we consistently observe good performance on similar deliveries, we can conclude that playing such deliveries is a batter's strength. Such detailed strength (/weakness) rules are far more expressive and valuable than simple statistics such as batting averages.

---

[1] https://www.espncricinfo.com/.

To collect the text commentaries associated with a given Test match, one has to first obtain the season and series in which this particular match is a part. In addition, match and innings IDs and associated URLs need to be formulated from ESPNCricInfo's archive. This information is used to acquire the text commentaries for a given match. This procedure is repeated for all the matches played between May 2006 and April 2019. Total text commentaries of 1,088,570 deliveries are collected spanning thirteen years and stored in a local database. The collected deliveries account for a total of 550 international Test cricket matches. The acquired data are stored in a MySQL database and can be accessed at https://bit.ly/3tOJHZ3. The python code to obtain this data can be accessed at https://bit.ly/3sjVD4W.

5.2 Challenges

In order to construct strength and weakness rules from the text commentary data, following are the main challenges:

Data representation. Every ball of text commentary comprises a maximum of 50 words and contains cricket technical vocabulary. The cricket technical vocabulary majorly overlaps with stop words in the conventional information retrieval application domain. This causes difficulty in adapting the off-shelf text data models in the present work. In addition, text data representation models suffer from sparsity problems (fewer words per document and a large vocabulary).

Rule definition. Strength and weakness rules are highly subjective and often debatable. Even experts differ with the individual's opinions about strengths and weaknesses. Given that there is no universal agreement, defining what constitutes a strength rule and a weakness rule itself is challenging. Note that such a definition must be agreeable to every stakeholder.

Computational method. Finding a suitable algorithm or computational method that constructs players' strength and weakness rules given the rule definition is another challenge.

6 Unigram and Bigram Modeling

In this section, we discuss the challenges and proposed steps for processing the text commentary data. Each text commentary can be divided into two parts: the structured part and the unstructured part. The structured part is located at the beginning of each commentary. It describes the exact over number, delivery number, name of the bowler, name of the batter, and outcome of the delivery. After this, a text commentary will optionally describe various bowling features such as line, length, and delivery speed. Some text commentaries will also describe the batter's response in terms of her footwork and shot selection. In the end, some deliveries have a subjective opinion of the commentator about how the batter performed. An example of short text commentary structure is presented below.

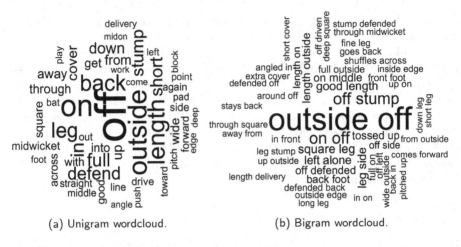

(a) Unigram wordcloud.　　　　　(b) Bigram wordcloud.

Fig. 3. Steve Smith's text commentary analysis.

Structured Text	Unstructured Text
75.3, Woakes to Smith, FOUR runs,	Back of a length, and a scudding pull skims over Root's head at mid-on!

Extraction of information from the structured part is a straightforward task. However, information extraction from unstructured part requires non-trivial efforts. The main challenges are:

- **Stopwords:** For an effective representation of text documents, stopword removal is performed as a preprocessing step in the traditional information retrieval context. A differentiating factor specific to text commentary is that majority of the technical words used in the cricketing domain are *stopwords* in the conventional text mining literature. A non-exhaustive list of technical stopwords are: off, on, room, across, behind, back, out, up, down, long, turn, point, under, full, open, good, great, away, etc.
- **Sparsity:** Cricket text commentary has a definite structure in which both bowler's action and batter's actions are described. Commentators, at times, focus either only on the bowler's action or only on the batter's action. Moreover, every document (commentary for a particular delivery) comprises a maximum of fifty words. This induces sparsity. Features employed in traditional text mining literature like term frequency and inverse document frequency (TF-IDF) are not suitable due to the sparsity of the data.

Cricket, like any other sport, has rich jargon. Frequency analysis of the data reveals that commentators frequently use technical words. Figure 3 presents the unigram and bigram (two words occurring together) word clouds [13] of the text commentaries where Steve Smith is mentioned as a batter. The importance of each unigram or bigram is shown with font size and color. Domain-specific technical vocabulary is dominantly observed in these word clouds. The high technicality of the vocabulary used, on most occasions, enables us to approach the problem in a more organized manner. Our analysis reveals that domain-specific feature space captures sufficient information from the short sentences and identifies whether the information is for the bowler or the batter.

To capture the most relevant information, we have used a combination of web resources [14] and the frequency counts of words in the corpus to come up with words (unigrams) most likely to capture the data. However, we found significant fault with many such cases. Consider two examples of short text commentary:

> Swings in from outside off, well left in the end as it scoots past off stump. (Swing signifies the type of ball)
>
> -
>
> Short ball over middle stump, Dhoni swings into a pull and takes it down to fine leg. (Swing signifies the way batter played the ball)

In both of these examples, the word *swing* is used differently; first concerning the bowler and second concerning the batter. Many such words like *leg, short,* etc., are used in both contexts.

There are also instances when a word changes meaning when combined with another word. For example, the word *short* usually refers to a short ball, but when it is used as in *short leg, short cover,* etc., it refers to field positions. Consider two examples of short text commentary:

> Short on the body, he gets up and nicely plays it to square leg. (Length of delivery)
>
> -
>
> Full outside off, Dhoni reaches out and pushes it to short cover. (Field position)

Such instances made us look into the possible usage of bigrams along with unigrams. Two words occurring together in a document are called bigrams. They carry more semantic meaning than single words. For example, *swing in, swing away, swing back,* and *late swing* are all bigrams that specifically address the swinging nature of the ball and removes the ambiguity of association with the batter. Bigrams are also helpful in the instances when a word changes meaning when combined with another word. For example, word *short* usually refers to a short ball, but when it is used as in *short leg, short cover, short midwicket,* etc., it refers to the field positions. Thus, bigrams can be used to differentiate between multiple meanings and contexts of a word. However, a significant problem is the identification of all relevant unigrams and bigrams. We build a set of relevant unigrams and bigrams using a combination of *unigram frequency,*

Table 1. Batting and bowling features.

Category	Feature (Feature Description)
	Batting Features
Outcome	**0, 1, 2, 3, 4, 5, 6** runs, **out** (Outcome of a delivery - runs or wicket)
Response	**Attacked** (Batter plays aggressive shots or exhibits strength)
	Defended (Batter blocks or leaves the ball)
	Beaten (Batter plays poor shots or exhibits weakness)
Footwork	**Front foot** (Stance decision of a batter for full length deliveries)
	Back foot (Stance decision of a batter for short length deliveries)
Shot area	**Third man, Square off, Long off, Long on, Square leg,** and **Fine leg** (Region where the batter plays the shot)
	Bowling Features
Length	**Short** (Bowler pitches the ball closer to himself)
	Full (Bowler pitches the ball closer to the batter)
	Good (Bowler pitches the ball between full and short)
Line	**Off** (Ball travels on the off-stump line or outside the off-stump line)
	Middle (Ball travels on the middle-stump line)
	Leg (Ball travels on the leg-stump line or outside the leg-stump line)
Type	**Spin** (Bowler bowls slow deliveries which turn sharply after pitching)
	Swing (Bowler bowls fast deliveries which have movement in the air)
Speed	**Fast** (Speed of ball upon release: more than 100 kph)
	Slow (Speed of ball upon release: less than 100 kph)
Movement	**Move-in** (Ball moves towards the batter)
	Move-away (Ball moves away from the batter)

bigram frequency, *A glossary of cricket terms* [2], and *The Wisden Dictionary of Cricket* [14]. The glossary and dictionary are the points of reference for cricket-specific unigrams and bigrams. Finally, we represent each text commentary as a set of unigrams and bigrams.

7 Feature Extraction

Unigram and bigram representations of text commentary cannot be directly used for strength and weakness rule extraction. We have identified a total of 19 batting features (batter facing the delivery is associated with these features) and 12 bowling features (bowler bowling the delivery is associated with these features) to represent each text commentary. Nineteen features are identified that characterize batting. These are *0 run, 1 run, 2 run, 3 run, 4 run, 5 run, 6 run, out, beaten, defended, attacked, front foot, back foot, third man, square*

---
[2] https://es.pn/1bAFI9H.

Table 2. Examples of identifying unigrams and bigrams for batting features.

Category	Batting Features	Unigrams and Bigrams
Response	Defense	leave, defend, block, leave alone
	Attack	drive, whip, punch, whack, great timing
	Beaten	miss, struck pad, beat, edge, lbw, poor shot
Footwork	Front	front foot, step out, come down
	Back	back foot, step back, hang back
Shot Area	Third man	third man, late cut, gully, back cut
	Square off	square, cover, point, upper cut, square drive
	Long off	mid off, long off, straight drive, off drive
	Long on	mid on, long on, on drive
	Square leg	short leg, square leg, sweep, hook
	Fine leg	fine leg, long leg, leg glance, paddle sweep

Table 3. Examples of identifying unigrams and bigrams for bowling features.

Category	Bowling Features	Unigrams and Bigrams
Length	Short	short, bouncer, short pitch, back length
	Full	full, overpitch, full toss, toss up, blockhole
	Good	length, good length, length delivery
Line	Off	outside off, pitch off, off stump, from off
	Middle	straight ball, straight line, middle stump
	Leg	down leg, wide leg, outside leg, leg stump
Type	Spin	spin, turn, googly, doosra, legspin, offspin
	Swing	swing in/away, late swing, reverse swing
Movement	Move In	move in, swing in, angle in
	Move Away	move away, swing away, angle away

off, long off, long on, square leg, and *fine leg.* We give a brief description of each of these features with their feature categories in Table 1. Twelve features are identified that characterize bowling. These are *good, short, full, off, leg, middle, spin, swing, fast, slow, move-in,* and *move-out.* We give a brief description of each of these features with their feature categories in Table 1.

All these features are discrete-valued. To transform each text commentary to this feature space, we have defined a mapping from unigrams and bigrams to this feature space. Each feature is represented as a *set* of unigrams and bigrams such that the identified set corresponds to the feature in question. For the batting features and bowling features, the corresponding examples of unigrams and bigrams are given in Tables 2 and 3, respectively. The complete list can be accessed at https://bit.ly/3sjVD4W. This unigram/bigram to feature mapping is obtained by consulting cricket experts. Corresponding to these features, 19 (batting features) and 12 (bowling features) sets of unigrams and bigrams are obtained. *This method of obtaining features has addressed the stop word related problem. The sparsity is addressed by mapping unigram and bigram of the text commentary only to these features.*

Finally, each delivery is represented as a set of extracted bowling and batting features, similar to the set of items representing a transaction in ARM (Example: *fullLength legStump fast attacked*). This is the input for ARM.

8   Mining Strength and Weakness Association Rules

In this section, we provide a computational definition of the strength/weakness rule and use ARM to construct strength/weakness rule of individual player given the definition.

Definition 1. *Rule. In the association rule $A \implies B$, when A comprises a set of bowling features and B comprises a batting feature.*

Definition 2. *Strength Rule of Batter. In Definition 1, when B or batting feature of the player (batter) corresponds to <u>attacked</u>.*

Definition 3. *Weakness Rule of Batter. In Definition 1, when B or batting feature of the player (batter) correspond to <u>beaten</u>.*

Whenever a batter exhibits strength on a delivery, it is a weakness for the bowler, and the inverse is also true. Therefore, the bowler's strength and weakness are defined in terms of the batters' batting features she is bowling. A bowler exhibits strength (or weakness) when the opponent batter's batting feature is beaten (or attacked).

Definition 4. *Strength Rule of Bowler. In Definition 1, when B or batting feature of the opponent players (batters) corresponds to <u>beaten</u>.*

Definition 5. *Weakness Rule of Bowler. In Definition 1, when B or batting feature of the opponent player (batters) corresponds to <u>attacked</u>.*

For constructing the strength and weakness association rules, we use the apriori algorithm [1]. The parameters on which the strength of the association of $A \implies B$ is dependent are - (i) *Support* is an indication of how frequently A and B appear in the dataset, (ii) *Confidence* is an indication of how often the rule is true, i.e., the conditional probability of occurrence of B given A, and (iii) *Lift* is the rise in the probability of having B with the knowledge of A being present over the probability of having B without any knowledge about the presence of A. Lift value greater than 1 signifies high association between A and B. In this work, the support for the analysis is varied from 0.001 to 0.1 and the confidence for the analysis is set at 0.5. The analysis has resulted in some interesting results, giving insights into player's strengths and weaknesses.

The results of the strength and weakness analysis for batter Steve Smith against all bowlers in Test matches are presented in Table 4. The first strength

Table 4. Identified strength and weakness association rules for batter Steve Smith.

Association Rule (A ⟹ B)	Support(%)	Confidence(%)	Lift
Strength Rules			
{shortlength, slow} ⟹ {attacked}	2.6	72.1	1.6
{legstump} ⟹ {attacked}	2.5	60.1	1.3
{fast, middlestump} ⟹ {attacked}	2.7	53.9	1.2
{fulllength, middlestump} ⟹ {attacked}	2.0	51.4	1.1
Other Rules			
{goodlength} ⟹ {defended}	10.6	68.7	1.4
{fast, offstump} ⟹ {defended}	19.0	64.4	1.3
{fast, shortlength} ⟹ {backfoot}	9.2	91.4	1.9
{fulllength, offstump} ⟹ {frontfoot}	8.5	81.9	1.6
{fast, offstump} ⟹ {0run}	22.8	82.2	1.2
{fast, offstump} ⟹ {squareoff}	11.2	50.4	1.4
{legstump, slow} ⟹ {squareleg}	17.8	86.9	2.3
{legstump, movein, spin} ⟹ {fineleg}	0.01	100	23.7

rule of Steve Smith is - *Smith attacks slow and shot-length deliveries.* With our confidence threshold, no weakness rule is obtained for Steve Smith.

Similarly, we can obtain rules other than strengths and weaknesses by choosing the consequent of the association rule as other batting features such as footwork, shot area, and outcome. We present these rules for batter Steve Smith in Table 4. Similar strength and weakness analyses can be performed for the bowlers as well. The code and result of ARM analysis for more than 250 players are provided in https://bit.ly/3rj6k6c.

9 Conclusion

We presented an application of association rule mining for learning the strength and weakness rules of cricket players from the text commentary data. We provided computational definitions for capturing the strength and weakness rules. We fully utilized the ball-by-ball description of the game's proceedings during the Test matches. We established that association rule mining is a suitable method for the computation of strength and weakness rules. The constructed rules will be helpful for analysts, coaches, and team management in building game strategies.

The possible direction for future research is to include the external factors like playing conditions (age-of-ball, pitch condition, weather condition) and match situations (day of the match, inning of the match, session of the day) in the proposed method.

References

1. Agrawal, R., Imielinski, T., Swami, A.: Mining association rules between sets of items in large databases. In: SIGMOD 1993 (1993)
2. Satou, K., et al.: Finding association rules on heterogeneous genome data. In: Pacific Symposium on Biocomputing, pp. 397–408 (1997)
3. Hsieh, N.: An integrated data mining and behavioral scoring model for analyzing bank customers. Expert Syst. Appl. **27**, 623–633 (2004)
4. Brijs, T., Goethals, B., Swinnen, G., Vanhoof, K., Wets, G.: A data mining framework for optimal product selection in retail supermarket data: the generalized PROFSET model. In: KDD 2000 (2000)
5. Puchun, W.: The application of data mining algorithm based on association rules in the analysis of football tactics. Int. Conf. Robots Intell. Syst. (ICRIS) **2016**, 418–421 (2016)
6. Liao, S., Chen, J., Hsu, T.: Ontology-based data mining approach implemented for sport marketing. Expert Syst. Appl. **36**, 11045–11056 (2009)
7. Sun, J., Yu, W., Zhao, H.: Study of association rule mining on technical action of ball games. Int. Conf. Measur. Technol. Mech. Autom. **3**, 539–542 (2010)
8. Raj, K.A., Padma, P.: Application of association rule mining: a case study on team India. Int. Conf. Comput. Commun. Inform. **2013**, 1–6 (2013)
9. Umamaheswari, P., RajaRam, M.: A novel approach for mining association rules on sports data using principal component analysis: for cricket match perspective. IEEE Int. Adv. Comput. Conf. **2009**, 1074–1080 (2009)
10. Behera, S.R., Agrawal, P., Awekar, A., Vedula, V.S.: Mining strengths and weaknesses of cricket players using short text commentary. In: 2019 18th IEEE International Conference On Machine Learning And Applications (ICMLA), pp. 673–679 (2019)
11. Behera, S.R., Vedula, V.S.: Mining temporal changes in strengths and weaknesses of cricket players using tensor decomposition. In: ESANN (2020)
12. Behera, S.R., Saradhi, V.V.: Stats aren't everything: learning strengths and weaknesses of cricket players. In: Brefeld, U., Davis, J., Van Haaren, J., Zimmermann, A. (eds.) MLSA 2020. CCIS, vol. 1324, pp. 79–88. Springer, Cham (2020). https://doi.org/10.1007/978-3-030-64912-8_7
13. Steinbock, D.: TagCrowd. http://www.tagcrowd.com/blog/about/ Accessed 19 Nov 2020
14. Rundell, M.: The Wisden Dictionary of Cricket, vol. 67, 3rd edn. A.& C Black, London (2009)

Learning to Describe Player Form
in the MLB

Connor Heaton[(✉)] and Prasenjit Mitra

The Pennsylvania State University, State College, PA 16802, USA
{czh5372,pmitra}@psu.edu

Abstract. Major League Baseball (MLB) has a storied history of using
statistics to better understand and discuss the game of baseball, with
an entire discipline of statistics dedicated to the craft, known as *sabermetrics*. At their core, all *sabermetrics* seek to quantify some aspect of
the game, often a *specific* aspect of a player's skill set - such as a batter's ability to drive in runs (RBI) or a pitcher's ability to keep batters
from reaching base (WHIP). While useful, such statistics are fundamentally limited by the fact that they are derived from an account of *what*
happened on the field, not *how* it happened. As a first step towards alle-
viating this shortcoming, we present a novel, contrastive learning-based
framework for describing player *form* in the MLB. We use *form* to refer
to the way in which a player has impacted the course of play in their
recent appearances. Concretely, a player's *form* is described by a 72-
dimensional vector. By comparing clusters of players resulting from our
form representations and those resulting from traditional *sabermetrics*,
we demonstrate that our *form representations* contain information about
how players impact the course of play, not present in traditional, publicly available statistics. We believe these embeddings could be utilized
to predict both in-game and game-level events, such as the result of an
at-bat or the winner of a game.

Keywords: Machine Learning · Player Valuation

1   Introduction

As the sport of baseball grew in popularity, fans, players, and managers desired
a more pointed way of discussing, and arguing over, the game. The more math-
ematically inclined fans realized that they could use statistics to describe how
players have historically performed, and how those performances have translated
in to advantages for their team - and thus, *sabermetrics* was born[1].

While *sabermetrics* have undoubtedly changed how players, fans, and front
offices alike interact with the game - introducing new statistics, such as WAR,
OPS+, SIERRA, and BABIP among others, and inspiring new strategies, such
as the defensive infield shift, offensive launch angles, etc. - such statistics are

---

[1] A somewhat simplified history.

U. Brefeld et al. (Eds.): MLSA 2021, CCIS 1571, pp. 93–102, 2022.
https://doi.org/10.1007/978-3-031-02044-5_8

fundamentally limited in their descriptive power by the fact that they are derived from an account of *what* happened on the field, not *how* it happened.

To see why a description of *what* happened is less desirable than a description of *how* it happened, consider two at-bats: one between *pitcher A* & *batter B*, and another between *pitcher X* & *batter Y*. In the former, *pitcher A* got ahead in the count 0-2, but *batter B* battled back to a full-count, eventually hitting a ball to deep right-field and reaching first base comfortably. For the latter, *pitcher X* fell behind 2-0 in the count, before *batter Y* hit a dribbler down the third base line and beat the throw to first. The most simple way of describing the two at bats would be to say a single was recorded in both cases, which would do nothing to differentiate between the two at bats. Information could be included about how many pitches were thrown in each at-bat, but that still doesn't tell the whole story. For example, it wouldn't convey that *batter B* was able to battle back from an 0-2 count and reach base or the way in which either pitcher sequenced their pitches. Furthermore, it would not convey that *batter B* had power-hit a fly-ball to deep-right nor that *batter Y* had the speed to beat out the throw to first.

Typically, *sabermetrics* have been used to describe some aspect of a player's game over a relatively large time-scale. Intuitively, in a statistical sense, this makes sense - they are statistics derived from a sample population, and the larger the sample population, the more *accurate* the computed sample statistic will be with respect to describing the population at large. The interpretations of these *sabermetrics* often "break down" when working with a small number of samples. For example, it would not make much sense to use batting average or WHIP to describe the players participating in the at-bats mentioned above. *Pitcher A* and *pitcher B* will have a WHIP of ∞ while *batter X* and *batter Y* will have a batting average of 1.000. They aren't incorrect, however - they accurately describe *what* happened, but do little to reveal *how* it happened. For this reason, we believe it is sub-optimal to derive a description of a player's short-term performance using traditional *sabermetrics*.

In 2015, Statcast systems were added to all 30 MLB stadiums [2]. These systems record highly detailed information about many aspects of the game including player positioning in the field, thrown pitch types, pitch velocity, pitch rotation, hit distance, batted ball exit velocity, and launch angle, among others, for every pitch thrown in every game. Analysis of this Statcast data has already influenced how the game is understood, drawing more attention to batters' launch angle, for example. We believe new insights can be found by analyzing Statcast data as a sequence of records instead of records in isolation.

2   Related Work

For an extended description of the many *sabermetrics*, we direct the interested reader toward *Understanding sabermetrics* by Costa, Huber, and Saccoman. Below, we describe similar work towards obtaining player representations and related work in machine learning (ML).

2.1   (batter|pitcher)2vec

The (batter|pitcher)2vec model was proposed in 2018, motivated by recent advances in natural language processing (NLP) [1]. Player embeddings were learned by modeling at-bats - Given an ID for the batter and pitcher taking part in an at-bat, the model was asked to learn embeddings that describe each player and can be used to predict the result of said at-bat. The model was trained using MLB at-bats from 2013 through 2016. Once an embedding was learned for each player, the author demonstrated how they can be used to make predictions as to the result of an unseen at-bat with more accuracy than previous methods.

2.2   Transformers, BERT, and Image-GPT

The *transformer* architecture rose in popularity thanks in large part to its use in the BERT language model [5,9]. The motivating principal behind BERT is the notion that the meaning of words can be inferred by analyzing the context in which they naturally appear, and the transformer architecture, along with a special training regimen, enable BERT to do just that.

To learn the language, BERT browses the internet and performs two tasks when it comes across a piece of text: 1) Masked Language Modeling (MLM) and 2) Next Sentence Prediction (NSP). MLM is essentially BERT creating fill-in-the-blank questions for itself. For example, if BERT comes across the text "I love you," it may create a fill-in-the-blank question in the form of "I love ____." By analyzing the context surrounding the blank, the model is likely to fill the blank with "you." Instead, if the fill-in-the-blank question were "I go to the gym every day. I love ____," the context may induce the model to fill the blank with "exercise." By learning to fill in the blank correctly, BERT is learning to infer from the context the meaning associated with different words.

The NSP task helps BERT learn the emergent meaning associated with various sequences of characters. Given two sentences, the model is asked to make a binary prediction as to whether or not these sentences appeared next to each other "in the wild." For example, if the example above was separated and given to the model as two sentences in "I go to the gym every day" and "I love exercise," the model would be expected to respond affirmatively. By repeatedly performing this test, the model will begin to understand the semantics emerging from the sequence of words and characters - if you do something every day, you likely "love" it, and the "gym" is associated with "exercise," for example.

Upon seeing the success BERT and similar models had working with natural language, Chen et al. noted that their MLM training objective closely resembled that of Denoising Autoencoders, which were originally designed to work with images, and explored the extent to which transformers could be used to learn image representations using a similar training scheme [3]. Instead of learning to "fill in the blank" as BERT would, this model, dubbed *Image-GPT*, would learn to impute the missing pixels in a corrupted image. In much the same fashion that BERT understands language as a collection of characters and words and learns their meaning by analyzing the context in which they appear, *Image-GPT* perceives images as a collection of pixels with varying intensities of red, green, and blue, and learns the role they play in the emergent semantics of the image by analyzing the context in which they appear.

BERT and *Image-GPT* demonstrate that when paired with an appropriate training objective, transformers can be effective learners of atomic-element representations by leveraging the context in which these atomic-elements appear. Here, we use *atomic-element* to refer to the lowest unit of information the model is capable of expressing or understanding - for BERT, groups of English characters are the *atomic-elements*, while pixel values are the *atomic-elements* for *Image-GPT*. Furthermore, they demonstrate how the same model that learned these atomic-element representations also learns how to discern an emergent meaning when these representations are viewed in conjunction with one another.

2.3   Contrastive Learning

Contrastive Learning is a training scheme often used in Computer Vision (CV) applications where a model's training objective is to minimize a contrastive loss objective among a batch of sample records [4]. The motivating theory behind contrastive learning is that similar inputs should result in similar outputs from a representation-learning model - in our application, similar sequences of at-bats should be described with similar *form* vectors. When learning via self-supervised contrastive loss, for example, the model is given two different *views* of a single image, and encouraged to produce similar outputs [7]. Furthermore, the output produced by two *views* of the same image are expected to be dissimilar to outputs resulting from views of different source images. The different *views* are often obtained by a combination of randomly cropping, rotating, resizing, inverting, or otherwise distorting the source image.

The self-supervised contrastive loss objective is given in Eq. 1, where $I \equiv \{0, 1, ..., 2N - 1\}$ is the set of indices in the batch, $j(i)$ is the *positive* sample(s) for record i, $\cdot$ is the inner product, $\tau \in \mathbb{R}^+$ is a scaling temperature value, and $a \in A(i)$ is the set including the *positive* and *negative* samples for record i [6]. Record j is a considered *positive* sample for record i if it is derived from the same source image, otherwise it is considered a *negative* sample.

$$L^{self} = \sum_{i \in I} L_i^{self} = -\sum_{i \in I} log \frac{exp(z_i \cdot z_{j(i)}/\tau)}{\sum_{a \in A(i)} exp(z_i \cdot z_a/\tau)} \qquad (1)$$

3   Our Method

The principal motivation behind our work towards describing player *form* is very much the same as that of contrastive learning - players who impact the game in similar ways should be described using similar *form* vectors. We do not have ground truth player *form* labels (vectors), but we do know the same batter at two very close points in time should be described similarly. In the sections that follow, we describe how data was collected, our player *form* model was trained, and discrete player forms were obtained.

3.1 Data Collection and Organization

While data was originally collected by the Statcast system, we use the Python package `pybaseball`[2] to collect data used for our study and populate a local `sqlite3` database. We collected two types of data using this package: 1) pitch-by-pitch data and 2) season-by-season statistics. Pitch-by-pitch data was collected for the 2015 through 2018 seasons, and contains information such as pitch type, batted ball exit velocity, and launch angle among others. Season-by-season statistics were collected for the 1995 season through 2018, and contain position-agnostic information such as WAR and age in addition to position-specific information such as WHIP for pitchers and OPS for batters.

Each record in our pitch-by-pitch table is accompanied by three key values- 1) *game_pk*, 2) *AB_number*, and 3) *pitch_number*. The *game_pk* is a unique value associated with each game played in the MLB. Within each game, each at-bat has a corresponding *AB_number*, and each pitch thrown in an at-bat an associated *pitch_number*. By using these three pieces of information, we can completely reconstruct the sequence of events which constitute an MLB game. A summary of our collected dataset is given in Table 1.

Table 1. Dataset summary

# Games	9,860
# PA	750k
# Pitches	2.9M
# Batters	1,690
# Pitchers	1,333

3.2 Describing In-game Events

Typically, one would use terms like *single*, *home run*, or *strikeout* to describe the outcome of an at bat. Using this terminology to describe the outcome of at-bats to our model would be insufficient, however, as it tells an incomplete story. For example, did other runners advance on the play?

For this reason, we describe the outcome of a pitch in terms of the **change** in the *gamestate*, where the *gamestate* refers to 1) ball-strike count, 2) base occupancy, 3) number of outs, and 4) score. These changes in *gamestate* will constitute the vocabulary that our model will learn to understand. In total, we identify 325 possible changes in *gamestate* and the result of any thrown pitch can be described by one of these changes in *gamestate*. We colloquially refer to these *gamestate* changes as *gamestate deltas*. From our pitch-by-pitch table, we also have information describing the thrown pitch and batted ball which induced this change in the game state, such as pitch type, pitch rotation, location over the plate, and batted ball distance and launch angle among others.

In aggregate, the *gamestate deltas* describe *what* happened and *how*, but do not describe *who* was involved. We describe the pitcher, batter, and historical matchup between the two using traditional sabermetrics.

---

[2] https://github.com/jldbc/pybaseball.

Table 2. Supplemental statistics at different time scales.

	Batter	Pitcher	Matchup
Career	167	141	137
Season	137	137	137
Last 15	137	137	N/A
This Game	137	137	137

We use statistics derived from four different temporal scales when describing the pitcher, batter, and matchup between the two. A summary of these supplemental features are given in Table 2.

When presenting this information to the model, the 1,541 supplemental features are projected to a lower dimension such that roughly half the data at each input index describes the *gamestate delta* and the other half describes the *players* involved in the at-bat, thrown/batted ball, and stadium.

3.3 Player Form Learning

We seek to describe player *form* - how a player has impacted the game in their recent appearances - so we must identify a *window* of activity (consecutive appearances) we wish to describe for each player. Once this *window* is identified, we can then create two *views* (sets of consecutive appearances) of the player's influence on the game in this *window* of activity. These two *views* describe the same player over a relatively small period of time; so they should induce similar outputs from our player *form* model. Furthermore, *views* from the same *window* of activity for the same player should be dissimilar to *views* derived from *windows* of activity of other players, and even other *windows* for the same player.

For batters, we define a *window* of activity as a sequence of 20 consecutive at-bats for that batter. Then, for each *window* of activity, we derive the first *view* as the first 15 at-bats in the *window*, and the second *view* as the final 15 at-bats in the window. For pitchers, we define a *window* of activity as a sequence of 100 consecutive at-bats for which they pitched, and a *view* as 90 at-bats. That is, the first 90 at-bats in the *window* serve as the first *view* while the final 90 at-bats serve as the second *view*. Batters have an average 4.2 plate appearances per game[3], and starting pitchers face an average of 23.3 batters per start from 2015-2018[4], so *view* sizes were selected such that each view covered *roughly* four games per player.

Present in each input sequence will also be a special *[CLS]* token, which will be used in a similar fashion as BERT's *[CLS]* token. That is, our model will learn to process the input data such that the processed *[CLS]* embedding will sufficiently describe the entirety of the input.

Our model describes players over a short period of time, i.e., 15 at-bats, while (batter|pitcher)2vec describes players over a much larger time scale, four seasons. However, we would still be able to describe players over a much larger time-scale

---

[3] https://fivethirtyeight.com/features/relievers-have-broken-baseball-we-have-a-plan-to-fix-it/.

[4] https://blogs.fangraphs.com/starting-pitcher-workloads-have-been-significantly-reduced-in-2020/.

by viewing consecutive sequences of 15 at-bats in the aggregate, making our model much more versatile - the same model can be used to derive a description of a player over the course of 15 at bats, or four seasons.

Model Architecture. We use a multi-layer, bidirectional transformer encoder, based on the original implementation used in BERT [5,9]. Our model consists of 8 transformer layers, 8 attention heads in each layer, and a model dimension of 512. Our model learns embeddings to describe many aspects of the input data, including *gamestate deltas* , stadiums , player positions , pitch types , and pitch locations over the plate . The remaining information at each input index is derived from a two-layer projection of the supplemental player inputs, described in Sect. 3.2, and real-valued attributes of the thrown pitch and batted ball.

Additionally, the model learns embeddings, which help position the inputs with respect to one another, such as the at-bat number within the *window* and the pitch number within said at-bat. Separate models are trained to describe pitcher and batter *forms* with no shared weights.

Training. We use two tasks to train our model: 1) Masked Gamestate Modeling (MGM) and 2) Self-supervised Contrastive Learning. The MGM task is akin to MLM, with roughly 15% of *gamestate delta* tokens in the input sequence masked and the model asked to impute the missing values. In addition to learning the relation between *gamestate delta* tokens - e.g., three consecutive balls are often shortly followed by a fourth - the model also learns the relation between different types of batters and pitchers participating in the at-bat. For example, if the supplemental inputs describe a shutdown pitcher, poor batter, and pitcher-friendly stadium, the corresponding *gamestate delta* is likely to be to the pitcher's benefit.

The self-supervised contrastive learning task is used to train our model to induce representations that are similar for *views* from the same *window* and dissimilar for *views* of from different *windows*. Concretely, our model produces a 72-dimensional representation for each *view*, which is used in computing the self-supervised contrastive loss. An example of how the model processes a batch of inputs is presented in Fig. 1.

We use an Adam optimizer with $\beta_1 = 0.9$, $\beta_2 = 0.999$, and learning rate of $5e^{-4}$. When learning to describe batters, our model is trained using a batch size of 78 for 90,000 iterations, with 7,500 of the iterations being warm-up. A pitchers' *form* is described by a larger number of at-bats, so we train our pitcher model using a batch size of 36 for 35,000 iterations with 2,500 iterations of warm-up.

3.4   Discretizing Player Forms

We compute a *form* representation for all players in the starting lineup at game-start for all regular season games from 2015–2018. Then, to identify players who have impacted the game in a similar capacity at various points in time, we perform agglomerative clustering with Ward linkage on the form representations

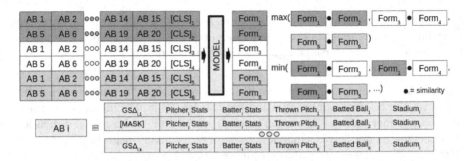

Fig. 1. Example of how our model processes a batch of data while learning to describe batters. Each record in the batch consists of 15 at-bats and a special *[CLS]* token, and each at-bat consists of one or more pitches. For each pitch, the model is given statistics describing the pitcher and batter involved, metrics describing thrown pitch type and batted ball (when applicable), and embeddings describing the stadium and the resulting *gamestate delta*. The model is asked to predict the masked *gamestate delta* tokens using the context in which the masked token appears. Once processed by the model, the embedding for the *[CLS]* assumed to describe the 15 corresponding at-bats. These embeddings are projected to a 72-dimension space before being used to compute the self-supervised contrastive loss.

to obtain discrete form ID's [8]. For a point of comparison, we follow a similar clustering process using traditional *sabermetrics* to describe players. That is, the players' corresponding supplemental inputs, mentioned in Sect. 3.2, without the *in-game* split. We perform Principal Component Analysis on the statistics used to describe each type of player prior to clustering.

4   Results

While a more thorough analysis is required to better understand the representations produced by our model, comparing clusters of players derived from traditional sabermetrics and from *form representations* can give an intuition as to the information contained in the representations.

Figure 2 presents a comparison of cluster membership over time for four batters: Bryce Harper, Mike Trout, Giancarlo Stanton, and Neil Walker. Harper and Trout are somewhat similar, high impact outfielders, while Stanton can tend to be more of a streaky power hitter, and Walker is perhaps more of a utility infielder. In analyzing the plot describing *stat-clusters* in Fig. 2, we see minimal overlap between Harper and Trout. This is an undesirable representation of form, as in our estimation, Harper and Trout tend to impact the game in a similar way. Conversely, we seem to notice a strong association between Harper and Trout in the plot describing their *form-clusters* in Fig. 2.

Figure 3 presents a comparison of cluster membership over time for four starting pitchers: Gerrit Cole, Alex Wood, Trevor Bauer, and Justin Verlander. Cole had rather poor performances throughout 2016 and some of 2017 before

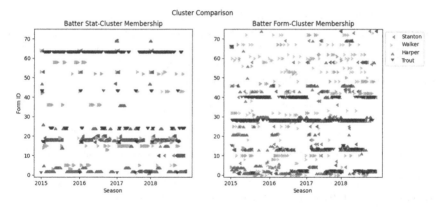

Fig. 2. Discrete batter forms at game-start for games in the 2015 through 2018.

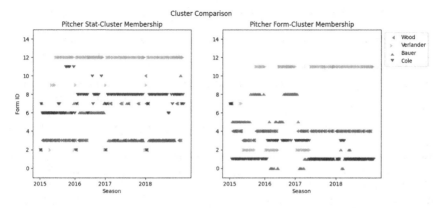

Fig. 3. Discrete pitcher forms at game-start for games in the 2015 through 2018.

snapping back in to All-Star form with Houston in 2018 and 2019. In looking at Cole's *stat-clusters* in Fig. 3, we see that he is consistently mapped to cluster 8 from 2016 onward. This would seem to be an undesirable to describe how he impacted the game, then, as he clearly impacted the game in very different ways in 2016 & 2017 versus 2018. While at the moment we cannot say for certain what signal is contained in our *form representations* we see they describe 2016 Cole differently than 2018 Cole.

5 Conclusion and Future Work

We believe this work serves as a strong starting point in a line of work towards a new way of describing how MLB players - and athletes in other sports - impact the course of play, in a manner not contained in existing, publicly available statistics. Moving forward, we would like to gain a stronger understanding of the contents of the produced *form representations* and how they can be leveraged towards specific ends, such as predicting the result of an at-bat, the winner of an MLB game, or the occurrence of an injury. Furthermore, it would be interesting to take a closer look at the embeddings learned by our model. It would be interesting to explore the relation between different stadiums, for example, from the perspective of both the batter and pitcher.

References

1. Alcorn, M.A.: 2vec: statistic-free talent modeling with neural player embeddings. MIT Sloan Sports Analytics Conference (2016)
2. Casella, P.: Statcast primer: baseball will never be the same (2015). https://www. mlb.com/news/statcast-primer-baseball-will-never-be-the-same/c-119234412. Accessed 20 June 2021
3. Chen, M., Radford, A., Child, R., Wu, J., Jun, H., Luan, D., Sutskever, I.: Generative pretraining from pixels. In: International Conference on Machine Learning, pp. 1691–1703. PMLR (2020)
4. Chen, T., Kornblith, S., Norouzi, M., Hinton, G.: A simple framework for contrastive learning of visual representations. In: International conference on machine learning, pp. 1597–1607. PMLR (2020)
5. Devlin, J., Chang, M.W., Lee, K., Toutanova, K.: Bert: pre-training of deep bidirectional transformers for language understanding. arXiv preprint arXiv:1810.04805 (2018)
6. Khosla, P., et al.: Supervised contrastive learning. arXiv preprint arXiv:2004.11362 (2020)
7. Misra, I., Maaten, L.V.D.: Self-supervised learning of pretext-invariant representations. In: Proceedings of the IEEE/CVF Conference on Computer Vision and Pattern Recognition, pp. 6707–6717 (2020)
8. Rokach, L., Maimon, O.: Clustering methods. In: Maimon, O., Rokach, L. (eds.) Data Mining and Knowledge Discovery Handbook. Springer, Boston, MA (2005). https://doi.org/10.1007/0-387-25465-X_15
9. Vaswani, A., et al.: Attention is all you need. arXiv preprint arXiv:1706.03762 (2017)

Low Cost Player Tracking in Field Hockey

Henrique Duarte Moura[✉] [iD], Leonid Kholkine, Laurens Van Damme,
Kevin Mets, Christiaan Leysen, Tom De Schepper, Peter Hellinckx,
and Steven Latré

Department of Computer Science, University of Antwerpen - imec, IDLab,
Antwerpen, Belgium
henrique.duartemoura@uantwerpen.be

Abstract. In the paper, we describe the technical details of a multi-player tracker system using tracking data obtained from a single low-cost stationary camera on field hockey games. Analyzing the tracking data of the players only from the transmitted video opens a multitude of applications that allows the cost of technology to be reduced. This method does not depend on the cooperation of the players (by using sensors) or their teams (by sharing data with a third party). The approach taken in this paper uses a variety of computer vision and tracking techniques. Making player tracking data more accessible lowers the barrier to entry for sports research and increases the period during which advanced analysis methods can be applied. The proposed system runs the full pipeline at 3 fps on a computer with a simple graphics card.

Keywords: Computer vision · field hockey video analysis · player tracking

1 Introduction

Artificial Intelligence (AI) impacts many aspects of sports. Its application can provide pre- and post-game reports, online summaries, and performance analysis personalized to specific targets, such as athletes, coaches, media, and fans. Many challenges still exist involving data collection (e.g., merging sensor and video data) and processing (e.g., large volumes of high-quality video data). Tracking players is key to analyze game strategies, player and team performance. It involves two steps: identification of in-field players and tracking them in time.

AI is widely used to track players using video data. Most studies consider football [1], soccer [2,3], basketball [4,5], and ice hockey [6] games. Most of them require expensive hardware around the pitch, sensors attached to the players or the ball, and manual annotation. Sensors could simplify tracking. However, there

This work was funded by the DAIQUIRI project, cofunded by imec, a research institute founded by the Flemish Government. Project partners are Ghent University, InTheRace, Arinti, Cronos, VideoHouse, NEP Belgium, and VRT, with project support from VLAIO under grant number HBC.2019.0053.

U. Brefeld et al. (Eds.): MLSA 2021, CCIS 1571, pp. 103–115, 2022.
https://doi.org/10.1007/978-3-031-02044-5_9

are some challenges using sensors: (a) not all teams wear them, (a) there is no suitable sensor to use in the ball, in most cases, (c) its use needs approval from the sports federation, (d) the sensor may not have an open API for online access, and besides that (e) the opposing team has little interest in sharing its data.

Multiple-object tracking (MOT) solutions benefit from the high quality of state-of-art object detection algorithms, popularizing the tracking-by-detection approach. This type of approach allows very simple, but accurate tracking methods to be applied, and depends mainly on the use of bounding boxes or detection masks as input to high-speed trackers. However, tracking players remains challenging due to frequent occlusions, abrupt movements, and environmental conditions (lighting, shadows, etc.). Moreover, players in one team wear the same uniform, making them more difficult to distinguish. In addition, players' body shape variations and poses, motion blur, and the presence of the reserve players and spectators alongside the pitch make the players hard to be tracked reliably. Thus, many existing tracking methods fail in this field.

We show in this paper a player detection and tracking method inspired by recent progress in deep learning (DL). Our method operates on a sequence of frames from a stationary camera. We develop the full field hockey video analysis pipeline. The different modules are designed with performance in mind to allow efficient processing of high-definition video. In this paper, we make three contributions. First, we present a complete pipeline that can (i) identify which area of the image corresponds to the field; (ii) detect the people in the image and select only the players on the pitch; (iii) exclude goalkeepers and referees because they are not tracked; (iv) identify which players correspond to which team; and finally (v) track the movement of these players on the pitch. Second, a comparison of two different approaches for each module described before. Third, a technique that combines the tracking by similarity with a merging stage. In contrast to existing approaches that solely focus on one aspect of the pipeline, our proposal yield insights into which points need improvement in the current state-of-the-art algorithms.

The paper is organized as follows. Related work is listed in Sect. 2, while the architecture is presented in Sect. 3. The experimental setup and results are discussed in, respectively, Sects. 4 and 5. Finally, Sect. 6 concludes this work.

2   Related Work

Several works on player detection and tracking make use of computer vision algorithms, tracking heuristics, and DL. Here, we discuss the main approaches.

Detection Methods: Originally, feature maps associated with classifiers are used to identify the players, such as the Deformable Part Model [7,8] and the histogram of oriented gradients (HOG) features [9]. Gaussian mixture model (GMM) can separate background and foreground [10]. Those methods work well for offline processing but depend on pre-selected features to identify the objects. Newer methods profit from the advances in DL using detection networks to identify the player or the ball [11–14]. Other solutions identify the pitch using the dominant color of the background, morphological filtering [15,16], or more complex color segmentation approaches [17] but suffer from shadows and lighting variation. One can also apply a deep semantic segmentation network using semantic cues (the field surface, lines, etc.) [18]. However, the hockey pitch has few semantic cues.

Trackers: Most modern trackers follow the tracking-by-detection paradigm, where an object detector first finds all objects of interest in each individual frame before a tracking algorithm deals with the problem of associating the objects in consecutive frames [11,19–26]. A common approach is to use a Kalman filter (KF) to forecast random variables (e.g. position or speed) at a specific timestamp [8]. Several proposals are based on this filter, such as Simple online and real-time tracking (SORT) [27], DeepSORT [11], and MF-SORT [24]. The association between frames can use appearance and motion features [13], the bounding boxes' intersection over union (IoU) in consecutive frames [28], visual aspects of players [29] and geometric cues [26] can be added in the matching between video frames. Particle filter [30] and k-shortest paths (KSP) tracking [31,32] are alternatives to KF. To improve the tracking due to occlusions, ensemble methods are used. For example, simple trackers can be sampled from a set of trackers using Markov Chain Monte Carlo (MCMC) [33]. However, this method needs manual feature engineering and is slow to run online. Deep networks were also applied to solve the tracking problem. Long Short-Term Memory (LSTM)s can concatenate high-level visual features produced by a convolutional neural network (CNN)s with region information to track the players [12]. The long-term behavior of the players can be extracted using deep hierarchical networks [4]. Siamese network [34] composes a correlation filter used to discriminate between images and their translations in consecutive frames. Despite the improvements, the DL algorithms are slower than filters. When two players are close to each other, their identities can easily be switched. To address this problem, researchers have explored appearance models [35,36], motion models [37,38], or a mix [32].

Other Approaches to Detection: Other tracking methods also still exist that do not require video input. For example, Yurko et al. [1] used RFID tags, but it requires a large amount of hardware to be installed on-site, as well as the cooperation of both teams for the installation of the RFID chips on their players.

Summary: Most of the current approaches focus only on one aspect: detection or tracking. Our solution provides a complete pipeline that works with images captured by a camera. These images are processed for the identification of players and the field and subsequent tracking of in-field players. Our approach, described in the following sections, uses tracking-by-detection, where we balance the system performance vs the result's quality to process high-quality video.

3 Proposed Solution

In this section, we describe our modular video processing pipeline, shown in Fig. 1. It identifies and tracks field hockey players using a low-cost camera as an

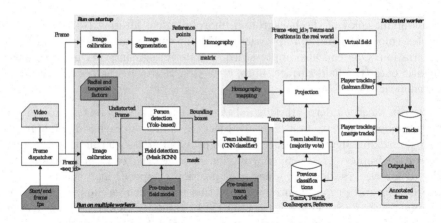

Fig. 1. Proposed pipeline

input. The main components are *field detection, player detection, team labeling,* and *tracking* modules. The camera streams the video, which is captured by the system frame by frame. An image flows in the pipeline from left to right. Each frame is forwarded to a worker that detects the players. There are two processes depending on the execution stage of the system: (1) "Run on startup" module runs at initialization and are shown at the top of the figure, and (2) after startup, the system runs modules in "Run on multiple workers". These stages are explained below. "Run on startup" and "Dedicated worker" run in the same worker, because they don't compete for resources. During start-up, the first frames are used to generate the homography matrix, which is used to convert the pixel coordinates (image) in coordinates in the virtual field, i.e., coordinates measured in meters in a Cartesian system [39, § 2.1.2]. As there are few reference points in a field hockey pitch, several frames are captured to compute a robust position of the reference point, improving the homography's quality. After this step, the workers that perform the detection are activated. A dispatcher selects the worker (e.g., via round-robin) to receive a frame, which has a unique sequential identification number that allows the results to be sorted in the tracking step. The image calibration corrects the received image (e.g., removes distortions), which depends on parameters of the camera, lens type, and resolution. Next, a module detects people in the (corrected) image, which, combined with the field detector, identifies the players inside the pitch. In-field players are also tracked. We will explain below the main modules.

Field Detection: We tested two ways to detect the field: (1) using Mask region-based CNN (R-CNN) network [40,41], which obtain a polygon that represents the limits of the pitch; and (2) using instance segmentation based on Mask R-CNN and Hough transform to detect the pitch lines, the goals, and the penalty mark. With the lines identified by the segmentation, the system can say which are the external lines of the pitch that demarcate the limits of the field.

Fig. 2. Result from the pipeline

Player Detection: We tested two different approaches: (1) based on Yolo v5, which outputs the bounding box of the detected players; and (2) based on Mask R-CNN [40] that segments the image on a pixel-to-pixel basis. The former is less complex, thus it smaller and faster. However, with the finer granularity of the second solution's output, it can show better results in occlusion cases (due to being able to detect a person based on only a part).

Team Labeling: The images of all the people in the field are sent to a module that classifies them into two teams, referees, keepers, and unknown. We also tested two approaches. The first uses visual cues (characteristics). As the images of some players are very small, like one can see in Fig. 2, we cannot use more sophisticated methods such as identifying faces or reading texts on the player's jersey. A CNN is used for feature extraction, *i.e.*, find the important characteristics of the players, and classify the detected people into both teams. The second method is based on a clustering method and separates players belonging to team 1 from those from team 2 using density-based spatial clustering of applications with noise (DBSCAN) [42,43]. The labels outputted by DBSCAN are used to split the player detection into two teams and non-players (the outliers). We use DBSCAN for two reasons: (a) few hyperparameters need to be configured and (b) the inherent ability of the method to deal with outliers (referees and keepers).

Tracking: The pixel coordinates obtained by the player detection module are converted to the coordinates of the virtual field. We tested two methods to track the players. The first uses bipartite matching [44,45], which joins elements from two sets (subsequent images) while keeping the cost of the edges (similarity metric) as low as possible. A simple metric is a Euclidean distance between the coordinates on frames $t-1$ and t. The results are improved using the predicted position on t of detection on $t-1$. This prediction uses simple motion equations.

The second method uses KF as a corrective predictor filter by estimating the process's hidden state that predicts where the player is in the next frame. Ideally, in both cases, if those predictions are accurate, the distance will be zero. The changes between consecutive frames are small. For example, using a 4000×3000 pixels image at 30 frame-per-second (fps), one meter corresponds to 72 pixels in our video, and a person running at 12 m/s moves 29 pixels between two consecutive frames. Thus, the similarity can be (1) the distance between the center of the predicted and the detected bounding box or (2) the IOU of these two boxes, as there will always be some overlap. For any of the two forms, the assignment problem can be written, respectively, as the minimization of the sum of the distances or the maximization of the sum of the IOU. Due to occlusions, player overlapping, and conflicts, the tracking algorithm can break the track (it considers that a new player has been identified, spawning a new track). To reduce this problem, an additional module has been added to combine old tracks with newly created tracks, which is based on [32,46] but adapted to run online.

4   Experimental Setup

The pipeline runs on a machine with 32 MB of RAM, 4 Intel(R) Xeon(R) Silver 4108 CPU @ 1.80 GHz, and one GeForce GTX 1080 Ti. The machine also runs Ubuntu 20.04 LTS with Python 3.8 and PyTorch 1.5.0. The camera is a Go Pro Hero7 Black running with 1080p at 30 fps.

Player Detection: The first player detector is based on Yolo v.5 [47], with pre-trained parameters trained with 5000 COCO val2017 images [48]. We trained the two-class classifier (person or background) on a private dataset (900 annotated images taken from field hockey videos filmed with a GoPro Hero 8). The second detector uses Mask R-CNN, trained with 900 annotated frames. The network parameter was initialized with pre-trained values of 50-RESNET.

Field Detection: The field detector based on Mask R-CNN was trained using the same dataset described. To assist the detection mechanism, we superimpose each frame with a 5-pixel-wide blank border. We calculate the convex hull of the network's output. The second method uses image segmentation with fully convolutional networks for semantic segmentation (FCN) [49] based on the implementation in [50]. We added new backbone models based on layer residual nets (RESNET) -18, -34, -50, and -101. The best results were obtained using RESNET-101, which also showed good results in [51]. The network was trained using 120 images annotated by the authors.

Team Labeling: The classifier requires that labeled data about the teams is available before the match. The classifier is a multi-layer network composed of two convolution layers (CL) and four fully connected layers (FC), which use ReLU as activation. The CL are followed by Max Poll layers with $kernel = (2,2)$ and $stride = 2$. The second method does not need previous training. It assembles clusters based on visual characteristics. The outliers are the goalkeepers and the referees, who use jerseys of different colors from both teams. Notice that DBSCAN cannot distinguish the referees from the goalkeepers.

Tracking: We consider only the last-second window for prediction. The KF's hidden state corresponds to the position, speed, and acceleration of the bounding box's coordinates. Our approach models its transitions as constant acceleration.

5   Experimental Results

Figure 2 shows an output generated by the pipeline. We clearly see that (1) the identified players are marked with bounding boxes in the image, with players and others who are out of the field being excluded by the tracking, and (2) the positioning of the players in the image is converted into a virtual field at the top left of the figure. In the virtual field, the area indicated in green corresponds to the visual field captured by the camera. Below we discuss each module.

Player Detection: We tested two flavors: *v5s* and *v5m*. The results for *v5m* are, in general, better than *v5s* (F1 score 81.1% vs. 79.3%). This is expected because *v5m* has a bigger network, which can capture more nuances. However, we opt to use *v5s* due to its faster running time. Thus, from here onward, we only show results with Yolo *v5s*. The detection module takes on average 60.590 ± 0.944 ms to run with the Yolo-based player detection, while the Mask R-CNN module runs in 2.445 ± 0.009 s. Thus the Yolo-based module is $40\times$ faster than the Mask R-CNN module, which is a much bigger network. In both methods, one important parameter that controls the number of detected people is the threshold used to select if detection is a person or not. Choosing the right threshold is hard. If it is too high, it may cause a lot of people in the image to not be detected. The current threshold is set to 0.5 for both methods. Most of the cases where detection problems occur refers to players that were positioned far away from the camera. We also argue that using two cameras, one behind each goal, solves the detection problems in our footage, except occlusion.

Field Detection: Using the CNN, we obtained a 98.9% accuracy with a mean IoU of 72.8% for the entire test set. Analyzing the average IOU values per class, we see the worst result is the identification of the shooting circle (curved line), followed by the lines inside the pitch. The shooting circle is actually composed of a line parallel to the goal line closed by curved edges. The algorithm confuses the straight part with the rest of the lines in the field. On the other hand, the internal field lines do not have visual cues capable of distinguishing one from the other. The distinction between them is purely based on distance. We leave for future work the incorporation of factors capable of distinguishing these lines in the segmentation. The CNN-based field detection on average takes 0.217 ± 0.021 s to run, while the image segmentation runs in 1.384 ± 0.005 s. It is $6\times$ faster than the segmentation method, as it uses a smaller network and the segmentation involves more complex operations. It is key that the identified field mask produced by the detector follows the lines that define the pitch as close to perfection as possible, to exclude players who wait near the outer lines. Both algorithms tested in this section showed good adherence to these lines in the plane close to the camera. However, the more distant lines, particularly the bottom line of the pitch, are not well recognized because they are quite blurred, making the task difficult even for the authors who made the filming. The use of two cameras positioned on opposite sides of the field will again improve the result since the algorithm only has to deal with the nearest lines.

Team Labeling: The main advantage of the CNN-based method is that it has higher accuracy (98% vs. 69.2%). We ran this method over a video with 2800 frames for 5 different videos, from which we created a dataset with about 10,000 annotated images of people in the pitch. The dataset was divided into train and test sets in a proportion of 6:4. The second method uses clustering based on DBSCAN. To configure the hyperparameter ϵ, DBSCAN searches the suitable value during the startup. The running time during clustering averages 1.812 ± 0.0230 ms. This method is about 20× faster than using CNN. However, this method does not work well due to the assumption that there are always two teams in the image and that the number of players is much greater than that of non-players. If these conditions are not met, the algorithm fails completely. Another problem is related to the features used by DBSCAN. In our case, we use color histograms to characterize the players. These histograms can present great variations due to lighting, making the similarity metric values quite different for players of the same type, leading to classification errors. This is aggravated if the teams use uniforms with similar colors. The use of more complex identification methods with DBSCAN increases the runtime that makes it similar to the use of identification via CNN, which showed higher accuracy than DBSCAN.

Tracking: We tested two methods to track the players: bipartite matching and Kalman-based tracker. The first approach takes 383.447 ± 0.170 ms, while the second takes 3.466 ± 1.010 ms (110× faster). The last stage of the pipeline's processing path consists of merging tracks. In Fig. 3, we see in the 3D representation of each of the tracks (as a curve) generated by the tracking process. The X and Y axes represent the coordinates in the virtual field (relative to the width and depth of the pitch), while the Z-axis corresponds to the frame where the detection was made. Over time, each curve grows upwards on the Z-axis and the position (x, y) consists of the location of the player for a given z frame. Figure 4 shows the tracks after merging. Thirty-two tracks were altered out of 46. The method took 11.4 ms on average per loop (the standard deviation was $229\,\mu$s). The merging mechanism presents problems for joining tracks with a large gap in the detection (*e.g.* tracks 15, 33, and 40 correspond to the same player in Fig. 4). However, they were not joined because the interval without detection was higher than the limit defined in the system. If this threshold is too small, a short period where the player is not detected or is occluded disconnects the tracks. However, if it is too large, tracks from different players can be connected. In our example, the merging modules fail in only one case due to a lack of player detection. In the other cases, occlusion and collision were the causes that lead

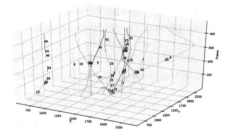 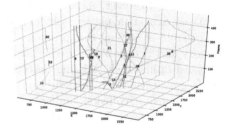

Fig. 3. Only the simple tracking   **Fig. 4.** Merged tracks

to the disconnected tracks. This problem may be reduced (or even solved) using temporal correlation via attribute matching as proposed in [2], which can be tested in future work.

System's Accuracy: We analyze each frame in a 01:30 min video, comparing it with human-provided ground truth. The results obtained with Yolo are better than with Mask R-CNN, where the accuracy is 93.8% and 70.9%, respectively. Both methods show two problems: (1) detect fewer players; or (2) detect more players than the total amount in the pitch. Those occur because: (a) the detection algorithm cannot recognize the player; (b) occlusion; and (c) duplication, *i.e.*, detection generates two bounding boxes for the same player. Yolo shows more over-detection cases, and because Mask R-CNN uses segmentation to generate the detection mask, it produces fewer duplication errors since the mask generation unites the parts into a consistent whole. In Yolo, it is necessary to regulate the overlapping of bounding boxes manually. The main error found in our studies is the algorithm provides two bounding boxes for different parts of the player's body or, when two players collide, the algorithm produces multiple detection. Some collisions can be solved by the tracking module. Offline methods provide better results than online methods because offline can use future tracking points [11,27]. Online can be improved by enhancing tracking, using multiple cameras with different fields of view, or using a small delay in the transmission. However, the problem posed by occlusion is still an open topic.

6 Conclusion

Our solution uses the tracking-by-detection paradigm: the object detector first finds all objects of interest in a frame, and the tracking algorithm associates these objects in consecutive frames. We created a full pipeline that was tested on field hockey videos. Two approaches were tested for each of the main modules, and their performance is compared and discussed in Sect. 5. The player detection module directly influences the pipeline output's quality. The better the detection, the easier the tracking module work, as fewer players are missing or occluded. However, some problems cannot be solved by the detection module alone, *e.g.*, if a player is hidden by another player, the detection module is incapable of solving this problem. Thus, it is necessary that the system has memory and is capable of predicting the existence of this hidden player, which is a hard online task. Missing detection causes a large number of ID switches and fragmentation, which significantly degrades the tracking quality, especially during occlusion, collision, and crossings. Future work will consider better movement patterns forecasting and ball tracking, which is much harder than in tennis (little obstruction/high contrast) and soccer (larger ball). Player identification can be improved by identifying the jersey number (not on footage) and by using extracted player features in team labeling.

References

1. Yurko, R., et al.: Going deep: models for continuous-time within-play valuation of game outcomes in American football with tracking data. J. Quant. Anal. Sports **16**(2), 163–182 (2020)
2. Sabirin, H., Sankoh, H., Naito, S.: Automatic soccer player tracking in single camera with robust occlusion handling using attribute matching. IEICE Trans. Inf. Syst. **98**(8), 1580–1588 (2015)
3. Linke, D., Link, D., Lames, M.: Football-specific validity of TRACAB's optical video tracking systems. PloS one **15**(3), e0230179 (2020)
4. Zheng, S., Yue, Y., Hobbs, J.: Generating long-term trajectories using deep hierarchical networks arXiv preprint arXiv:1706.07138, 2017
5. Macdonald, B.: Recreating the game: using player tracking data to analyze dynamics in basketball and football. In: Harvard Data Science Review, vol. 2, no. 4 (2020)
6. Vovk, V., Skuratovskyi, S., Vyplavin, P., Gorovyi, I.: Light-weight tracker for sports applications. Signal Process. Symposium (SPSympo). IEEE **2019**, 251–255 (2019)
7. Felzenszwalb, P., McAllester, D., Ramanan, D.: A discriminatively trained, multiscale, deformable part model. In: IEEE Conference on Computer Vision and Pattern Recognition, vol. 2008 pp. 1–8. IEEE (2008)
8. Lu, W.-L., Ting, J.-A., Little, J.J., Murphy, K.P.: Learning to track and identify players from broadcast sports videos. IEEE Trans. Pattern Anal. Mach. Intell. **35**(7), 1704–1716 (2013)
9. Cheshire, E., Halasz, C., Perin, J.K.: Player tracking and analysis of basketball plays. In: European Conference of Computer Vision (2013)
10. Csanalosi, G., Dobreff, G., Pasic, A., Molnar, M., Toka, L.: Low-cost optical tracking of soccer players. In: Brefeld, U., Davis, J., Van Haaren, J., Zimmermann, A. (eds.) MLSA 2020. CCIS, vol. 1324, pp. 28–39. Springer, Cham (2020). https://doi.org/10.1007/978-3-030-64912-8_3
11. Wojke, N., Bewley, A., Paulus, D.: Simple online and realtime tracking with a deep association metric. In: IEEE International Conference on Image Processing (ICIP), vol.2017, pp. 3645–3649. IEEE (2017)
12. Ning, G., Zhang, Z., Huang, C., Ren, X., Wang, H., Cai, C., He, Z.: Spatially supervised recurrent convolutional neural networks for visual object tracking. In: IEEE International Symposium on Circuits and Systems (ISCAS), vol. 2017, pp. 1–4. IEEE (2017)

13. Khan, G., Tariq, Z., Khan, M.U.G.:Multi-person tracking based on faster R-CNN and deep appearance features. In: Visual Object Tracking with Deep Neural Networks. IntechOpen (2019)
14. Komorowski, J., Kurzejamski, G., Sarwas, G.: Footandball: integrated player and ball detector arXiv preprint arXiv:1912.05445 (2019)
15. Tong, X., Liu, J., Wang, T., Zhang, Y.: Automatic player labeling, tracking and field registration and trajectory mapping in broadcast soccer video. ACM Trans. Intell. Syst. Technol. (TIST) **2**(2), 1–32 (2011)
16. Gu, L., Ding, X., Hua, X.-S.: Online play segmentation for broadcasted American football TV programs. In: Aizawa, K., Nakamura, Y., Satoh, S. (eds.) PCM 2004. LNCS, vol. 3331, pp. 57–64. Springer, Heidelberg (2004). https://doi.org/10.1007/978-3-540-30541-5_8
17. Hung, M.-H., Hsieh, C.-H., Kuo, C.-M., Pan, J.-S.: Generalized playfield segmentation of sport videos using color features. Pattern Recogn. Lett. **32**(7), 987–1000 (2011)
18. Homayounfar, N., Fidler, S., Urtasun, R.: Sports field localization via deep structured models. In: Proceedings of the IEEE Conference on Computer Vision and Pattern Recognition, pp. 5212–5220 (2017)
19. Leal-Taixé, L., Canton-Ferrer, C., Schindler, K.: Learning by tracking: Siamese CNN for robust target association. In: Proceedings of the IEEE Conference on Computer Vision and Pattern Recognition Workshops, pp. 33–40 (2016)
20. Schulter, S. Vernaza, P. Choi, W. Chandraker, M.: Deep network flow for multi-object tracking. In: Proceedings of the IEEE Conference on Computer Vision and Pattern Recognition, pp. 6951–6960 (2017)
21. Sharma, S., Ansari, J.A. Murthy, J.K., Krishna, K.M.: Beyond pixels: leveraging geometry and shape cues for online multi-object tracking. In: 2018 IEEE International Conference on Robotics and Automation (ICRA), pp. 3508–3515. IEEE (2018)
22. Fang, K., Xiang, Y., Li, X., Savarese, S.: Recurrent autoregressive networks for online multi-object tracking. In: 2018 IEEE Winter Conference on Applications of Computer Vision (WACV), pp. 466–475. IEEE (2018)
23. Xu, Y., Zhou, X., Chen, S., Li, F.: Deep learning for multiple object tracking: a survey. IET Comput. Vis. **13**(4), 355–368 (2019)
24. Fu, H., Wu, L., Jian, M., Yang, Y., Wang, X.: MF-SORT: simple online and real-time tracking with motion features. In: Zhao, Y., Barnes, N., Chen, B., Westermann, R., Kong, X., Lin, C. (eds.) ICIG 2019. LNCS, vol. 11901, pp. 157–168. Springer, Cham (2019). https://doi.org/10.1007/978-3-030-34120-6_13
25. Ciaparrone, G., Sánchez, F.L., Tabik, S., Troiano, L., Tagliaferri, R., Herrera, F.: Deep learning in video multi-object tracking: a survey. Neurocomputing **381**, 61–88 (2020)
26. Nasseri, M.H., Moradi, H., Hosseini, R., Babaee, M.: Simple online and real-time tracking with occlusion handling arXiv preprint arXiv:2103.04147 (2021)
27. Bewley, A., Ge, Z., Ott, L., Ramos, F., Upcroft, B.: Simple online and realtime tracking. In: IEEE International Conference on Image Processing (ICIP), vol. 2016, pp. 3464–3468. IEEE (2016)
28. Bochinski, E., Eiselein, V., Sikora, T.: High-speed tracking-by-detection without using image information. In: 2017 14th IEEE International Conference on Advanced Video and Signal Based Surveillance (AVSS), pp. 1–6. IEEE (2017)
29. Manafifard, M., Ebadi, H., Moghaddam, H.A.: A survey on player tracking in soccer videos. Comput. Vis. Image Understand. **159**, 19–46 (2017)

30. Murray, S.: Real-time multiple object tracking-a study on the importance of speed arXiv preprint arXiv:1709.03572 (2017)
31. Berclaz, J., Fleuret, F., Turetken, E., Fua, P.: Multiple object tracking using k-shortest paths optimization. IEEE Trans. pattern Anal. Mach. Intell. **33**(9), 1806–1819 (2011)
32. Liang, Q., Wu, W., Yang, Y., Zhang, R., Peng, Y., Xu, M.: Multi-player tracking for multi-view sports videos with improved k-shortest path algorithm. Appl. Sci. **10**(3), 864 (2020)
33. Kwon, J., Lee, K.M.: Tracking by sampling trackers. In: 2011 International Conference on Computer Vision, pp. 1195–1202. IEEE (2011)
34. Valmadre, J., Bertinetto, L., Henriques, J., Vedaldi, A., Torr, P.H.: End-to-end representation learning for correlation filter based tracking. In: Proceedings of the IEEE Conference on Computer Vision and pattern Recognition, pp. 2805–2813 (2017)
35. Shitrit, H.B., Berclaz, J., Fleuret, F., Fua, P.: Tracking multiple people under global appearance constraints. In: International Conference on Computer Vision, vol. 2011, pp. 137–144. IEEE (2011)
36. Kang, T., Mo, Y., Pae, D., Ahn, C., Lim, M.: Robust visual tracking framework in the presence of blurring by arbitrating appearance-and feature-based detection. Measurement **95**, 50–69 (2017)
37. Liu, J.: Carr, P., Collins, R.T., Liu, Y.: Tracking sports players with context-conditioned motion models. In: Proceedings of the IEEE Conference on Computer Vision and Pattern Recognition, pp. 1830–1837 (2013)
38. Li, Z., Gao, S., Nai, K.: Robust object tracking based on adaptive templates matching via the fusion of multiple features. J. Vis. Commun. Image Represent. **44**, 1–20 (2017)
39. Szeliski, R.: Computer Vision: Algorithms and Applications. Springer, London (2010). https://doi.org/10.1007/978-1-84882-935-0
40. He, K., Gkioxari, G., Dollár, P., Girshick, R.: Mask R-CNN. In: Proceedings of the IEEE international conference on computer vision, pp. 2961–2969 (2017)
41. Abdulla, W.:Mask R-CNN for object detection and instance segmentation on Keras and TensorFlow (2017). https://github.com/matterport/Mask_RCNN
42. Schubert, E., Sander, J., Ester, M., Kriegel, H.P., Xu, X.: DBSCAN revisited, revisited: why and how you should (still) use DBSCAN. ACM Trans. Database Syst. (TODS) **42**(3), 1–21 (2017)
43. Ester, M., Kriegel, H.-P., Sander, J., Xu, X., et al.: A density-based algorithm for discovering clusters in large spatial databases with noise. KDD **96**(34), 226–231 (1996)
44. Kuhn, H.W.: The Hungarian method for the assignment problem. Naval Res. Logistic. Q. **2**(1–2), 83–97 (1955)
45. Munkres, J.: Algorithms for the assignment and transportation problems. J. Soc. Ind. Appl. Math. **5**(1), 32–38 (1957)
46. Zhou, X., Koltun, V., Krähenbühl, P.: Tracking objects as points. In: Vedaldi, A., Bischof, H., Brox, T., Frahm, J.-M. (eds.) ECCV 2020. LNCS, vol. 12349, pp. 474–490. Springer, Cham (2020). https://doi.org/10.1007/978-3-030-58548-8_28
47. Ultralytics: YOLOv5 in PyTorch, January 2021. https://github.com/ultralytics/yolov5/tree/v4.0
48. Lin, T.-Y., et al.: Coco common object in context - 2017 dataset. https://cocodataset.org/

49. Long, J., Shelhamer, E., Darrell, T.: Fully convolutional networks for semantic segmentation. In: Proceedings of the IEEE Conference on Computer Vision and Pattern Recognition, pp. 3431–3440 (2015)
50. Shah, M.P.: Semantic segmentation architectures implemented in pytorch (2017). https://github.com/meetshah1995/pytorch-semseg
51. He, K., Zhang, X., Ren, S., Sun, J.: Deep residual learning for image recognition. In: Proceedings of the IEEE Conference on Computer Vision and Pattern Recognition, pp. 770–778 (2016)

PIVOT: A Parsimonious End-to-End Learning Framework for Valuing Player Actions in Handball Using Tracking Data

Oliver Müller[1](✉), Matthew Caron[1], Michael Döring[1,2], Tim Heuwinkel[1], and Jochen Baumeister[1]

[1] Paderborn University, Paderborn, Germany
{oliver.mueller,matthew.caron,michael.doering,tim.heuwinkel,
jochen.baumeister}@uni-paderborn.de
[2] SG Flensburg-Handewitt, Flensburg, Germany

Abstract. Over the last years, several approaches for the data-driven estimation of expected possession value (EPV) in basketball and association football (soccer) have been proposed. In this paper, we develop and evaluate PIVOT: the first such framework for team handball. Accounting for the fast-paced, dynamic nature and relative data scarcity of handball, we propose a parsimonious end-to-end deep learning architecture that relies solely on tracking data. This efficient approach is capable of predicting the probability that a team will score within the near future given the fine-grained spatio-temporal distribution of all players and the ball over the last seconds of the game. Our experiments indicate that PIVOT is able to produce accurate and calibrated probability estimates, even when trained on a relatively small dataset. We also showcase two interactive applications of PIVOT for valuing actual and counterfactual player decisions and actions in real-time.

Keywords: expected possession value · handball · tracking data · time series classification · deep learning

1 Introduction

Team handball, hereafter simply referred to as handball, is an action-packed invasion sport that is considered to be one of the fastest in the world. Although it is a high-scoring sport, the task of objectively assessing the impact that individual decisions and actions have on the overall game remains, nonetheless, challenging.

Despite the fact that several data-driven approaches to value player contributions in various team sports, such as basketball and association football (soccer), have been proposed over the last years [2,3,5,6,10,12,13], none of these approaches can, due to the unique characteristics defining this highly dynamic game [18], easily be applied to handball. For instance, compared to football, handball is played on a smaller field, generates way more goals (between 20 and 35 goals), and most of the action takes place around the goal area (6-m line).

© The Author(s), under exclusive license to Springer Nature Switzerland AG 2022
U. Brefeld et al. (Eds.): MLSA 2021, CCIS 1571, pp. 116–128, 2022.
https://doi.org/10.1007/978-3-031-02044-5_10

Rule-wise, handball shares many common characteristics with basketball while being, however, much more physical. Lastly, and most importantly, the data revolution has yet to happen in handball. In truth, there are currently no official providers that collect event data for handball, and only recently, some European handball leagues have started implementing tracking systems.

Against this background, we propose PIVOT – i.e., a framework for valuing player actions in handball purely based on tracking data. To the best of our knowledge, PIVOT is the first expected possession value (EPV) approach for handball. By leveraging deep neural networks and spatio-temporal features, our framework can predict the probability of a team scoring in the immediate future, given all players' and the ball's actual and past positions on the court. Since our framework does not require additional event data (annotations) and learns in an end-to-end fashion – i.e., without complex ensembles of specialized sub-models for evaluating different facets of the game – we argue that this approach is more parsimonious than existing approaches. Furthermore, our empirical experiments reveal that PIVOT produces accurate and calibrated probability estimates, even when trained with only a limited amount of data. In close collaboration with SG Flensburg-Handewitt[1], a top-tier German first division team and former EHF Champions League winners, we also showcase two interactive applications of PIVOT for valuing actual and counterfactual player decisions and actions in real-time.

2   Related Work

Over the last years, the evaluation of players' individual decisions and actions has gained increased attention in invasion sports, especially basketball and football. Driven by the increased availability and quality of in-game data, several statistical and machine learning approaches have been proposed to estimate the value of various offensive and defensive actions – i.e., with and without the ball. In the following, we concentrate on approaches that are primarily based on tracking data (as opposed to event data, like in [1,4]).

Concentrating on basketball, Cervone et al. introduced a concept known as expected possession value (EPV) which refers to the number of points the attacking team is expected to score at the end of a given possession [2,3]. The EPV of a given possession is computed by a multi-resolution process as the weighted average of the ball carrier's predicted probability of making a specific action and the estimated value of each of these potential actions. The model distinguishes between discrete actions like passing or shooting (referred to as macro-transitions) and continuous actions like moving with the ball (referred to as micro-transitions). The latter type of actions is derived from optical tracking data and the former from annotated events based on the tracking data.

Focusing merely on passes in football, Power et al. developed an approach for evaluating the risk – i.e., the likelihood of making a successful pass – based on the potential reward – i.e., the likelihood that a pass made will result in a shot

---
[1] https://www.sg-flensburg-handewitt.de.

within the next 10 s [10]. To do so, they used a logistic regression classifier to estimate both likelihoods given micro features – e.g., speed of players, distance to the nearest opponent, pressure applied to passer and receiver – tactical features – e.g., build-up, counter-attack, unstructured play – and formation features (high, medium or low block). These features were derived from both tracking and event data. Based on the risk and reward models, they propose several new metrics such as passing plus/minus and dangerous passes.

Spearman proposed an off-ball scoring opportunity model that, given data about the current position and velocity of all players and the ball, can predict the probability that a football player not currently in possession of the ball will score with the next on-ball event [13]. To estimate this probability, the model has to estimate three distinct probabilities: (1) the probability that the attacking team passes to each possible point on the field, (2) the probability that the team can control the ball at each of those possible locations, and (3) the probability that the team scores from these locations. The parameters of these separate models are estimated using tracking and event data, and, at prediction time, their outputs are combined to produce a single off-ball scoring opportunity metric.

Recently, Fernandez et al. developed what is, arguably, the most holistic approach to EPV in football [5,6]. This framework, which is based on tracking and event data, comprises a series of sub-components, each targeted at evaluating a specific type of action – e.g., passes, ball drives, shots. These sub-components are implemented either through specialized machine learning models – e.g., deep neural networks for extracting spatio-temporal features from tracking data – or through handcrafted algorithms developed by domain experts. According to the authors, the main advantage of this decomposition approach is the increased interpretability of the individual components of the framework.

Sicilia et al. proposed an end-to-end learning approach for estimating the probability and value of individual actions in basketball [12]. Their deep learning architecture learns a joint function incorporating all available spatio-temporal information at once. More specifically, they combine (1) a recurrent neural network trained on a multivariate time series of the positions of all players and the ball and (2) an embedding of player identities to predict the terminal action – e.g., field goal, turnover, foul – of a given possession. Based on these terminal action probabilities and the long-term averages of points per action, the expected value of individual actions can be determined. Like all other approaches, the framework requires the availability of linked tracking and event data.

3   The PIVOT Framework

Our proposed framework, named PIVOT, builds on the end-to-end learning idea presented by Sicilia et al. [12] while however, only requiring tracking data and minimal data preparation. Therefore, we argue that our framework is more parsimonious than existing EPV estimation approaches and, as a result, more suitable for practical applications in handball.

3.1   Features

We represent a game G as a sequence of frames $[f_1, f_2, ..., f_n]$, where n is the total number of frames in a game. Each frame f is a tuple comprised of a timestamp (only used for indexing) and the (x, y) coordinates of the ball, the seven home team players, and the seven away team players. When a player is substituted, G is updated so that the incoming player's data is stored in the columns formerly occupied by the outgoing player.

Instead of using the entire sequence of frames from the beginning of the game up to a given point in time t, we only focus on a sliding window composed of p frames. Hence, our features are represented by the fixed-length two-dimensional array $X_t = [f_{t-p}, ..., f_{t-2}, f_{t-1}, f_t]$, where X_t contains the spatio-temporal distribution of the ball and all players present on the field during a given window (Fig. 1). Thereby, this array accounts for the obvious temporal dependency of positions between neighboring frames. Moreover, it also has the advantage of having a fixed length – i.e., a requirement for many machine learning algorithms.

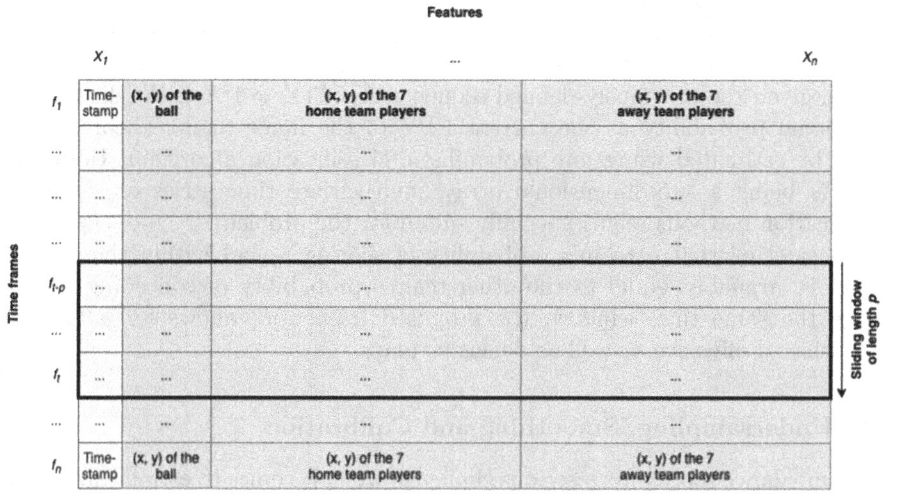

Fig. 1. Representation of (parts of) a game by a fixed-length two-dimensional array capturing the spatio-temporal distribution of the ball and all players present on the field during a given time window.

3.2   Response Variable

Our response variable, or target, is the binary variable Y_t which indicates whether the home team will score a goal in the immediate future. It takes the value 1, if the home team scores a goal within the next k frames $[f_{t+1}, ..., f_{t+k}]$; otherwise it takes the value 0.

Recall that our tracking data does not contain any event annotations – e.g., goals, shots, passes. Hence, in order to construct the target variable, we implemented a simple rule-based approach capable of determining the exact frame of a goal from raw tracking data. The algorithm is illustrated in Fig. 2 and executed for each frame of the game during the data preparation phase.

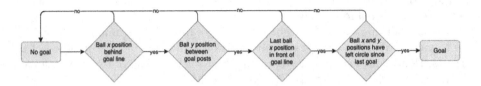

Fig. 2. Rule-based approach for determining the exact frame of a goal from tracking data.

3.3 Learning Task

Given the above-defined features and labels, our learning task is to predict, at frame t, the probability that the home team will score a goal within the next k frames, given the previously-defined sequence X_t: $P(Y_t = 1|X_t)$. We define this conditional probability as the current EPV of the home team. Theoretically, it can be estimated using any probabilistic classification algorithm. However, with X_t being a two-dimensional array, multivariate time series or sequence classification methods seem especially suited for the problem.

Considering that a team's probability of scoring a goal within the next k frames is, arguably, equal to the other team's probability of conceding a goal within the same time window, the proposed framework allows for a holistic evaluation of offensive as well as defensive plays.

3.4 Undersampling, Smoothing and Calibration

Class imbalance represents a serious challenge when it comes to estimating EPV. Hence, various techniques, such as over or undersampling [14], have been proposed to overcome this problem. However, applying such sampling techniques to a training set tends to cause bias in the estimated class probabilities for unseen observations – i.e., an issue that is especially severe when using neural networks for probability estimation [11]. With only 2.5% of the frames in our dataset being positive, we address this problem by implementing the following three steps.

First, we perform undersampling by randomly deleting a share of the training observations that did not result in an immediate goal – i.e., the majority class. The amount of undersampling is a hyperparameter that should be tuned empirically. In our experiments, decreasing the negative class by a factor of 0.9 showed to be effective.

Second, we use a loss function with label smoothing instead of a conventional loss function to train our networks. More specifically, we smooth the standard one-hot encoded vector with ones and zeros using the Label Smoothing Cross-Entropy loss function [9]. In short, this decreases the values of the ones by a small amount and, respectively, increases the zeros by a small amount; therefore, preventing the network from becoming overconfident in its predictions. The parameter epsilon (ϵ) of the Label Smoothing Cross-Entropy function is another hyperparameter that should be tuned for a given dataset. In our experiments, we stuck to the default value – i.e., $\epsilon = 0.1$.

Finally, we calibrate the raw probability estimates generated by our classifiers using the method proposed by [11], which is based on a Bayesian framework and takes the class imbalance and undersampling ratios into account. A classifier is said to be well-calibrated when the predicted probability of a class matches the expected frequency of that class. Some statistical models, such as logistic regression, are naturally calibrated; others, especially neural networks, tend to be uncalibrated and overconfident – i.e., they typically output probabilities close to 0 or 1. While calibration is often unnecessary for discrete classification problems, it becomes critical when exact probability estimates are required. The estimation of EPV represents such a case.

4 Experiments

In this section, we demonstrate that with the help of real-world data, PIVOT can generate accurate and calibrated probability estimates. We also show that using the latest deep learning architectures for time series classification, namely Transformers, can substantially improve predictive accuracy over standard Convolutional Neural Networks (CNN) or Long Short-Term Memory networks (LSTM).

4.1 Dataset

In the 2019/20 season, the German elite handball league (Liqui Moly HBL) started rolling out a sensor-based tracking system capable of collecting location data at a frequency 20 Hz (or frames per second). Through a collaboration with the team SG Flensburg-Handewitt, we obtained ball and player tracking data for a total of 15 games (the season was ended prematurely due to the COVID-19 pandemic). We performed minimal data cleaning by removing all observations with coordinates outside the field – e.g., players sitting on the bench – or timestamps associated with events taking place before/after the game or during the halftime break. Furthermore, we rotated the data for the second halftime by 180 °C so that the home team always plays from left to right and the away team from right to left. Finally, we augmented the dataset by mirroring each game; therefore, enabling us to train the classifier on both the home and away team data.

After the above transformations, our dataset contained more than 2 million observations (frames), each composed of 32 variables. To derive the features and labels described in Sect. 3, we applied a sliding window with window length p, horizon k, and stride one and split the data into training (approx. 70%), validation (approx. 15%), and test (approx. 15%) sets. For the following experiments, we set k to 60 frames (3 s) – i.e., a decision based on domain knowledge and discussion with the club – and experimented with various p ranging from 20 to 60 frames (1–3 s).

4.2 Network Architectures

Theoretically, the framework outlined in Sect. 3 could be instantiated with any machine learning classifier capable of producing probability estimates. However, because of the sequential nature of our features, one would have to flatten the two-dimensional arrays before feeding them into a standard classification model – e.g., logistic regression or random forest. Hence, to maintain the original structure of the data, we tackle this problem by using time series classification models that can handle two-dimensional feature arrays. All of the three following models were implemented using the TSAI[2] library and trained for 10 epochs with early stopping regularization with a patience of 3 and a minimum delta of 0.005 (AUC) on the validation set.

First, we implemented the Fully Convolutional Network (FCN) architecture proposed by Wang et al. [16]. We chose this relatively simple model as a baseline for gauging the performance of the more complex architectures, as it proved to be a strong benchmark for end-to-end time series classification in prior experiments [16]. The FCN architecture comprises three convolution blocks, each followed by a batch normalization layer and a ReLU activation layer. Following these convolution blocks, the features are fed into a global average pooling layer, and a linear classification layer produces the final label. The default TSAI values were used for all hyperparameters – i.e., filter size, kernel size, stride, and padding.

Second, we tested a recurrent neural network, more specifically, the LSTM architecture introduced by Hochreiter and Schmidhuber [8]. The main advantage of LSTMs is their capability to model long-term dependencies in sequences, which might enable the detection of patterns in build-up plays. We chose this architecture as it is close to the architecture used by Sicilia et al. [12], which inspired our work. Akin to Sicilia et al. [12], we stacked three LSTM layers with hidden states of size 32, followed by a dropout layer ($\delta = 0.2$) and a linear classification layer.

Third, we used a transformer-based architecture, namely the Time Series Transformer (TST) by Zerveas et al. [17]. The TST architecture uses only the encoder layers of the original Transformer architecture [15]. We selected this architecture as it has outperformed many other models in recent experiments by a significant margin while requiring only relatively few training samples [17]. Our TST network has three stacked encoder layers, each consisting of a multi-head self-attention layer (128), dropout ($\delta = 0.2$), batch normalization, a feed-forward layer, dropout ($\delta = 0.2$), and batch normalization. The outputs of the encoder

---

[2] https://github.com/timeseriesAI/tsai.

layers are then flattened, another dropout ($\delta = 0.2$) is applied, and the results are fed into a linear classification layer.

4.3   Results

Table 1 summarizes the results of our experiments. Following [4,12], we evaluate the predictive performance of our models using the probability scoring metrics AUC, Brier Score (BS), and Brier Skill Score (BSS). For the BSS, we use a naive model, which predicts the base rate of the positive class (in our case 2.5%) as the probability for every observation in the test set, as the reference model [7]. The results provide strong empirical evidence for the superiority of the TST model over the other models. For instance, for the window length 20, TST outperforms the FCN in terms of BSS by 30% and the LSTM by 40%. Regarding the window length p, our results suggest that windows of 20 or 40 frames – i.e., 1 or 2 s – work best. It seems that longer windows introduce noise into the learning process, which is probably due to the dynamic and fast-paced nature of handball. Conversely, longer windows may work best for sports like football.

Table 1. Predictive performance for different neural network architectures and sliding window lengths. For AUC and Brier Skill Score values closer to 1 are better; for the Brier Score values closer to 0 are better. Best results in bold.

Model	Window	AUC	Brier Score	Brier Skill Score
FCN	20	0.808	0.027	0.222
FCN	40	0.810	0.027	0.225
FCN	60	0.761	0.028	0.185
LSTM	20	0.845	0.028	0.190
LSTM	40	0.827	0.026	0.230
LSTM	60	0.836	0.027	0.214
TST	20	**0.909**	**0.023**	**0.318**
TST	40	0.882	0.024	0.284
TST	60	0.884	0.025	0.278

In addition to probability scoring metrics, we used calibration plots to assess the accuracy of our EPV estimates. For a perfectly calibrated model, when considering all frames with a predicted EPV of x%, one would expect that x% of these frames actually resulted in a goal. Figure 3 shows the calibration plot for PIVOT, suggesting that the model is well-calibrated for probabilities below 50%, but underestimates situations with true high goal probabilities, which might be a result of the label smoothing.

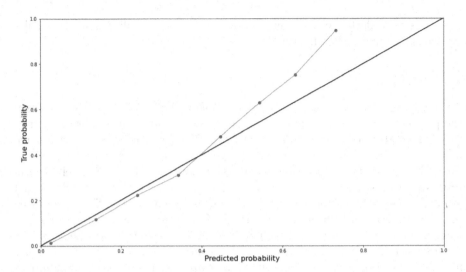

Fig. 3. Calibration plot for PIVOT. The model is well-calibrated for EPV values below 0.5, but underestimates high goal probabilities.

5   Applications

In this section, we showcase two exemplary applications built on top of PIVOT, which were co-created with members of the coaching staff of SG Flensburg-Handewitt.

5.1   Application 1: Augmented Instant Replay

Following the stock ticker idea of Cervone et al. [2], we can use PIVOT to calculate and monitor EPV in near real-time continuously. The resulting timeline, which we call *Augmented Instant Replay*, uncovers what in-game decisions have the most significant impact on EPV. Figure 4 shows the evolution of EPV during a possession of SG Flensburg-Handewitt in a 2019/20 league game against TSV Hannover-Burgdorf. After an unsuccessful attack from Hannover, Flensburg's goalkeeper Bergerud initiates a fast break, which results in a steep rise in EPV. Gottfridsson then quickly drives the ball towards Hannover's goal area. When he comes under pressure by Olson, the EPV drops momentarily but promptly recovers when Gottfridsson makes a successful pass to the right-winger Svan, who then finishes the possession with a successful falling jump shot.

Fig. 4. Development of EPV for an attack of SG Flensburg-Handewitt during a league match against TSV Hannover-Burgdorf.

5.2   Application 2: What-If

Another application that builds on top of PIVOT is a sensitivity analysis called *What-If.* Instead of only valuing plays that actually happened, it can be used to perform a counterfactual analysis of plays that could have happened. Using an interactive dashboard similar to a tactics board, an analyst can simulate and assess the expected value of any play or combination of moves by dragging the players and/or the ball around the court. The upper half of Fig. 5 depicts a moment from the match between Flensburg and Hannover when the right-back Rød, currently in possession of the ball, comes under pressure by Hannover's Garcia. The four arrows represent four different passing options along with their expected change in EPV. Passing to Gottfridsson or Johannessen would result in a loss of EPV, while passes to Svan or Golla would dramatically improve the chances of scoring in the near future. Of course, the latter two passing options are much riskier, which is not accounted for in the current version of the analysis. The bottom half of Fig. 5 shows another counterfactual analysis, this time focusing on off-ball moves. The heatmap around Rød visualizes how the EPV would change if the player moved to the respective locations (the size of the heatmap roughly spans the distance a player can reach within one second). The model suggests that Rød should run towards the right wing to increase the likelihood of Flensburg scoring a goal within the next three seconds.

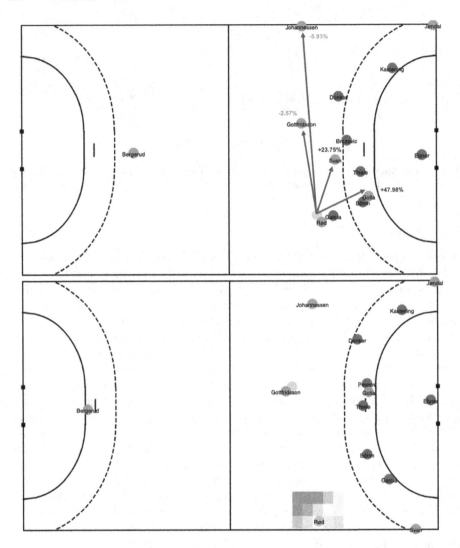

Fig. 5. Upper half: Change in EPV for four different passing options. According to the model, a pass from Rød to Svan or Golla would increase EPV, while a pass to Gottfridsson or Johannessen would decrease EPV. Bottom half: EPV surface for right back Rød. Red color indicates increase in EPV, blue color indicates decrease in EPV. According to the model, Rød should run towards the right wing. (Color figure online)

6 Conclusion and Outlook

This paper introduced PIVOT – i.e., a deep learning framework for estimating the expected value of possession in handball purely based on tracking data. Compared to existing approaches, PIVOT is less resource-intensive, as it does not require the availability of linked tracking and event data and learns in an end-to-end fashion, even with a limited amount of data.

As part of our future work, we aim to extend the framework with additional player features. Currently, our approach neither takes the identity nor skills of individual players into account. The reason for this is that our models were trained using only 15 games and, therefore, would easily overfit with such features (for SG Flensburg-Handewitt players). The situation would be even worse with players of opposing teams, as our models have seen them for a maximum of one game. Likewise, after collecting data for more games, we plan to integrate advanced spatial features. Examples include players' speed and direction of movement, their orientation on the field, the pressure put on a player, and their available passing options. Finally, we currently explore different ways for distributing overall EPV to the individual players involved in a play. A straightforward approach, which produced promising results in the first tests, would be to calculate the difference in EPV between the start and end of a player's ball possession. The obvious drawback of this approach is that it only values the actions of the ball-carrying player. An extension to off-ball players could be based on our What-If application. For each frame, one could calculate the difference in EPV between the estimated best possible action and the action taken.

References

1. Bransen, L., Van Haaren, J.: Measuring football players' on-the-ball contributions from passes during games. In: Brefeld, U., Davis, J., Van Haaren, J., Zimmermann, A. (eds.) MLSA 2018. LNCS (LNAI), vol. 11330, pp. 3–15. Springer, Cham (2019). https://doi.org/10.1007/978-3-030-17274-9_1
2. Cervone, D., D'amour, A., Bornn, L., Goldsberry, K.: POINTWISE: predicting points and valuing decisions in real time with NBA optical tracking data: a new microeconomics for the NBA. In: Proceedings of the 8th MIT Sloan Sports Analytics Conference (2014)
3. Cervone, D., D'Amour, A., Bornn, L., Goldsberry, K.: A multiresolution stochastic process model for predicting basketball possession outcomes. J. Am. Stat. Assoc. **111**(514), 585–599 (2016)
4. Decroos, T., Bransen, L., Van Haaren, J., Davis, J.: Actions speak louder than goals. In: Proceedings of the 25th ACM SIGKDD International Conference on Knowledge Discovery and Data Mining, pp. 1851–1861 (2019)
5. Fernández, J., Bornn, L., Cervone, D.: A framework for the fine-grained evaluation of the instantaneous expected value of soccer possessions. Mach. Learn. **110**(6), 1389–1427 (2021). https://doi.org/10.1007/s10994-021-05989-6
6. Fernandez, J., Bornn, L., Cervone, D.: Decomposing the immeasurable sport: a deep learning expected possession value framework for soccer. In: Proceedings of the 13th MIT Sloan Sports Analytics Conference (2019)
7. Hamill, T.M., Juras, J.: Measuring forecast skill: is it real skill or is it the varying climatology? Q. J. Roy. Meteorol. Soc. **132**(621C), 2905–2923 (2006)
8. Hochreiter, S., Schmidhuber, J.: Long short-term memory. Neural Comput. **9**(8), 1735–780 (1997)

9. Müller, R., Kornblith, S., Hinton, G.: When does label smoothing help? In: Advances in Neural Information Processing Systems, vol. 32 (2019)
10. Power, P., Ruiz, H., Wei, X., Lucey, P.: Not all passes are created equal. In: Proceedings of the 23rd ACM SIGKDD International Conference on Knowledge Discovery and Data Mining, pp. 1605–1613 (2017)
11. Dal Pozzolo, A., Caelen, O., Johnson, R.A., Bontempi, G.: Calibrating probability with undersampling for unbalanced classification. In: Proceedings of the 2015 IEEE Symposium Series on Computational Intelligence, pp. 159–166 (2015)
12. Sicilia, A., Pelechrinis, K., Goldsberry, K.: Deep-Hoops: evaluating micro-actions in basketball using deep feature representations of spatio-temporal data. In: Proceedings of the 25th ACM SIGKDD International Conference on Knowledge Discovery and Data Mining, pp. 2096–2104 (2019)
13. Spearman, W.: Beyond expected goals. In: Proceedings of the 12th MIT Sloan Sports Analytics Conference (2018)
14. Sun, Y., Wong, A.K.C., Kamel, M.S.: Classification of imbalanced data: a review. Int. J. Pattern Recognit. Artif. Intell. 23(04), 687–719 (2009)
15. Vaswani, A., et al.: Attention is all you need. In: Advances in Neural Information Processing Systems, vol. 30 (2017)
16. Wang, Z., Yan, W., Oates, T.: Time series classification from scratch with deep neural networks: A strong baseline. In: 2017 International Joint Conference on Neural Networks, pp. 1578–1585 (2017)
17. Zerveas, G., Jayaraman, S., Patel, D., Bhamidipaty, A., Eickhoff, C.: A Transformer-based Framework for Multivariate Time Series Representation Learning. arXiv preprint (2020). https://arxiv.org/abs/2010.02803
18. Zeuthen, K.: Team Handball: It's Not What You Think It Is, February 2002. https://www.washingtonpost.com/archive/lifestyle/2002/02/15/team-handball-its-not-what-you-think-it-is/09cee01c-9daa-4fdb-a17b-bb23fc60fd11/

Predicting Season Outcomes for the NBA

González Dos Santos Teno, Chunyan Wang, Niklas Carlsson,
and Patrick Lambrix[(✉)]

Linköping University, Linköping, Sweden
`Patrick.Lambrix@liu.se`

Abstract. Predicting game or season outcomes is important for clubs
as well as for the betting industry. Understanding the critical factors of
winning games and championships gives clubs a competitive advantage
when selecting players for the team and implementing winning strategies.
In this paper, we work with NBA data from 10 seasons and propose an
approach for predicting game outcomes that is then used for predicting
which team will be champion and which stages a team will reach in the
playoffs. We show that our approach has a similar performance as the
odds from betting companies and does better than ELO.

1 Introduction

In many sports, work has started on predicting game or season outcomes. From
an entertainment point of view, this is important considering the amount of
money spent on betting. For clubs, understanding the critical factors of winning
games and championships is important for creating a competitive team and
implementing winning strategies. This paper focuses on such predictions for the
National Basketball Association (NBA).

Most of the work on predicting game or season outcomes for the NBA uses box
score information. The Four Factors (effective field goal percentage, turnovers per
possession, offensive rebounding percentage, and free throw rate, e.g., [3,8]) which
have an offense variant and a defense variant, are used as a basis in [1,9]. In [6], 18
box score features and information about wins and losses were used for 778 games.
The Naive Bayes-based method reached 67% accuracy for game outcome. Several
neural networks were trained on data from 620 NBA games using 11 box score
statistics in [4]. The best networks had a prediction accuracy of 74%. A Maximum
Entropy principle-based approach used on data from 7 seasons obtained an accuracy of 74% [2]. In [10], data was collected from the NBA finals 1980–2017 and
22 mainly box score features were used. The most significant feature influencing
game outcome was deemed to be defensive rebounds. Other important factors were
three-point percentage, free throws made, and total rebounds. A method taking
into account team strength with attention to home court advantage and back-to-
back games is proposed in [5]. Different approaches tested on 8 seasons have a prediction accuracy between 66% and 72% for regular seasons and between 64% and
79% for playoffs. The progression of a basketball game is modeled by a Markov
model using play-by-play data in [12] and by a probabilistic graphical model based

U. Brefeld et al. (Eds.): MLSA 2021, CCIS 1571, pp. 129–142, 2022.
https://doi.org/10.1007/978-3-031-02044-5_11

on play-by-play data and tracking data in [7]. Play-by-play data is also used for learning stochastic models for substitutions. In all cases, the models are used for game outcome prediction. There is also work on predicting the outcome of basketball games in other leagues, but techniques may need adjustment to be transferable between leagues (e.g., [11]).

In this paper, we propose an approach for predicting which team will become NBA champion and to which stage of the NBA playoffs a team will proceed. The data that we use is from 10 seasons of NBA games and is presented in Sect. 2. We first introduce an approach for game outcome prediction (Sect. 3). This approach is then used to simulate NBA seasons and to derive frequencies over 10,000 simulations for teams reaching the different stages of the playoffs or become NBA champion (Sect. 4). We show that our approach has a similar performance as the odds from betting companies and significantly outperforms ELO. The paper concludes in Sect. 5.

2   Data Collection and Preparation

We gathered data from 10 complete NBA seasons from 2008–2009 to 2017–2018. All the extracted information comes from web-scraping https://www.basketball-reference.com/, a website specialized on NBA stats. The site includes box scores providing information relevant to a team's performance in a single game, including well-known performance measures such as points, assists, and rebounds, as well as performance data on team level and information on the current regular season record prior to a game. Also information about salaries, draft picks and performance during previous seasons is available.

Table 1 summarizes the kind of data that we used.[1] Team victory is the objective variable. It takes a value of 1 in case the team has won the current match. This is the value to be predicted by the different classification models. For the collected team data we have standardized the team names. Thus, the teams which have changed their denominations in the previous 10 seasons have been converted to their current team names, e.g., the New Jersey Nets are denoted as the Brooklyn Nets. Our approach for season prediction involves simulating the seasons using a game outcome model for each game and then updating the information for the next game. Therefore, we use only stats in the box scores that can be derived from the game outcome. This means that stats such as assists, blocks, and points are not used.

From the **box scores** we retained information about the games regarding which team is the home team, at which stage of the season the game is played and how many earlier games were played in that stage, how many wins and losses the team had up to the current game in the regular season or in a playoff round, whether the team won the last game, the number of wins and losses in the last 3, 8, 15 games, home games and away games, and whether the game is a back-to-back game. The latter is important as the performance of players usually decreases when playing consecutive games in such a short time period

---

[1] Explanations of all features can be found in the appendix.

[4]. The previous 3, 8, 15 games take into account the recent performance of the team. We also look at sequences of home and away games as teams often have road trips and time periods with many consecutive home games in a row.

For **team performance in previous seasons** we gathered information on the stage that the team reached, the regular season record, the offensive rating in terms of points scored per 100 possessions, and the defensive rating in terms of points allowed per 100 possessions. We also collected the Four Factors metrics.

The **performance of individual players** has an impact on the team performance. This is particularly true in sports such as basketball, where there are only five players per team on the court at each moment in time and the top players often play the majority of the game. Due to the top players' significantly impacting the outcome of games, many NBA teams prioritize trying to recruit two or three top players to their roster. These players are often referred to as the "Big Two" or the "Big Three", and are generally considered the most important players for team success. An example of a high impact player is Lebron James. Before arriving to the Cleveland Cavaliers in 2006 (after being drafted), Cleveland had never won the NBA championship and performed poorly on a regular basis. After his arrival, they reached the playoffs for 5 consecutive years until his move to Miami in 2010 with an NBA final in 2007. The team did not qualify for the playoffs again until his return to the team in 2014, when they played four consecutive finals and won the title in 2016. During his four years in Miami, he also made it to the finals each year (and won two championships), while forming a feared "Big Three" together with Dwyane Wade and Chris Bosh. We collected data about the performance of players using a variant of eWS48 which is an estimate of the number of wins contributed by a player per 48 min (total time played in a game without overtime). The average value in the league is around 0.100. We normalized this by multiplying by the minutes played during the season and divided by the total number of games in the season (82) and the number of minutes in a standard game (48). We then aggregated player performances to a team level. We used information on the mean eWS48 for returning players (staying with the team) and players leaving and joining the team.

The features related to **player salaries** represent how much a team pays their players, how this quantity relates to the salary cap imposed by the league, and the importance of key players based on how much they are paid. The total salary - salary cap ratio can be a critical factor, since spending more money usually leads to better players on the roster. However, if a team pays their players over the salary limit, they need to pay also a luxury tax, which could influence the team's future development. The importance of the salary of the top players can be exemplified by the fact that, according to https://hoopshype.com/salaries/, in the 2008–2009 season the Boston Celtics paid 61 MUSD, i.e., 77% of the salary, only to 3 players. In general, at least half of the teams during each of the seasons considered in this paper spent over 50% of the salary to 3 players.

The features for the **NBA draft picks** represent the draft picks made by the teams in the previous 5 years. The draft is organized in two rounds of (usually)

30 players. Usually, the earlier the player gets picked, the better his expected performance is. However, this has not always been the case, as several 1st draft picks left the league after a few years, due to injuries or poor performance.

3   Game Outcome Prediction

3.1   Methods

A first step in our approach is to compute a model for game outcome prediction. We used four different techniques: Logistic Regression (LR), Linear Support Vector Machines (LSVM), Random Forest (RF) and Multilayer Perceptron (MLP). For each of these techniques we did hyperparameter tuning to find the best fit to the data. Furthermore, when appropriate, we selected the features for the different algorithms that resulted in the best accuracy which is the ratio of correct predictions to all predictions or $(TP + TN)/(TP + TN + FP + FN)$, where TP is the number of true positives, TN the number of true negatives, FP the number of false positives and FN the number of false negatives. For every combination of hyperparameters and features, we fit the model and predict a season based only on the data from previous seasons, and report the averages using the 10 different resulting accuracies.

3.2   Results

For LR, we used a grid of values to tune the hyperparameter C, which stands for the inverse of regularization strength (see Fig. 1). The best accuracy was obtained by the model with C = 0.1, with a mean test accuracy score of 68.58%.

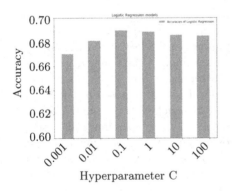
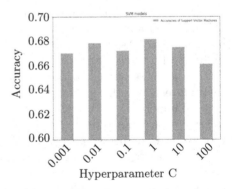

Fig. 1. Accuracies for the different models of LR, with different C.

Fig. 2. Accuracies for the different models of LSVM, with different C.

For LSVM, we tried to optimize the C parameter, which adds a penalty for each misclassified data point (see Fig. 2). The best accuracy was obtained by the model with C = 1, with a mean test accuracy score of 68.18%.

Table 1. Features.

Box score data per game	Home team
	Season stage
	Games played in Regular Season
	Wins in League Record
	Losses in League Record
	Games played in current play-offs round
	Wins in current play-offs round
	Losses in current play-offs round
	Won Last game
	Won Last Home game
	Won Last Away game
	Wins in previous 3, 8 and 15 games
	Wins in previous 3, 8 and 15 home games
	Wins in previous 3, 8 and 15 away games
	Back-to-back game
Team performance in previous season	Previous season furthest stage
	Previous season regular season record
	Previous season offensive rating
	Previous season defensive rating
	Offense Four Factors: eFG%, TOV%, ORB%, FT/FGA
	Defense Four Factors: eFG%, TOV%, DRB%, FT/FGA
Player performance in previous season	Staying players weighted mean eWS48
	Signed players weighted mean eWS48
	Leaving players weighted mean eWS48
Player Salaries	Total Salary
	Total Salary/Salary Cap Ratio
	Top-1 player salary ratio
	Top-2 players salary ratio
	Top-3 players salary ratio
	Top-5 players salary ratio
NBA draft picks	Previous season draft picks in positions 1 to 3
	Previous season draft picks in positions 4 to 10
	Previous season draft picks in positions 11 to 20
	Previous season draft picks in positions 21 to end of 1st round
	Previous season draft picks in 2nd round
	Previous 3 seasons draft picks in positions 1 to 3
	Previous 3 seasons draft picks in positions 4 to 10
	Previous 3 seasons draft picks in positions 11 to 20
	Previous 3 seasons draft picks in positions 21 to end of 1st round
	Previous 3 seasons draft picks in 2nd round
	Previous 5 seasons draft picks in positions 1 to 3
	Previous 5 seasons draft picks in positions 4 to 10
	Previous 5 seasons draft picks in positions 11 to 20
	Previous 5 seasons draft picks in positions 21 to end of 1st round
	Previous 5 seasons draft picks in 2nd round
Objective variable	Team Win

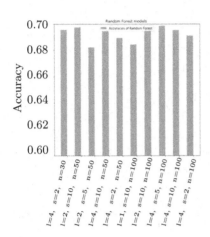

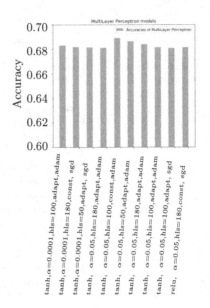

Fig. 3. Top 10 accuracies for the different models of Random Forest with different combinations of hyperparameters (min_samples_leaf, min_samples_split, and n_estimators).

Fig. 4. Top 10 accuracies for the different models of Multilayer Perceptron with different combinations of hyperparameters. (Models used: activation, tanh/relu, α, hidden_layer_size (hls), learning_rate, constant/adaptive, solver, adam/sgd).

For MLP, we used sets of different values for the different hyperparameters. We used single hidden layer networks with 50, 100, or 180 neurons in each layer. For the regularization term alpha (L2) we used 0.0001, 0.01, and 0.05. As activation functions we used hyperbolic tangent function, logistic sigmoid function and rectified linear unit function. The learning rate for the schedule for weight updates was kept constant at 0.001 or adaptive which kept the learning rate constant at 0.001 as long as training loss kept decreasing. Further, we used SGD and Adam for weight optimization. The best accuracy was achieved by the model with hyperbolic tangent function as the activation function, alpha = 0.05, a single hidden layer with 100 neurons, Adam solver and an adaptive learning rate (Fig. 4). This combination had a mean test accuracy score of 68.85%.

For RF, we used sets of different values for the different hyperparameters. For the number of estimators representing the number of trees in the forest we used the values 10, 15, 20, 30, 50 and 100. The minimal number of samples required to split a node was set to 2, 5 and 10, while the minimum number of samples in a leaf node was set to 1, 2 and 4. The top 10 accuracies are shown in Fig. 3. The best accuracy was achieved by the model with number of estimators = 100, minimum of samples in a leaf = 4 and minimum of samples in a split = 5. This combination got a mean test accuracy score of 69.88%.

The representative for RF obtained the best result. This was the model that we selected to use in the season simulations.

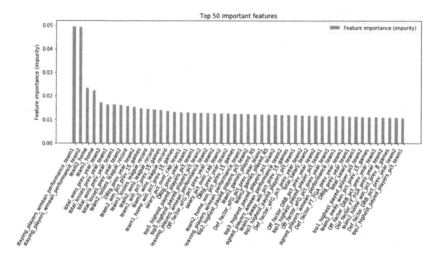

Fig. 5. Feature importance for chosen RF model.

In Fig. 5 we show the 50 most important features with respect to Gini impurity for the chosen model. The most relevant features are the performances during the previous season of the players that stayed with the team. Further, whether a team is the home team in a game is important. This suggests a home team advantage. The rest of the top-50 most important features have relatively similar values. Among these, there are wins and losses in the current and previous seasons. Regarding the last games, it is more important to look at the last-15 games than the other values we looked at (3 and 8). Further, there are some features related to the total salary of a team, the percentage over the salary cap and the salary of the top-2 and top-3 players. Also factors regarding team performance (offense and defense) from the previous years and regarding the performance of leaving and signed players appear in this top-50 list.

4   Season Simulation

We simulated 10 complete seasons from 2008–2009 to 2017–2018 using the chosen RF model. Since we had the actual schedule of the regular season from each year, we could simulate the calendar in the same order as it occurred in reality. For every season and every game in the calendar, we predicted the output probabilities of each team to win. During the simulation, we used these probabilities to draw a random number between 0 and 1 uniformly. If the draw landed between 0 and the probability of a team winning, the victory is assigned to the team, otherwise the win went to the opponent. Upon the assignment of the win we updated the values of the dynamic features in order to prepare the input for the upcoming games. Once the whole regular season was simulated, the playoffs started. At this stage, we simulated the playoff series as a means to pick the best team from each playoff matchup until a single team became the

Table 2. Predictions for the 2017–2018 season.

	Team	1st Round (Model)	Conf. Semifinals (Model)	Conf. Finals (Model)	NBA Finals (Model)	NBA Champion (Model)	Reality (furthest stage)	ELO season start	ELO season end
1	GSW	88.4	73.1	47.9	28.9	20.8	NBA champion	1752	1745
2	CLE	86.5	58.0	37.8	22.3	16.1	NBA finals	1650	1577
3	HOU	83.5	51.6	34.1	20.9	14.6	Conf. finals	1574	1704
4	TOR	85.5	56.1	36.9	20.8	10.4	Conf. semifinals	1532	1600
5	SAS	86.3	64.5	35.7	17.4	8.6	1st round	1617	1551
6	BOS	81.6	50.5	29.8	12.2	7.3	Conf. finals	1532	1580
7	NOP	79.8	57.0	29.8	9.6	4.1	Conf. semifinals	1488	1585
8	UTA	67.5	46.1	19.8	7.3	2.5	Conf. semifinals	1580	1663
9	OKC	65.9	30.8	15.6	6.0	2.2	1st round	1518	1611
10	POR	58.9	30.6	13.1	5.6	1.5	1st round	1531	1579
11	PHI	79.2	33.1	14.0	5.7	1.4	Conf. semifinals	1380	1641
12	WAS	59.0	26.1	12.4	4.8	1.2	1st round	1566	1499
13	MIA	86.6	37.5	13.5	4.4	1.2	1st round	1553	1497
14	IND	54.0	21.7	8.0	3.1	1.0	1st round	1503	1572
15	MIN	60.6	18.9	6.8	2.3	1.0	1st round	1474	1548
16	MIL	39.2	15.4	6.6	2.1	0.7	1st round	1508	1522
17	DET	36.6	12.9	5.3	1.7	0.6	9th East conf.	1457	1488
18	LAC	36.2	13.8	4.7	1.5	0.5	10th West conf.	1591	1506
19	CHO	39.7	10.9	3.7	1.1	0.4	10th East conf.	1473	1501
20	CHI	30.3	14.8	4.0	1.0	0.3	13th East conf.	1497	1317
21	NYK	22.8	8.9	2.8	0.8	0.3	11th East conf.	1407	1378
22	DEN	41.5	13.9	3.7	1.1	0.2	9th West conf.	1540	1587
23	DAL	21.4	6.4	1.7	0.4	0.2	13th West conf.	1441	1357
24	MEM	45.5	10.3	2.1	0.4	0.1	14th West conf.	1489	1322
25	SAC	50.4	10.5	2.4	0.4	0.1	12th West conf.	1421	1360
26	ORL	15.8	4.0	1.2	0.3	0.1	14th East conf.	1390	1335
27	BRK	16.2	4.2	1.2	0.3	0.0	12th East conf.	1405	1408
28	LAL	20.5	4.1	0.9	0.2	0.0	11th West conf.	1401	1486
29	ATL	17.9	4.0	0.8	0.2	0.0	15th East conf.	1486	1349
30	PHO	13.8	5.1	0.9	0.1	0.0	15th West conf.	1381	1277

NBA champion. This simulation process was repeated 10,000 times in order to obtain not only the winning frequencies of each team to become the NBA champion, but also for reaching the different stages of the competition. The whole simulation process was performed for every season 2008–2009 to 2017–2018. To keep consistency in our predictions, we trained our model only on the seasons previous to the one that we were simulating. Table 2 shows the results for the 2017–2018 season. The complete results for the 2008–2009 to 2017–2018 seasons are available at https://www.ida.liu.se/research/sportsanalytics/projects/conferences/MLSA21-basketball/. In addition to the predictions of our method, we have also added information about the teams' ELO at the start and end of the season. ELO data was obtained from https://projects.fivethirtyeight.com/complete-history-of-the-nba.

Table 3. Prediction success. For all stages, the first/second number is the number of correct predictions using our approach (first) and ELO (second) at the start of the season. For the NBA champion, the third number shows the success based on the pre-season odds. (*Two teams with same odds of which one was champion.)

Season	1st Round	Conf. Semifinal	Conf. Final	NBA Final	NBA Champion
2008–2009	13/12	6/3	3/1	1/1	0/0/0.5*
2009–2010	13/13	6/4	3/2	1/1	1/1/1
2010–2011	12/10	3/2	1/0	0/0	0/0/0
2011–2012	13/11	5/5	3/2	1/1	1/0/1
2012–2013	14/12	5/6	3/2	2/2	1/0/1
2013–2014	12/11	5/5	4/3	2/2	0/0/0
2014–2015	12/11	4/4	0/1	0/0	0/0/0
2015–2016	12/12	5/4	2/2	1/1	0/0/0
2016–2017	13/13	5/3	3/3	2/1	1/0/1
2017–2018	15/13	7/4	2/2	2/2	1/1/1
Total	129/118	51/40	24/18	12/11	5/2/5.5
out of	160	80	40	20	10

Table 3 shows the prediction success of the method over the 10 seasons. We say that a prediction is correct for a team and a season regarding one of the stages NBA Champion, NBA Final, Conference Final, Conference Semifinal and 1st Round, if the prediction score for the team reaching the stage is among the 1, 2, 4, 8, 16 highest, respectively, for the season. Further, we compare with the ELO at the start of the season and for the NBA Champions also with the pre-season odds at https://www.basketball-reference.com/. The Spearman correlation of our prediction scores and ELO at the start of the season for NBA Champion ranges from 0.71 to 0.96. For the other stages NBA Final, Conference Finals, Conference Semifinals and 1st Round, these ranges are 0.72 to 0.95, 0.71 to 0.95, 0.73 to 0.92 and 0.69 to 0.92, respectively (Table 4). The highest correlation for each stage is for the 2016–2017 season, while the lowest is for the 2017–2018 season. Note that for all stages our approach outperforms the ELO approach. We obtain the same predictions as the odds-based approach for all seasons except 2008–2009 where two teams had the same lowest odds.

Table 4. Spearman correlation between prediction score and ELO at start of season.

Season	1st Round	Conf. Semifinal	Conf. Final	NBA Final	NBA Champion
2008–2009	0.8432529	0.8525648	0.9086255	0.9178359	0.9181914
2009–2010	0.8868365	0.9048626	0.9370062	0.9313884	0.9361926
2010–2011	0.8196685	0.8908666	0.9139869	0.9081600	0.9253556
2011–2012	0.8265658	0.8661698	0.8985088	0.8830014	0.9045688
2012–2013	0.8792701	0.8787002	0.8971390	0.8662733	0.8859901
2013–2014	0.9031038	0.9065421	0.9143112	0.9048204	0.9203673
2014–2015	0.7259177	0.7872719	0.8261741	0.8330925	0.8301203
2015–2016	0.8700490	0.8929446	0.8981637	0.8956920	0.9083453
2016–2017	0.9209033	0.9202181	0.9565992	0.9540246	0.9622899
2017–2018	0.6908444	0.7329773	0.7199778	0.7292364	0.7118506

5 Conclusion

In this paper, we first proposed an approach for game outcome prediction that reached a mean accuracy of 69.88%. The most relevant features in the model are found to be the performances during the previous season of the players that stayed on the team as well as whether a team plays at home. Other important features are wins and losses in the current (last 15 games) and previous seasons, offensive and defensive performance from previous years, performance of signed and leaving players, and salary features. Second, we then used this approach to simulate 10 NBA seasons 10,000 times and computed frequencies for teams reaching different stages in the playoffs. We showed that the approach was equally successful in picking a Champion as the odds makers and consistently outperformed ELO for all playoff rounds (except one 2014–2015 round). Future work will investigate whether the approach is equally successful for other sports.

Appendix - Features

See Tables 5, 6, 7, 8, 9.

Table 5. Features - 1.

Box score data per game	
Home team	1 if team is home team, 0 if team is away team
Season stage	One of: regular season, 1st round, conference semi-finals, conference finals, NBA final
Games played in Regular Season	Amount of games played by the team up to, but not including the current game during regular season. The value is set to 82 during play-offs
Wins in League Record	Number of wins up to current game during the regular season. Not updated during playoffs
Losses in League Record	Number of losses up to current game during the regular season. Not updated during playoffs
Games played in current play-offs round	Number of games played by the team up to, but not including the current game during each play-off round. The value is reset to 0 at the beginning of each playoff round. The value is set to 0 during the regular season
Wins in current play-offs round	Number of wins by the team up to, but not including the current game during each play-off round. The value is reset to 0 at the beginning of each playoff round. The value is set to 0 during the regular season
Losses in current play-offs round	Number of losses by the team up to, but not including the current game during each play-off round. The value is reset to 0 at the beginning of each playoff round. The value is set to 0 during the regular season
Won Last game	1 if team won the last game; 0 otherwise
Won Last Home game	1 if team won the last home game; 0 otherwise
Won Last Away game	1 if team won the last away game; 0 otherwise
Wins in previous 3, 8 and 15 games	Number of wins during the previous 3, 8 and 15 played games by the team
Wins in previous 3, 8 and 15 home games	Number of wins during the previous 3, 8 and 15 played home games by the team
Wins in previous 3, 8 and 15 away games	Number of wins during the previous 3, 8 and 15 played away games by the team
Back-to-back game	1 if the team has played a game within the last 36 h; 0 otherwise

Table 6. Features - 2.

Team performance in previous season	
Previous season furthest stage	One of: not qualified for play-offs, 1st round loss, conference semi-finals loss, conference finals loss, NBA final loss or NBA champion
Previous season regular season record	Number of wins and losses during the previous regular season
Previous season offensive rating	Estimated amount of points scored in 100 possessions in the previous season
Previous season defensive rating	Estimated amount of points allowed in 100 possessions in the previous season
Offense Four Factors: eFG%, TOV%, ORB%, FT/FGA	Effective Field Goals percentage, Turnovers committed per 100 plays, Percentage of available Offensive Rebounds, Free Throws per Field Goal attempt
Defense Four Factors: eFG%, TOV%, DRB%, FT/FGA	Opponent effective Field Goals percentage, Turnovers caused on the opponent per 100 plays, Percentage of available Defensive Rebounds, Opponent Free Throws per Field Goal attempt

Table 7. Features - 3.

Player performance in previous season	
Staying players weighted mean eWS48	Weighted mean performance of the players that remained in the team from the previous season
Signed players weighted mean eWS48	Weighted mean performance of the players that joined in the team after the previous season
Leaving players weighted mean eWS48	Weighted mean performance of the players that left the team after the previous season

Table 8. Features - 4.

Player Salaries	
Total Salary	Sum of the salaries of all the players in the team
Total Salary/Salary Cap Ratio	Ratio between total salary payed by a team and the salary limit established by the league
Top-1 player salary ratio	Ratio between the salary of the top player and the total salary of the team
Top-2 players salary ratio	Ratio between the sum of the salaries of the top 2 players and the total salary of the team
Top-3 players salary ratio	Ratio between the sum of the salaries of the top 3 players and the total salary of the team
Top-5 players salary ratio	Ratio between the sum of the salaries of the top 5 players and the total salary of the team

Table 9. Features - 5.

NBA draft picks	
Previous season draft picks in positions 1 to 3	Number of draft picks in positions 1 to 3 during previous season
Previous season draft picks in positions 4 to 10	Number of draft picks in positions 4 to 10 during previous season
Previous season draft picks in positions 11 to 20	Number of draft picks in positions 11 to 20 during previous season
Previous season draft picks in positions 21 to end of 1st round	Number of draft picks in positions 21 to end of 1st round during previous season
Previous season draft picks in 2nd round	Number of draft picks in 2nd round during previous season
Previous 3 seasons draft picks in positions 1 to 3	Number of draft picks in positions 1 to 3 during previous 3 seasons
Previous 3 seasons draft picks in positions 4 to 10	Number of draft picks in positions 4 to 10 during previous 3 seasons
Previous 3 seasons draft picks in positions 11 to 20	Number of draft picks in positions 11 to 20 during previous 3 seasons
Previous 3 seasons draft picks in positions 21 to end of 1st round	Number of draft picks in positions 21 to end of 1st round during previous 3 seasons
Previous 3 seasons draft picks in 2nd round	Number of draft picks in 2nd round during previous 3 seasons
Previous 5 seasons draft picks in positions 1 to 3	Number of draft picks in positions 1 to 3 during previous 5 seasons
Previous 5 seasons draft picks in positions 4 to 10	Number of draft picks in positions 4 to 10 during previous 5 seasons
Previous 5 seasons draft picks in positions 11 to 20	Number of draft picks in positions 11 to 20 during previous 5 seasons
Previous 5 seasons draft picks in positions 21 to end of 1st round	Number of draft picks in positions 21 to end of 1st round during previous 5 seasons
Previous 5 seasons draft picks in 2nd round	Number of draft picks in 2nd round during previous 5 seasons

References

1. Baghal, T.: Are the "four factors" indicators of one factor? An application of structural equation modeling methodology to NBA data in prediction of winning percentage. J. Quant. Anal. Sports **8**(1) (2012). https://doi.org/10.1515/1559-0410.1355
2. Cheng, G., Zhang, Z., Kyebambe, M., Kimbugwe, N.: Predicting the outcome of NBA playoffs based on the maximum entropy principle. Entropy **18**(450), 1–15 (2016). https://doi.org/10.3390/e18120450
3. Kubatko, J., Oliver, D., Pelton, K., Rosenbaum, D.T.: A starting point for analyzing basketball statistics. J. Quant. Anal. Sports **3**(3) (2007). https://doi.org/10.2202/1559-0410.107
4. Loeffelholz, B., Bednar, E., Bauer, K.W.: Predicting NBA games using neural networks. J. Quant. Anal. Sports **5**(1) (2009). https://doi.org/10.2202/1559-0410.1156
5. Manner, H.: Modeling and forecasting the outcomes of NBA basketball games. J. Quant. Anal. Sports **12**(1), 31–41 (2016). https://doi.org/10.1515/jqas-2015-0088

6. Miljković, D., Gajić, L., Kovačević, A., Konjović, Z.: The use of data mining for basketball matches outcomes prediction. In: IEEE 8th International Symposium on Intelligent Systems and Informatics, pp. 309–312 (2010). https://doi.org/10.1109/SISY.2010.5647440

7. Oh, M., Keshri, S., Iyengar, G.: Graphical model for basketball match simulation. In: MIT Sloan Sports Analytics Conference (2015)

8. Oliver, D.: Basketball on Paper. Brassey's (2004)

9. Teramoto, M., Cross, C.L.: Relative importance of performance factors in winning NBA games in regular season versus playoffs. J. Quant. Anal. Sports 6(3) (2010). https://doi.org/10.2202/1559-0410.1260

10. Thabtah, F., Zhang, L., Abdelhamid, N.: NBA game result prediction using feature analysis and machine learning. Ann. Data Sci. 6(1), 103–116 (2019). https://doi.org/10.1007/s40745-018-00189-x

11. Zimmermann, A.: Basketball predictions in the NCAAB and NBA: similarities and differences. Stat. Anal. Data Min. 9(5), 350–364 (2016). https://doi.org/10.1002/sam.11319

12. Štrumbelj, E., Vračar, P.: Simulating a basketball match with a homogeneous Markov model and forecasting the outcome. Int. J. Forecast. 28(2), 532–542 (2012). https://doi.org/10.1016/j.ijforecast.2011.01.004

Individual Sports

Detecting Swimmers in Unconstrained Videos with Few Training Data

Nicolas Jacquelin[1,3]([✉]), Romain Vuillemot[1,3], and Stefan Duffner[2,3]

[1] École Centrale de Lyon, Lyon, Écully, France
[2] INSA Lyon, Villeurbanne, France
[3] LIRIS, UMR 5205 CNRS, Lyon, France
{nicolas.jacquelin,romain.vuillemot,stefan.duffner}@liris.cnrs.fr

Abstract. In this work, we propose a method to detect swimmers in unconstrained swimming videos, using a Unet-based model trained on a small dataset. Our main motivation is to make the method accessible without spending much time or money in annotation or computation while maintaining performances. The swimming videos can be recorded from various locations with different settings (distance and angle to the pool, light conditions, reflections, camera resolution), which alleviates a lot of the usual video capture constraints. As a result, our model reaches top-performances in detection compared to other methods. Every algorithm described in the paper is accessible online at https://github.com/njacquelin/swimmers_detection.

Keywords: Computer Vision · Swimming · Small Dataset · Segmentation · Detection

1 Introduction

Regarding swimmer analyses from competition videos, the main and most important aspect is to detect the swimmers in each frame. Although it is often not the terminal goal, a precise and reliable detection and localisation allows to perform further studies on swimming quality, helping the swimmers to improve their overall performance in a non-intrusive way. Therefore, a robust algorithm to effectively detect all swimmers of a race in a video is of utmost importance for both the athletes and their coach.

1.1 Problem Formulation

Swimmer detection in videos is the process of identifying the visible parts of the body in a picture. Detecting a swimmer in an image - and by extend in a video - may seem like a relatively easy task as state-of-the-art methods reach excellent results for human detection. However, the visible features in the environment of a pool are very different from those of daily-life walking and standing persons. A swimmer is mostly hidden under small and noisy waves, so a precise detection is much harder than for a normal human detection task. Therefore, an entirely different model has to be created to detect swimmers during competitions and training.

This task is far from trivial, due to the complexity of the environment: the pool. It is full of reflections and diffraction, affected by unpredictable waves creating many local deformations in the image. Moreover, the light on the water tends to saturate the camera sensor, or at least obfuscate the swimmers underneath. Apart from that, even recent deep learning methods [11,13,14] usually require a large amount of carefully labelled data which are not easily available. However, we argue that a dataset with tens of thousands of images is not accessible to everyone to train their data on due to their computational cost and time (not everyone has access to GPU servers).

This paper shows a way to alleviate these problems without requiring thousands of labelled images, making the detection process work even with rough, non-expert annotations. Our approach could be applicable to detect unusual objects which are not in common detection datasets or daily-life context (with unusual visual features). The main contributions of this paper are the following:

- a model for automatic and robust swimmers detection in competition videos outperforming state-of-the-art large-scale object detection models,
- a annotated swimmers dataset,
- a method to easily train the model which reaches high performances with few data.

1.2   Related Work

Several past research works tackle the problem of swimmers detection with a computer vision approach. First, we need to mention the work of Benarab et al. [1–3], who recently proposed several techniques pursuing the same detection goal as ours. An interesting aspect of their work is the absence of deep-learning methods: their computer vision algorithms are mostly based on color gradient and low-level techniques. Although it allows a faster speed inference, this choice leads to hand-crafted, pool-specific thresholds and a lack of overall generalisation (they always use the same 2 races as an example for their papers). In the end, they do not provide a model or a metric to compare results.

Woinoski et al. [16] proposed a method based on a swimmer dataset annotated by themselves on a selection of 35 race videos, collecting about 25 000 images in the process. Sadly, it was not released before the end of our work, so we could not use it. However, creating such a data collection is a great milestone for the community, and the authors also applied current object detection methods on these data. As a result, they provide the mAP 25 (mAP definition in Sect. 3) of their best model, based on Yolo-V3 [13], which reaches 70% (Section 5, Fig. 3 of [16]).

Hall et al. [9] propose a similar work, with an even larger dataset containing 327 000 images from 249 different races, but it appears they did not publish it. Their model is a 2-stage refinement method. They used tracking-based metrics, as opposed to the detection-based metrics we used.

1.3   Motivation

Detecting swimmers is an important part in automatic swimming video analysis, and it provides the basis for further, more detailed analyses.

Indeed, to estimate the swimmers positions in a pool from a race video, the detection in the 2D images is obviously required. Then, after a geometric projection into the coordinate system of the pool, it is possible to know the position of the swimmers in the pool plane, *i.e.* their distance in meters to the starting blocks and their lane. This whole detection and transformation process informs the swimmers relative position and rank, as well as their speed, speed variation, lap time etc. Furthermore, the number of swimming strokes during a length is also a metric of utmost importance to measure the swimming quality. To extract this information automatically, one needs to crop a sub-region surrounding them first, which is doable with a detection model.

Apart from these objective and quantifiable metrics, subjective and qualitative observations made by coaches are extremely precious for a swimmer. To perform them efficiently, coaches often need zoomed videos around their swimmers: such videos could either be extracted manually, by annotating the position on each frame, or be computed automatically as we propose in this paper. The extracted regions of interest and the automatic metrics mentioned before could greatly help the trainers to guide their swimmers. Automating this task would save a large amount of time allowing the coach to focus more on the technical aspect of swimming.

A good model is an important objective, but obtaining one with few data is rather challenging. Nowadays, there are many datasets with thousands or even millions of images of common objects [7,10], but some problems arise. First, the swimmer class is present in none of these public datasets. Second, not everyone can afford to train a model on such data collections since this is computationally expensive and time-consuming. Third, fine-tuning a robust generic model is not interesting if the distribution is too different from the daily-life context it was trained on, which is the case in swimming. Therefore, the use of small specialized well-crafted datasets gets more and more attention in many applications, especially if they allow the creation of good detection models. Finally, a detection model trained from few annotated data can then be enhanced by training with more unlabelled data, using common semi-supervised learning techniques like self-training [4] or knowledge distillation [8]. This new, better model could itself be used to get a better precision in the aforementioned applications.

2   Proposed Approach

State-of-the-art detection methods, like Yolo [12] and Faster-RCNN [14], require at least tens of thousands of precisely labelled images to train a model. Such a dataset is extremely time-consuming to create, and it requires a large amount of time to train a model in an optimal way.

In this paper, we propose an easily trainable real-time method that can be trained with a small dataset of 400 images. The input labels are bounding boxes, and the output can either be bounding boxes too, or a segmentation of the swimmers in an image. Despite these conditions, our solution gives excellent results and is usable in many different environments (inside/outside, pool/free water) and for a large variety of acquisition conditions (see Sect. 3). Further, it could easily be applied to other swimming-based sports like water polo.

2.1 Dataset Construction and Data Augmentation

The creation of a pertinent dataset is extremely important in order to get generalizable detection results with machine-learning based methods. To this end, we selected 12 international level competitions with openly available race videos with various points of view. This gave the dataset a great range of angle and size variation. For each competition, 8 races were selected, to represent the 4 main swimming styles performed by the 2 genders. One frame of these videos was saved every 3 s, resulting in 403 different images with a maximum of ten swimmers, where at least one of them is visible.

The swimmers bounding box annotation was made with the open-access tool LabelImg [6]. The main difficulty was to be consistent: the extremities (legs and arms) are often hidden under the water and not visible, but the annotation process needs to always highlight the same body parts. If for some images, the bounding boxes stop where the skin is not visible, and for other images they stop where the legs actually are (even if we cannot see them), that will cause divergence during the model training. Here, the decision was to frame the visible parts only so that the boxes are as small as possible around the athlete.

The data from 3 pools out of the 12 was used as test data and the 9 remaining as training data. The resulting dataset, that we called $Swimm^{400}$, was composed of 80 test images and 323 train images.

In addition to this carefully created dataset, we propose a specific data augmentation strategy in order to increase the trained models performance. It will also compensate the low quantity of images in $Swimm^{400}$.

Zoom-in/zoom-out: the main augmentation was the zoom in and out (Fig. 1, right column). Image crops are performed during training, such that the subjects occupy more space. Inversely, a neutral colour could be put around the reduced image, so that the swimmers look smaller. This helped the model to generalize its representation of swimmers independently from their size. $Swimm^{400}$ originally contains swimmers at different distances from the camera, but this data augmentation increased this benefit even more. Note that to allow batch training, the images were all resized to (256, 256) pixels after augmentation.

Side-switch: another important augmentation was the side-switch, seen in Fig. 1, bottom row, third column. This transform is extremely useful to avoid central overfitting: most images present in $Swimm^{400}$ tend to center the swimmer. The side-switch puts them on the side, preventing the model to only detect instances at the center.

Others: apart from these two transforms, other more common methods where used to train the model. The random left-right flip generalizes the swimmer direction to the model, by giving them the same chance to face each

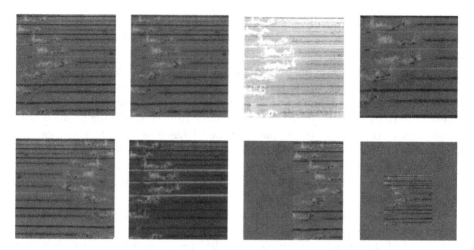

Fig. 1. The data augmentations used for the model training. From left to right, top to bottom: original image, blur, contrast and brightness change, crop, horizontal flip, hue change, side switch, zoom out.

side. The colour change (in HSV format, the hue is rotated by max. 45° so that the water can have any blue shade plus some green ones) generalizes to many skin, pool and water colors. The contrast and brightness random variations adapts the model to the many lighting conditions that can happen during a different competitions. Finally, Gaussian blur increases the overall robustness.

Of course, all these augmentations do not require any further annotation, as they are automatically generated during the training. The probability to trigger them is 50% each, except for color variation (30%) and side-switch (10%), as they both are stronger changes and thus might make the model diverge if used too much. These trigger probabilities work well for our study case, but may need to be slightly varied to adapt them to other detection problems.

2.2 Detection Model

We propose to train a relatively simple Convolutional Neural Network (CNN) using $Swimm^{400}$ and data augmentation. It is designed to be deep enough to learn the complex feature hierarchies and patterns of high variability in our data, but not too much to overfit on the small dataset. Finally, the real-time constraint is important according to the experts we worked with, which discards Faster-RCNN [14] and similar methods with multiple sub-image inference.

Bounding box regression vs. segmentation: bounding box regression-based approaches [11,13,14] all rely on the same principle. They transform a part of the image into a semantic vector, from which the model computes the probability of presence and position of the objects on the image. Learning this transformation and providing stable results requires large amounts of labelled training images.

On the other hand, fully-convolutional models like Unet [15] simply transform each pixel into a "1" or "0" response according to the objective. This relatively simpler task brings two main advantages. First, it requires fewer data because the overall task is not regression (of the bounding boxes), but a classification extended to the whole image. Second, the conversion of a pixel into a presence probability amounts to a segmentation, which is actually a task at a higher level than just a bounding box regression. Indeed, according to the object position and orientation, much space contained inside a bounding box can be background, but most of a segmentation area designates the searched instance. Thus a segmentation model provides an alternative, more precise description of the regions of interest, as it has the possibility to exclude the parts of the surrounding background.

Tiny-Unet: we propose a variant of the well-known Unet architecture [15] for our swimmer detection model. The original model is a residual autoencoder with blocs of 3 convolutions layers with the same number of filters before a downsampling (in the encoder) or upsampling (in the decoder). The following modifications have been performed: instead of 3 convolution layers between each down/up-sampling, only one is performed. The filters are also smaller, increasing from 8 up to 128 instead of 64 to 1024 for the original Unet. We will refer to our model as *tiny-Unet*. Due to its shallow architecture and low filters number, it is able to run at 40 frames per seconds (FPS) on a GTX 1080 NVIDIA GPU, therefore the model is a real-time detector for 25 FPS videos.

To convert the model's output heatmap into bounding boxes, a threshold is applied to said heatmap, and the remaining areas are extracted. A bounding box is created by finding the circumscribed rectangle around each of them. This further allows for a fair comparison with the benchmark methods in Sect. 3, each of them creating bounding boxes.

Box-to-Segmentation-Map Transformation: the Unet model requires segmentation heatmaps for training. In order to convert the bounding boxes from $Swimm^{400}$ into segmented data, an image with black background is created, and "filled" with white pixels inside the labelled boxes. Therefore, a pixel is 1 or 0 depending on whether there is or not a swimmer at the pixel. Multiple variants of this approach have been tested. Whiten inside the full box or only in the inscribed ellipsis; using smooth edges or hard edges. As shown in Table 1, the option giving the best result was to use the inscribed ellipsis with hard edges. As the boxes are reduced to approximate masks, we noticed that the model can be successfully trained even with mediocre and partly inconsistent annotation. This allows for a much quicker and less costly annotation process.

3   Experimental Results

First, we trained our tiny-Unet model on different variants of the box-to segmentation map strategy. The results are shown in Table 1.

This table clearly shows the superiority of shapes with hard edges. Smoothed ones tend to reduce the model convergence during training. Finally, filling an

Table 1. Detection performance of our model trained with different representations of the target heatmaps.

Training DSata	mAP 25	mAP 50
Ellipse Hard Edges	**72**	**45**
Rectangle Hard Edges	60	28
Ellipse Smooth Edges	21	5
Rectangle Smooth Edges	13	3

ellipse shape is better than filling the whole rectangle bounding box. An intuitive explanation could be that corner regions are less likely to contain pixels from the instance. In fact, the ellipse mask contains almost only the swimmer, and the remaining pixels can be understood by the model as regularisation. As the edges of a swimmer are fuzzy anyway, it probably does not differ much from a precisely-labelled pixel-wise mask.

To compare the results of tiny-Unet with current state-of-the-art methods, we trained two variants of Yolo on $Swimm^{400}$. The first version is YoloV3 [13], a deep model with a 2048 fully-connected layer after the convolutions. The second is Yolo-tiny, which is shallower. Moreover, it replaces the fully connected layer with a 1×1 convolution layer with 56 filters, in order to drastically reduce the number of parameters to train.

The 3 models are trained with $Swimm^{400}$ and the described data augmentation. The Adam optimizer is selected and starts with a learning rate of 10^{-3} with a decrease of 0.1 if the test loss plateaus more than 10 epochs. As the dataset is quite small, a batch size of 16 is chosen, and the loss is the Mean-Squared Error (MSE) in each case. For the Yolo-based models, the λ confidence training trick described in [12] Section 2.2 is followed.

To compare the models, the mean Average Precision (mAP) 25 and 50 are used, defined as:

$$mAP\ X = \frac{True\ Positives}{Positives} , \tag{1}$$

the "True Positives" being the detected bounding boxes with an Intersection over Union (IoU) of more than X% with the true box and "Positives" being the true number of boxes from the annotation. These metrics are not detection standards anymore (it is the COCO AP [5] which aims pixel perfect precision, which is nonsensical for swimmers with blurry edges under the water), but they are the closest to what real-world applications seek. Indeed, the precise delimitation of the swimmers' contour is not the priority here. The main objective of most applications is to obtain the overall position of the swimmers, for example to extract a sub-region around them. Thus, estimating the box barycenter and general size is enough, and therefore the mAP 25 and mAP 50 are good metrics. From Table 2, it appears that our tiny-Unet model outperforms by far the two others. Indeed, Yolo is a great model as long as enough data is available because

Table 2. Performance comparison for the different detection models. They are all trained with the same data, except for the first line. In bold, the best of a category. We observe that the original UNET architecture gives significantly worst results compared to tiny-Unet, as it overfits on the few data.

Model	mAP 25	mAP 50
Yolo (from [16])	70	-
Yolo	24	12
Yolo-tiny	31	20
Unet	39	25
Tiny-Unet	**72**	**45**

of its conversion from feature vectors to output tensors. On the other hand, tiny-Unet does not require such a transformation. This result is confirmed by testing the 3 models on the same videos: the tiny-Unet gives the best results. Moreover, with a video analysis, the tiny-Unet is much more stable between one frame and the next one.

The Yolo model trained on 25000 images from [16] gives results comparable to tiny-Unet trained on $Swimm^{400}$. It is not measured on the same benchmark though, thus we cannot assure which model exactly is superior. However, ours seems comparable to theirs with only a fraction of their amount of data and model size. In addition, it performs segmentation. Depending on the intended task, both the segmentation heatmap and the bounding boxes can be used, which is another advantage compared to the Yolo-based models.

Finally, tiny-Unet is extremely efficient in term of scalability. Being designed to be trained with small datasets, it is quite shallow and can run in real time (40 FPS) with not-so-recent GPUs (GTX 1080 NVIDIA GPU). Overall, the framework has been fairly optimized. The experts we interrogate can now the position of a swimmer in real time, but one swimmer at a time. With our detection model, we know the position of them all faster than real time, so more than 8 times faster than an expert, if there are 8 swimmers in the pool.

4   Discussions and Perspectives

The framework described in this paper is functional, but a few things can still be improved or modified to increase the overall performance. Also, despite having been proposed for swimming analyses, it can be generalized to other sports with low cost and small annotation time.

4.1   Improvements

The swimmers coordinates output by the framework could either be read as a segmentation area (the raw heatmap) or a bounding box (after the heatmap processing). The model is currently able to detect the parts of the swimmer that

Fig. 2. The raw segmentation output overlaid on the input image. Top-left: the overall detection quality is very good. Top-right: even swimmers in the pool that are not swimming can be detected. Bottom-left: sometimes the blobs are too close and merge (circled in red); to solve this issue, the buoys lines are detected and they mask out the segmentation map, dividing the merged blobs into several. Bottom-right: the farthest swimmers are often not visible even by a human eye if the camera is too low compared to the pool (misdetections circled in red). Before filming, one should consider going as high as possible (within the limits of the room) to avoid this problematic behavior. (Color figure online)

are outside of the water, but it does not detect any body part in particular. It results in an imprecise detection whose barycenter can vary from the shoulders to the hips. To alleviate this problem, we are currently creating another small dataset with the same images as $Swimm^{400}$, but this time only the swimmers head is annotated. By training a model to detect the head only, we will obtain a higher robustness. This might be incorporated into a 2-stage detector similar to Faster-RCNN [14], the first stage being the raw detector described in this paper. Having this second stage will also potentially remove most of the few false positives. Figure 2 shows a few detection results of our model, and illustrates its limits.

4.2   Generalization to Other Sports

The detection process is quite general and easy to handle. For sports with atypical objects that are not present in usual datasets, our annotation and detection process can be reused and adapted. Indeed, the low quantity of data is enough for most detection tasks if the background does not change too much (a pool, a sport field etc.) as the model will more easily understand what actually matters. In our context we did not mention the rotation augmentation because it was not relevant. Though, it might be in other contexts.

Its performances could be improved with the creation of a bigger dataset (and then the use of a bigger model), but the main point of this paper was to prove that powerful specific analysis tasks can be achieved at low cost without large computational and human resources.

Acknowledgement. We thanks Renaud Jester form Ecole Centrale de Lyon and David Simbada & Robin Pla from the FFN (French Swimming Federation) for their contributions and expertise through project NePTUNE. Also thanks to Méghane Decroocq for proofreading the article. This work was funded by the CNRS.

References

1. Benarab, D., Napoléon, T., Alfalou, A., Verney, A., Hellard, P.: A novel multi-tracking system for the evaluation of high-level swimmers performances. Baltimore, United States, May 2014
2. Benarab, D., Napoléon, T., Alfalou, A., Verney, A., Hellard, P.: Optimized swimmer tracking system by a dynamic fusion of correlation and color histogram techniques. Optics Commun. **356**, 256–268 (2015)
3. Benarab, D., Napoléon, T., Alfalou, A., Verney, A., Hellard, P.: Optimized swimmer tracking system based on a novel multi-related-targets approach. Optics Lasers Eng. **89**, 195–202 (2016)
4. Chapelle, O., Zien, A., Schölkopf, B.: Semi-Supervised Learning. MIT Press, Cambridge (2006)
5. COCO: Coco detection metric (2021). https://cocodataset.org/#detection-eval
6. DarrenL: Labelimg , December 2018. https://github.com/tzutalin/labelImg
7. Deng, J., Dong, W., Socher, R., Li, L.J., Li, K., Fei-Fei, L.: ImageNet: a large-scale hierarchical image database. In: 2009 IEEE Conference on Computer Vision and Pattern Recognition, pp. 248–255 (2009)
8. Gou, J., Yu, B., Maybank, S.J., Tao, D.: Knowledge distillation: a survey. Int. J. Comput. Vision **129**(6), 1789–1819 (2021)
9. Hall, A., et al.: The detection, tracking, and temporal action localisation of swimmers for automated analysis. Neural Comput. App. **33**, 1–19 (2021)
10. Lin, T.Y., et al.: Microsoft COCO: Common objects in context (2015)
11. Liu, W., et al.: SSD: single shot multibox detector. In: Leibe, B., Matas, J., Sebe, N., Welling, M. (eds.) ECCV 2016. LNCS, vol. 9905, pp. 21–37. Springer, Cham (2016). https://doi.org/10.1007/978-3-319-46448-0_2
12. Redmon, J., Divvala, S., Girshick, R., Farhadi, A.: You only look once: Unified, real-time object detection (2016). http://www.poker-edge.com/stats.php
13. Redmon, J., Farhadi, A.: Yolov3: an incremental improvement (2018)
14. Ren, S., He, K., Girshick, R., Sun, J.: Faster R-CNN: towards real-time object detection with region proposal networks (2016)
15. Ronneberger, O., Fischer, P., Brox, T.: U-net: convolutional networks for biomedical image segmentation (2015)
16. Woinoski, T., Bajić, I.V.: Swimmer stroke rate estimation from overhead race video (2021)

Imputation of Non-participated Race Results

Bram Janssens[(✉)] and Matthias Bogaert

Ghent University, 9000 Ghent, Belgium
{bram.janssens,matthias.bogaert}@ugent.be

Abstract. Most current solutions in cycling analytics focus on one specific race or participant, while a sports-wide system could render huge
benefits of scale, by automating certain processes. The development of
such a system is, however, heavily inflicted by the large number of non-
participations as most riders do not compete in all races. Therefore,
value imputation is required. Most popular value imputation techniques
are developed for cases where part of the data is fully observed, which
is not the case for cycling race results. While some methods are adapted
to situations without complete cases, this is not the case for the cross-
sectional imputation algorithm suggested by multiple previous studies
(i.e., KNN imputation). We therefore suggest an adaptation to the KNN
imputation algorithm which uses expert knowledge on race similarity in
order to facilitate the deployment of the algorithm in situations without complete cases. The method is shown to be the most performant
predictive model and does this within a competitive computation time.

Keywords: Sports Analytics · Scouting Analytics · Missing Value
Imputation · Predictive Modeling

1 Introduction

Cycling analytics has grown as a field of study, with researchers exploring a
range of possible applications. All these applications are, however, very narrowly
scoped with a focus on a specific race's outcome (e.g., [11]) or on the performance
of one specific athlete (e.g., [10]). While these solutions are useful, they limit
the usability of the systems derived from them. This is a missed opportunity
since athlete performance is even more interesting in relation to other athletes'
performances and fans and coaches often desire predictions of more than one
specific race.

The reason behind these scoped solutions, lays in the nature of the used data.
Not all riders compete in all races, which results in a an extreme number of
missing values. These missing values are extremely common, as most riders only
compete in a selected number out of the hundreds of youth races available on the
calendar. This results in a high number of missing values on a year-by-year result
basis, but the problem also persists when aggregating results across the youth

U. Brefeld et al. (Eds.): MLSA 2021, CCIS 1571, pp. 155–166, 2022.
https://doi.org/10.1007/978-3-031-02044-5_13

career, as many riders ride a similar program compared to their previous season. This results into highly specific setting, where generally no complete cases are observed. Most imputation methods are not adapted to this specific situation. Existing solutions to handle the absence of complete cases, like mean imputation or Multivariate Imputation by Chained Equations [24], result in over-extensive computation times or heavy reduction in data variability. The disadvantages of these solutions, might have dissuaded researchers to come up with a sports-wide system.

We therefore suggest a solution which deploys the K-nearest neighbor (KNN) imputation algorithm [23] on subgroups of races, which due to their similarity in used route attract the same riders. This results in both complete cases being observed and more quality imputations. The method is proven to give the most accurate predictions when combined with a random forest regressor.

The remainder of this study is structured as follows. Section 2 discusses advances made in cycling analytics and discusses current solutions in missing value imputation, followed by the used methodology in Sect. 3. Section 4 elaborates on the performance and outcome of the various techniques, while we end with a concluding remark and a critical note in Sect. 5.

2   Literature Overview

This section discusses current advances in literature. Section 2.1. describes how the interest in cycling analytics increased in recent years. Nonetheless, this growth in academic interest did not lead to an sports-wide analytical system as the nature of the data, with an abundance of missing values inhibits this. Current solutions on value imputation are therefore discussed in Sect. 2.2.

2.1   Cycling Analytics

In recent years, there has been an emergence of cycling-related data analytical studies. While some studies use analytical approaches to facilitate recreational and commuter cycling [14], less efforts have been made to harness the power of predictive analytics to boost rider and team performances. Initial introductions towards analytical methods in the field were made by [9]. The authors were able to predict a cyclist's heart rate at various moments in the training ride using a long short-term memory (LSTM) model. The study can be regarded as a proof-of-concept, indicating the feasibility of predictive models in the field of cycling.

This work was quickly followed by a range of studies who focused on practical applications to the cycling community. For example, [11] developed a real-time analytical system to estimate power performance of professional riders at the Tour de France (deployed on 2017 edition) based on GPS and wind sensor data. This would allow fans to have reliable estimates of the performance of athletes during the race. Another interesting study by [2] built a model which predicted the average velocity of a stage, the difference between the average stage velocity and the velocity of a rider and, finally, the head-to-head wins between two riders in a stage, using open data from procyclingstats.com. This popular information-tracking website was also used in other relevant studies. For example, [12] proved it was feasible to predict race rankings based on previous race rankings scraped from the procyclingstats.com website, while [11] was capable to predict individual rider performance in key mountain stages using a combination of private training data and the open data available on the procyclingstats.com website. These studies, and the wide usage of the website among fans, has clearly established the procyclingstats.com website as the go-to source for open cycling data. The field remains to be developed with recent studies (e.g., [3]) being developed out of collaborations with top-tier teams. Current developments are resulting in-race applications such as race tactics and nutrition schemes [3].

While data is freely available, the nature of the data inevitably leads to missing values. Riders do not participate in all races, as they select which races suit their specific skill set the most. This is further complicated by geographical orientation, as non-professional athletes often do not have the means to travel across half the globe. This dispersion has led many studies in cycling analytics to focus on the prediction of a specific race [12], or on a specific rider [11]. This solution enables modelers to select the considered features in such a way that the number of missing values are limited. The usage of such specific scopes, however, limits the applicability of most analytical approaches as no sports-wide system can be developed, such as the detection of young rider talents, or a general race prediction system.

2.2   Missing Value Imputation

Two broad types of imputation methods exist: single imputation and multiple imputation [16]. While single imputation uses the single outcome of a method to impute the value, multiple imputation methods average the outcome across multiple imputed samples, which theoretically ensures a better incorporation of uncertainty about this value. Nevertheless, single imputation methods have been proven capable of outperforming multiple imputation methods [10].

An interesting related field of research, are recommender systems (RS). Whereas value imputation focuses on estimating unknown values in the training, testing, and deployment sets, do RS focus on estimating unknown values in the user-rating matrix. While both fields show a clear overlap, there is still a large distinction. RS solely try to estimate the unknown values, while value imputation methods need a way to transfer the learned practices towards unseen data, used for testing and/or deployment. Accordingly, we observe many popular RS techniques like matrix factorization [21] to be unsuited for missing value imputation in a predictive pipeline.

The three most popular single imputation methods are: mean imputation, regression imputation, and KNN imputation [10]. Mean imputation replaces the non-observed values with the mean of the observed values of the variable and is commonly used due to its simplicity [4,20]. Regression imputation uses a regression model, which can be any type of regressor, to predict the missing values, by using the complete cases as training set and the missing cases as deployment set. KNN imputation [23] is similar to regression imputation as it also uses the neighbors of the missing case from the complete cases to see which average value the k nearest neighbors have. The k nearest neighbors are defined by a selected distance measure (in our case the Euclidean distance). It distinguishes itself from regression imputation as no explicit predictive model is fit. Note how each imputation technique can easily be adapted for usage on categorical variables by using the mode instead of the mean or by using classification techniques instead of regression techniques.

An issue with above mentioned methods is that most need to be adjusted when dealing with extreme missingness rates [20]. Mean imputation can be directly implemented, as no complete cases are needed. This ease-of-use might explain the popularity of the method despite the large reduction in variance. Regression imputation and KNN imputation, on the other hand, need complete cases to estimate missing values.

Multivariate Imputation by Chained Equations (MICE [24]) is a solution proposed to handle this issue for regression imputation. The method starts by randomly assigning observed data as imputation of the unobserved data. However, it is stored which values were unobserved. One feature's missing values are then imputed by a regression model which uses the other features' values (actually observed + imputed values) as independent features and uses the observed values as dependent values in the training set. This done for each feature, and imputed values are updated during a number of iterations. The computational time is the largest drawback to the method, as the iterative nature causes the regression imputation method to be very time-consuming.

KNN imputation has no adaptation that handles situations without complete observations. This translates to the situation where KNN imputation is only used in situations where complete cases are observed. This is a missed opportunity for several analytical systems as the algorithm is identified as the best imputation method for predictive modeling [10]. Therefore, we suggest an adaptation to the method which uses expert knowledge to group related races together. By doing so, KNN imputation becomes feasible as no incomplete cases are observed for the grouped races. In this study, we focus on the imputation of youth race results to predict a rider's performance in his professional career. Before explaining this adaptation, the used data and features-to-be-imputed are discussed.

3   Methodology

3.1   Data

As a case study, we will develop a system to predict a young rider's expected future performance. The used data was collected from the procyclingstats.com (PCS) website, which keeps track of all youth results. A list of popular youth competitions was created, and for each of these races all the available results in the period 2005–2020 were scraped, as almost no youth results were available prior to 2005. These scraped results were used as the basis of the independent variables. Given the scarcity of results in earlier years, we decided to only select riders who turned professional in the years 2010–2019. Before 2010, we observed the riders to have too little observed race results (i.e., less than 40 observations), leading to heavy time-based sample bias. Riders who turned professional in 2020 or 2021 were also not selected, as they did not yet have two full years of observed dependent period. Overall, this resulted in a sample of 1,060 athletes. The goal of our model is to predict the performance during a period in the rider's professional career, based on the results he achieved as youth competitor. This implies that, for instance, when modelling a rider turning professional in 2018, all his results up until 2017 will be used as input of the independent variables, while results from 2018 onwards will be used as input for the dependent variable.

The dependent variable was defined as the PCS points scored in the first two years as a professional athlete. This definition closely follows the regulations of the Union Cycliste Internationale (UCI; international cycling federation), which state that starting professional athletes (defined as competing in one of the top two tier levels) should be awarded contracts of at least two years. By measuring their performance during these two years, we can directly measure the return on investment of the hiring team. This limited time window also filters out potential negative effects of bad talent development. The option for PCS points rather than the official UCI points is inspired by the fact that this points system has remained stable during the entire period 2010–2020, while the current UCI ranking system only dates back to 2016. The ranking is also often used in cycling analytics by other researchers [18, 25].

3.2 Feature Engineering

We created a large set of independent variables (in total 242), which represent both the general rider performance (aggregate features), as well individual rider performance in one particular race. These race-specific features especially lead to large missing rates. Nonetheless, they cannot be disregarded as this gives information about a rider's talent. For example, it could be that a sprinter is more likely to score points straight away compared to climber of cobbled classics specialist. To incorporate individual race results, we included information on best past race result, and best past time difference, as finishing in the same group as the race winner can be regarded as a better result than achieving a largely distanced top-10 placement. When a rider did not finish the race, he received the placing of the last finishing rider plus one. Race participation is included as well, acting as imputation indicator. For stage races, number of stage victories, and best stage result are reported as well. Aggregate features were computed as well, both with a focus on one of the U23 (aged 19–22) and Junior (aged 17–18) categories, or averaged across both youth categories. Fully disclosed information on the set of used features can be obtained when contacting the authors.

3.3 Suggested KNN Adaption

The resulting sample contains a very high number of missing values, with only 49.57% of all the possible feature values observed. The observed rate for the race-based features (besides participation) only ranges between 5 and 40%, indicating that race-based features (e.g., best result) have 60 to 95% missing values. Note that the overall observed rate of 49.57% is inflated by the fully observed aggregate and participation features. The reason for this high missingness is related to the selection decision of the racer and the coach (i.e., races are chosen that fit with the capacities of the rider and the team), as well as the geographical location. This results in an atypical situation in which no single complete case is observed in the data, this while most analytical models can only be used with complete datasets [13].

As discussed in Sect. 2.2., current solutions for missing value imputation in situations without complete cases either result in reduced data variability or are extremely time-consuming. Therefore, we suggest an alternative method for value imputation, where we group the races based on domain knowledge into groups that do have complete cases on which KNN imputation can be applied.

In total, eight categories were created. A first category is the Big Tour category, which are races that take place during a period of over a week and over varied terrain. Diverse riders with good recuperation skills excel in the overall classification of this type of race. The importance of the races also attracts riders from quite wide geographical origins and the longitude and importance of the races make it more interesting for some to solely focus on stage victories rather than the overall classification. A related category is the Stage Race Climb category of French stage races over very hilly terrain, attracting many riders from France and neighboring countries. Both categories consist of U23 stage races, Junior stage races are categorized in the Stage Race Junior category, which is more diverse. This due to the fact that Juniors have more limited calendar options. Regarding the one day races, we also followed a similar method, with the One Day Junior races forming one category, and the U23 races divided into Cobbles and Hilly U23. Cobbled races are quite unique as they are the sole type of races which favor more heavy riders, while also being located in and near Belgium. This as opposed to the hilly one day races, which are one a hilly terrain,

Table 1. Average results

	Victory ratio U23	Evolution Wins	Omloop der Vlaamse Gewesten best result	Paris-Roubaix U23 best result	Tour de l'Isard best result	Tour d'Alsace best result
Rider 1	0.238	1.608	6	3	**70**	88
Rider 2	0.006	0.884	**6**	8	3	5
Rider 3	0.082	0.589	60	96	1	**5**
Rider 4	0.000	0.000	**60**	77	70	**88**

favoring more light-weight riders, while also being primarily located in Italy. All other races are categorized as Rest.

By using the KNN algorithm on each feature group, rather than across all features, complete cases are observed as the similarity of the race program attracts some riders to complete the fully considered race program. This has also has the advantage that we only use the most relevant features for imputation. Table 1 provides a simplified example of our proposed imputation method. Note that the imputed values are highlighted in bold. From this examples, it is clear that no rider competed in all four races, which would render the base KNN imputation method infeasible as no complete cases are observed. In addition, it also uses a more scoped and better-informed approach. For instance, the imputation-relevant information to predict the result of a rider in Omloop der Vlaamse Gewesten will be mainly situated in the Cobbles group (Paris-Roubaix U23 in this case), while the Stage Race Climb group will contain very limited relevant information. The benefit of our method is nicely reflected for rider 2. He has a highly similar profile to rider 3, which would probably be his nearest neighbor. However, compared to rider 3, he also performs quite well on the cobblestones, as is reflected by his 8th place in Paris-Roubaix U23. This makes rider 1 a better candidate for being rider 2's nearest neighbor in the cobbles group, rendering an imputed value of 6, rather than of 60.

3.4 Experimental Set-up

We will compare our suggested approach to both the mean imputation technique and the Multivariate Imputation by Chained Equations (MICE) technique. For the MICE methodology, we set the number of iterations at 10, acting as a trade-off between computational time and reaching of convergence. As base regressor, we chose random forest [1] due to the algorithms capacity to handle non-linear relationships as well as its good performance without parameter tuning [6]. Previous research [5] also concluded that recursive partitioning methods are recommended over standard applications of MICE. Do note that this implementation is essentially the same as the MissForest implementation by [22] The number of considered neighbors (K) is set to 5 for our KNN adaptation.

The three imputation methods will be compared to each other with regard to both the speed of execution as well as the performance in a predictive modeling pipeline. Besides the imputation step, this pipeline will also include a feature selection step, as a large number of 242 features were considered compared to the maximal sample size of 1,060 athletes, and a regression algorithm. These result in the sequence imputation - feature selection - regression being deployed.

A very popular feature selection method is the Boruta algorithm [15]. The base algorithm used is random forest and the method is based on the idea of 'shadow variables'. These are created by replacing the actual feature values with random permutations of these values. When the shadow variable's variable importance is not significantly different than the actual variable importance, it is decided that the feature in question is not needed and can be excluded from the eventual feature list. Since Gini-based variable importance rankings are unreliable, we use SHAP-based [17] feature importances.

As regression algorithm, we will deploy random forest regression [1]. This algorithm was selected in our experimental set-up as it is very robust and performs well without heavy parameter tuning. The number of trees was set sufficiently large at 500 and the number of random predictors to select at each tree split was set at the square root of the number of predictors.

As a season follows the subsequent one and riders compete against each other in the same season, rather than act as individualistic competitors, one can safely say that the assumption of independent and identically distributed data is clearly violated. This influences our test design, as a traditional cross-validated approach is not adequate in this situation. Rather, we will follow a rolling window approach where all available information is used up until the moment of prediction [26]. In order to have an unbiased estimation of performance, we use five different periods for testing: starting years 2015–2019. Note that the validation period is only used for hyperparameter tuning and that the combined training and validation period is eventually used for fitting the final model.

Each fold is evaluated against a range of performance measures. The Root-Mean-Squared-Error (RMSE) calculates how exact the method can predict the points scored per participant. This is, however, not the main goal, as teams rather want the best riders to be ranked on top. Therefore, the Spearman rank correlation between actual results and predicted results is calculated as well, indicating how consequent the best riders are ranked on top [8]. Another interesting way of dividing professional athletes is by grouping them into the top 10%, top 25%, or top 50% buckets of all athletes [19]. A good way of measuring the performance of this binned continuous scale, is accuracy within one [7] as this filters out the oversensitivity to misclassifications near the arbitrary cut-off. This adaption to the traditional accuracy measure also accounts ordered predictions as correct if they deviate only one class from the actual class.

Of special interest to the professional teams, is the absolute top bin of the top-10% riders. These riders are the ones they want to contact by preference. By considering this bin as the desired class, we can deploy the traditional binary classification performance measures. A popular measure based on the top decile bin, is the lift. By calculating how much more actual top 10% riders there are in the suggested bin, than on average in the dataset, one can derive how much better the model is compared to randomly contacting riders. It is clear that this measure is highly sensitive to the used cut-off of 10% contacted. This is even more worrisome as it is very feasible that the teams won't contact 10% of all riders as their teams simply aren't large enough to contract so many riders. A more complete measure is the average precision, which considers different cut-off rates.

$$RMSE = \sqrt{\frac{1}{N} \sum_{i=1}^{N} (true_i - predict_i)^2} \qquad (1)$$

$$Spearman = \frac{1 - 6\sum_{i=1}^{N} d_i}{N^3 - N} \qquad (2)$$

$$Lift = \frac{Precision\ contacted\ top\ decile}{actual\ rate} \qquad (3)$$

$$Average\ Precision = \sum_{n}(Recall_n - Recall_{n-1})Precision_n \qquad (4)$$

4 Results

Table 2 depicts the average results of the machine learning pipelines across all five folds. KNN scores best on 3 out of 5 performance measures (i.e., RMSE, Spearman correlation, and average precision), with competitive scores on the other 2 measures. This suggests the KNN method as the imputation method which is most useful in the predictive pipeline.

Table 2. Grouped KNN imputation

	RMSE	Spearman	Accuracy within one	Average precision	Lift
KNN	**282.89**	**0.5213**	0.8359	**0.3714**	3.2121
Mean	294.44	0.4799	**0.8437**	0.3232	2.9264
MICE	291.36	0.5107	0.8393	0.3681	**3.5996**

A final argument in method selection can be the time required to come up with suggested rider rankings. The computation time of the imputation step per fold is depicted in Table 3. Whereas the grouped KNN and mean imputation methods take only a couple of seconds, does the chained equation regression step take almost 10 h for the calculation of the largest imputed dataset. This time will probably only further increase with the addition of additional riders to the dataset. As fast imputation allows quick interpretation of new youth race results, this could potentially hinder teams in moving fast with regard of the contacting of a new interesting prospect. Therefore, grouped KNN and mean imputation are

Table 3. Computation time imputation methods (in seconds)

Fold	Train/val/test size	KNN imputation	Mean imputation	MICE
2015	401/80/112	1.92	0.06	13025.15
2016	481/112/110	1.59	0.03	15035.95
2017	593/110/117	2.46	0.06	20488.19
2018	703/117/131	2.75	0.03	26363.01
2019	820/131/109	3.46	0.03	32997.33

suggested above chained equation regression imputation. Overall, our suggested KNN imputation adaptation gives the best results when included in a predictive modelling pipeline, while being highly competitive in terms of computation time.

To see whether our approach can be effectively used to detect future star riders early on, we deployed the technique on the riders who turned professional during the years 2020 and 2021. Interestingly, we observe several prospects in our suggested top-10 who have already showed some good form at the professional level. For instance, Tom Pidcock already finished in the top-5 in the Strade Bianchi and Amstel Gold Race, some of the most important races on the calendar, and won the Brabantse Pijl against a top tier field of participants. Stefan Bisegger also already won a stage in the World Tour Paris-Nice stage race.

5   Conclusion

In this paper we developed a method to impute race results to riders who did not participate. The method leveraged expert knowledge about the similarity between certain youth races, ending up with complete cases for each subgroup, enabling the deployment of the KNN imputation algorithm. The used race groups were Stage Race Junior, One Day Junior, Cobbles, Hilly U23, Big Tour, Stage Race Climb, ITT, and Rest.

The proposed method was shown to yield the best results when included in a predictive modelling pipeline, compared to the traditional mean imputation and MICE solutions. This top performance was achieved within a competitive computation time. We demonstrated that the detection of young cycling talents based on youth race results is feasible despite the tendency of the observed data to have many missing values. The suggested rider rankings have a strong relation to the actually observed rider rankings.

An avenue for future research might be the inclusion of more various regression algorithms. While the adapted KNN is shown to yield the most accurate eventual results, it could be that this is due to a beneficial interplay between the imputation method and the base regressor. The used methodology should therefore be evaluated for other algorithms in the future.

Our method was only deployed onto one specific case, namely the detection of young cycling talents. However, we would like to point out that a similar grouping can be made with regard to professional races, or even amateur races, making predictive analytic systems feasible for a wide range of applications by using the grouped KNN method.

References

1. Breiman, L.: Random forests. Mach. Learn. **45**(1), 5–32 (2001)
2. De Spiegeleer, E.: Predicting cycling results using machine learning (2019)
3. de Leeuw, A.-W., Heijboer, M., Hofmijster, M., van der Zwaard, S., Knobbe, A.: Time series regression in professional road cycling. In: Appice, A., Tsoumakas, G., Manolopoulos, Y., Matwin, S. (eds.) DS 2020. LNCS (LNAI), vol. 12323, pp. 689–703. Springer, Cham (2020). https://doi.org/10.1007/978-3-030-61527-7_45

4. Dolatsara, H.A., Chen, Y.J., Evans, C., Gupta, A., Megahed, F.M.: A two-stage machine learning framework to predict heart transplantation survival probabilities over time with a monotonic probability constraint. Decis. Support Syst. **137**, 113363 (2020)

5. Doove, L.L., Van Buuren, S., Dusseldorp, E.: Recursive partitioning for missing data imputation in the presence of interaction effects. Comput. Stat. Data Anal. **72**, 92–104 (2014)

6. Fernández-Delgado, M., Cernadas, E., Barro, S., Amorim, D.: Do we need hundreds of classifiers to solve real world classification problems? J. Mach. Learn. Res. **15**(1), 3133–3181 (2014)

7. Gaudette, L., Japkowicz, N.: Evaluation methods for ordinal classification. In: Gao, Y., Japkowicz, N. (eds.) AI 2009. LNCS (LNAI), vol. 5549, pp. 207–210. Springer, Heidelberg (2009). https://doi.org/10.1007/978-3-642-01818-3_25

8. Gauthier, T.D.: Detecting trends using Spearman's rank correlation coefficient. Environ. Forensics **2**(4), 359–362 (2001)

9. Hilmkil, A., Ivarsson, O., Johansson, M., Kuylenstierna, D., van Erp, T.: Towards machine learning on data from professional cyclists. arXiv preprint arXiv:1808.00198 (2018)

10. Karetnikov, A.: Application of Data-Driven Analytics on Sport Data from a Professional Bicycle Racing Team. Eindhoven University of Technology, The Netherlands (2019)

11. Kataoka, Y., Gray, P.: Real-time power performance prediction in Tour de France. In: Brefeld, U., Davis, J., Van Haaren, J., Zimmermann, A. (eds.) MLSA 2018. LNCS (LNAI), vol. 11330, pp. 121–130. Springer, Cham (2019). https://doi.org/10.1007/978-3-030-17274-9_10

12. Kholkine, L., De Schepper, T., Verdonck, T., Latré, S.: A machine learning approach for road cycling race performance prediction. In: Brefeld, U., Davis, J., Van Haaren, J., Zimmermann, A. (eds.) MLSA 2020. CCIS, vol. 1324, pp. 103–112. Springer, Cham (2020). https://doi.org/10.1007/978-3-030-64912-8_9

13. Kowarik, A., Templ, M.: Imputation with the R package VIM. J. Stat. Softw. **74**(7), 1–16 (2016)

14. Kumar, A., Nguyen, V.A., Teo, K.M.: Commuter cycling policy in Singapore: a farecard data analytics based approach. Ann. Oper. Res. **236**(1), 57–73 (2014). https://doi.org/10.1007/s10479-014-1585-7

15. Kursa, M.B., Rudnicki, W.R.: Feature selection with the Boruta package. J. Stat. Softw. **36**(11), 1–13 (2010)

16. Little, R.J., Rubin, D.B.: Statistical Analysis with Missing Data, vol. 793. Wiley, Hoboken (2019)

17. Lundberg, S.M., Lee, S.I.: A unified approach to interpreting model predictions. Adv. Neural Inf. Process. Syst. **30**, 4765–4774 (2017)

18. Miller, J., Susa, K.: Comparison of anthropometric characteristics between world tour and professional continental cyclists. J. Sci. Cycl. **7**(3), 3–6 (2018)

19. Lehmus Persson, T., Kozlica, H., Carlsson, N., Lambrix, P.: Prediction of tiers in the ranking of ice hockey players. In: Brefeld, U., Davis, J., Van Haaren, J., Zimmermann, A. (eds.) MLSA 2020. CCIS, vol. 1324, pp. 89–100. Springer, Cham (2020). https://doi.org/10.1007/978-3-030-64912-8_8

20. Piri, S.: Missing care: a framework to address the issue of frequent missing values; the case of a clinical decision support system for Parkinson's disease. Decis. Support Syst. **136**, 113339 (2020)

21. Ranjbar, M., Moradi, P., Azami, M., Jalili, M.: An imputation-based matrix factorization method for improving accuracy of collaborative filtering systems. Eng. Appl. Artif. Intell. **46**, 58–66 (2015)

22. Stekhoven, D.J., Bühlmann, P.: MissForest-non-parametric missing value imputation for mixed-type data. Bioinformatics **28**(1), 112–118 (2012)

23. Troyanskaya, O., et al.: Missing value estimation methods for DNA microarrays. Bioinformatics **17**(6), 520–525 (2001)

24. Van Buuren, S., Groothuis-Oudshoorn, K.: mice: multivariate imputation by chained equations in R. J. Stat. Softw. **45**, 1–68 (2010)

25. van Erp, T., Sanders, D., Lamberts, R.P.: Maintaining power output with accumulating levels of work done is a key determinant for success in professional cycling. Med. Sci. Sports Exerc. **53**(9), 1903–1910 (2021)

26. Vomfell, L., Härdle, W.K., Lessmann, S.: Improving crime count forecasts using Twitter and taxi data. Decis. Support Syst. **113**, 73–85 (2018)

Sensor-Based Performance Monitoring in Track Cycling

Michaël Steyaert⬤, Jelle De Bock⬤, and Steven Verstockt$^{(\boxtimes)}$⬤

Ghent University-imec, IDLab, Ghent, Belgium
{Michael.Steyaert,Jelle.DeBock,Steven.Verstockt}@UGent.be

Abstract. Research has not found its way yet to the track cycling madison discipline. Currently, training files are collected from cycling computers, after which the data is interpreted in a mainly subjective manner, based on the domain knowledge of a coach. The goal of this paper is twofold. Starting with the automated detection of madison handslings from cadence, acceleration and gyroscope data, all other data corresponding to a single handsling can easily be obtained. The second goal concerns the calculation of statistics on rider performances during a handsling. We present two madison handsling performance assessment use cases. The first use case exposes imbalances within a madison rider pair, whereas the second use case employs power data to monitor the effort a single rider puts into the handsling.

Keywords: Sports analytics · Cycling rider performance · Track cycling · Madison

1 Introduction

The past decade, sports analytics significantly gained momentum in almost any discipline. When it comes to the spectators of a competition, storytelling allows a more immersive experience. One example is the use of data-driven race summaries, as described by [5]. In the field of performance analysis, the authors of [1] developed an XGBoost machine learning model to predict the outcome of cycling road races. Using data about rider performances, rider profile, relevant races and the target race profile, a prediction is made on the first 10 finishers for the target race. Among all research in cycling, track cycling has only been studied to a limited extend. Therefore, our goal is to contribute to track cycling research by presenting insightful results on the madison discipline, complemented with inspiration for potential future research topics.

Studies in track cycling are often focused on one of its multiple disciplines. For example, extensive research has been performed in pacing strategies for the individual pursuit discipline [4]. Data-driven rider scouting for the Olympic omnium race, introduced by [2], is another insightful study. Nevertheless, research has not found its way yet to the madison discipline. In current analysis of this discipline, required data is typically extracted from data files generated by a cycling

U. Brefeld et al. (Eds.): MLSA 2021, CCIS 1571, pp. 167–177, 2022.
https://doi.org/10.1007/978-3-031-02044-5_14

computer. Afterwards, handsling events are manually extracted from the file and the corresponding data is interpreted by a coach. The results presented in this paper are twofold. First and foremost, efficiently providing a coach with data corresponding to madison handslings would eliminate the current time-consuming and error-prone artisanal approach. The second part of the study is dedicated to performance monitoring of madison handslings, objectifying the current feedback provided to the riders and allowing a coach to only perform an in-depth analysis of handslings that require additional attention. During the study, multiple data streams were collected. Performance data, i.e. speed, cadence, heart rate and power, was extracted from training files. Furthermore, MetaMotion R[1] motion sensors were attached to arms and wrists of riders during madison training sessions, recording acceleration and gyroscope data. Two training sessions were recorded for a madison rider pair of professional, experienced and beginner level, thus six training sessions in total.

In the remainder of this paper, Sect. 2 will provide a short introduction to the madison discipline. The first results are presented in Sect. 3 and concern the automated detection of madison handslings. Afterwards, Sect. 4 will deal with the performance of riders during a madison training session or race by means of two use cases. Finally, Sect. 5 concludes this paper and provides inspiration for future work.

2   What is Madison?

Among the different track cycling disciplines, madison belongs to the relay category. A madison race consists of multiple teams composed of two riders. At all times, one rider of each team is considered to be actively racing and typically located on the lower part of the track. This rider is denoted as the active rider in what follows. The other rider, denoted as the inactive rider, is located on the upper part of the track, riding with much lower speed and waiting for the active rider. Once the active rider of a team catches up with the corresponding inactive rider, the inactive rider steers down towards the active rider. When the active and inactive rider are located next to each other, the speed of the active rider is transferred to the inactive rider by means of a handsling. This event is often called a change.

When it comes to racing format, the official madison race distance as defined by the Union Cycliste Internationale (UCI) is 50 km, i.e. 200 laps on a 250 m track. Every tenth lap, the first active rider of a team at the finish line earns five points, while the second, third and fourth rider earn three, two and one points respectively. One exception is the last sprint lap, in which the rewarded points are doubled. In addition, a team can escape the front of the bunch and catch up with the back of the bunch, which is called lap gain. In this case, the team is rewarded with 20 additional points. Of course, if a team loses a lap, the team loses 20 points. The goal is, as a team, to gain as much points as possible by the end of the race.

[1] https://mbientlab.com/metamotionr/.

3 Handsling Detection

From the collected data streams, i.e. performance and motion data, typical patterns occurring during a madison handsling can be exploited, in order to automate the detection of these handslings. The suitability of cadence data for this task is presented in Sect. 3.1. Afterwards, Sect. 3.2 discusses the potential of correlation in arm motion of a rider pair during a handsling.

In order to test/evaluate the proposed methodologies we collected data from 6 training sessions - 2 for each level of experience (beginner, experienced and professional). Each training session consists of 2 parts (i.e. there was a period of rest during the entire training session). The duration of the training sessions was between 20 and 45 min. Beginners had shorter training sessions (20–30 min.) and experienced/professional riders had longer sessions (30–45 min.). Beginners and experienced riders performed trainings at normal training speed, focusing on learning the madison technique (beginners) and practicing it (experienced riders). Professionals did trainings on normal training speed and race speed and focused on practicing madison technique and timing handslings at preferable moments (e.g. spring laps).

3.1 Performance Data

Typically, a training session is recorded using a cycling computer retrieving data from multiple connected sensors. Most commonly, speed, heart rate, cadence and power values are recorded. When it comes to track cycling, the bikes have a fixed gear. This causes the cadence data only to be dependent on the speed of the rider and the gear installed on the bike. Because speed is often recorded using GPS signals, which are often of low quality on an indoor track, solely cadence data was used for madison handsling detection in this study. For simplicity, data was recorded from rider pairs using the same gear. Consequently, the absolute values of cadence can be compared in a meaningful way. When different gears are used, cadence values can be converted using a gear ratio chart.

Using the properties of the madison discipline, it can be assumed that the cadence values of the active and inactive rider only intersect when a handsling occurs. However, small deviations from this assumption can easily be captured by a check for cadence values not to cross twice in a limited amount of time. Detection of madison handslings can now easily be implemented by searching for intersections in cadence values throughout the training session. Each intersection can be associated with a handsling, where the rider with a downward trend in cadence becomes the inactive rider after the handsling and the rider with an upward trend becomes the active rider. More formally, timestamp t corresponding to the cadence value intersection point can be described as:

$$\exists\, t : C_{t-1}^{inactive} \leq C_{t-1}^{active} \wedge C_t^{inactive} \geq C_t^{active} \tag{1}$$

Detecting madison handslings and assigning them with a fixed duration will capture the entire handsling only when the fixed duration spans the duration of the effective handsling. On average, a duration of five seconds suffices, but is not a silver bullet. In a more ideal case, it is possible to detect the start and end time of a handsling and derive the duration dynamically. Important to see is the increasing cadence of the inactive rider through the intersection, while the cadence of the active rider decreases. Defining an appropriate threshold over the rolling covariance between these two cadence time series allows the extraction of start and end time of a madison handsling in a rule-based manner.

As explained before, the duration of a handsling can significantly vary. In the recorded training sessions the average duration was approximately 5 s. When speed of the bunch is slow, the duration will typically be longer (approx. 7 s) and when speed of the bunch is high, the duration will typically be shorter (approx. 3–4 s). Fixing it at an average of 5 s means information loss for handslings that last longer. Possible problems this causes is that handslings of a rider pair that always has long handslings cannot fully be analysed, while the fact that their handslings last long probably implies potential improvements. Furthermore, a fixed duration also implies that the duration of handslings can not be compared as a statistic.

3.2   Motion Data

During the recorded training sessions, riders were equipped with acceleration and gyroscope sensors, attached to the arms and wrists. The orientation of these motion sensors is specified in Fig. 1. One sensor yields six different data streams. The acceleration x-axis of the sensor captures upward and downward movements, while the y-axis captures the inward and outward movements. Finally, the z-axis describes the forward and backward movements. Gyroscope data is generated using the same orientation. Thus, the x-axis corresponds to the inward and outward rotations, while the arm moves forward and backward rotating around the y-axis. Lastly, the z-axis corresponds to the sideways upward and downward rotations. The remainder of this section describes the automated detection of handslings using the generated motion data.

Dynamic Time Warping. A potential technique to automatically detect handslings is Dynamic Time Warping (DTW), which was originally developed to align sequences of spoken words [3]. Two sequences, $a = [a_1, a_2, ..., a_n]$ and $b = [b_1, b_2, ..., b_m]$ can be aligned by matching the items of one series to the items of the other series, such that the sum of euclidean distances between each matched pair of items is minimal. By selecting a reference handsling sequence, a sliding window over the motion data time series can be used to extract handslings from the training session. Whenever the calculated DTW distance falls below a predefined threshold, the subsequence within the sliding window can be marked as handsling. Note that it is possible for consecutive window distances to fall below the threshold. In this case, the window corresponding to the minimum distance will be associated with the handsling.

Fig. 1. Placement and orientation of the motion sensors on the arm and wrist of the rider.

The main drawback of the DTW approach is the $O(NM)$ time complexity, where N is the length of the reference sequence and M is the length of the query sequence. Clearly, in this case, $M = N$ can be assumed, resulting in quadratic time complexity. It should be noted that $M = N$ is limited to the size of the sliding window. Nevertheless, this comparison is made multiple times, for the entire training session, i.e. using a window sliding over the motion data time series. This increases the time complexity to $O(N^2 S)$, where S is the length of the time series.

Rule-Based. Clearly, the time complexity of DTW is significant for longer training sessions. In case handslings should be detected in real time, one desires as little delay as possible. Therefore, an approach similar to cadence-based handsling detection can be used as an alternative. A high degree of correlation in arm movements is achieved during a handsling, while correlation in between handslings is low to non-existent. Transforming the motion data provides the opportunity to detect handslings by using the average value of the transformation as a threshold. This transformation can be performed as follows:

$$\phi_{y,t} = var\left(cov_{y^{(1)}_{t,t+\Delta t}, y^{(2)}_{t,t+\Delta t}}\right) \qquad (2)$$

$$\psi_{y,t} = \phi_{y,t} - \overline{\phi_y} \qquad (3)$$

The variance at timestamp t in Eq. 2 is calculated over the rolling covariance between timestamps t and $t + \Delta t$ for the motion data time series under consideration, denoted by $y^{(r)}$ for rider r. $\overline{\phi_y}$ in Eq. 3 is both the global average of the transformation and detection threshold of the rule-based detection approach.

Discussion and Results. As an illustration, the previously discussed approaches are applied to one of the recorded training sessions. After discussing the DTW approach on motion data, the result of applying the rule-based approach on the same data is presented. The use of cadence data for automated handsling detection concludes this section.

An example of the DTW approach is provided in Fig. 2, where the upper part of the figure shows motion data of three handslings, generated by rotations over the y-axis for a gyroscope attached to the right arm of a rider. The lower part of the figure contains the sliding window DTW distance. The implementation uses a time window of 800 time units, i.e. 16 s as motion data is recorded 50 Hz. The step size of the sliding window is fixed at 200 time units, i.e. 4 s. Data corresponding to a manually picked high quality handsling is used as reference sequence. Important to mention is that the DTW approach does not require a new reference handsling when it comes to detecting all handslings from a training session. A handsling should be selected once and can be used for multiple training sessions. Manually labeled start and end timestamps of handslings are indicated by a vertical green and red line respectively. It is clear that by fixing the threshold value at a DTW distance of 800, handslings can be detected. Including multiple time series in the DTW distance calculation does not yield higher accuracy and is thus not found useful. For the considered training session, all handslings were detected (i.e., no false negatives). It should be noted, however, that this approach is vulnerable to false positives when arm or wrist motion from a rider outside of a handsling context becomes too similar to the reference sequence (i.e., 1 false positive was detected at the end of the session by the DTW caused by a gesture similar to handsling). Nevertheless, this typically occurs at the very beginning or end of a session, for example when riders get on or off their bikes. These events can easily be filtered out by limiting the data under consideration to the actual madison training session. The performance for the other five sessions is similar.

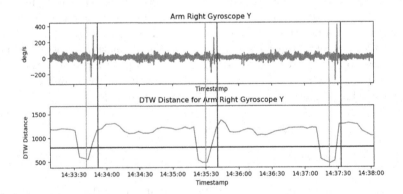

Fig. 2. Right arm gyroscope data for rotations over the y-axis (top) and the sliding window DTW distance, together with the detection threshold (bottom).

For the rule-based motion data approach, Eq. 2 is calculated over the rolling covariance between timestamp $t - 100$ and $t + 100$. Similar to the DTW approach, gyroscope data over the y-axis generated by the arms is used. Figure 3 shows the original data in the upper plot. In the lower plot, the red and green lines show the transformed data and detection threshold respectively. Intersections between the green and red line indicate the start and end of the handsling detection. This approach is vulnerable to false positives in case both riders move their arms in a way correlation occurs outside of a handsling context. In the training session under consideration all handslings were correctly detected (i.e., no false negatives). Nevertheless, one false positive is raised at the end of the session, when the madison training session is already over. Again, the majority of false positives can be eliminated for this approach by limiting the data to the essence of the training session. The performance for the other five sessions is similar.

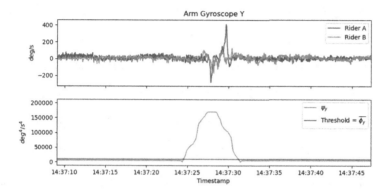

Fig. 3. Gyroscope data generated over the y-axis during a handsling (top) and the corresponding peak with threshold value used to detect this handsling (bottom).

Finally, patterns in performance data, more specifically cadence data, can be exploited when detecting madison handslings. Calculating the rolling covariance over 25 s (performance data is typically recorded 1 Hz), Fig. 4 shows how handslings can be detected by setting a threshold at 25% of the maximum rolling covariance value. The intersections of the threshold with the rolling covariance denote the start and end timestamps of the handslings within a training session. This approach yields perfect accuracy for all training sessions where cadence values only cross during a handsling. By filtering out all cases where the cadence of the inactive rider peaks above the cadence of the active rider for at most two seconds and only using intersection points of at least 80 RPM, all false positives were eliminated from the collected training session data. Such filtering is required for example at the very beginning of a training session where riders are riding next to each other at the same speed, before starting the actual madison training session.

In conclusion, detecting madison handslings using cadence covariance yields perfect accuracy and suffices when only performance data is analysed. Although, DTW and rule-based approaches on motion data might more easily generate false positive results, these can often be eliminated by only considering the essential part of the training session. The motion data is especially useful when the arm technique of riders is analysed. Similar to cadence-based handsling detection, the rule-based motion data approach allows flexible start and end timestamps. In contrary, the DTW approach uses a fixed window size, but can be used in a more individual approach and only needs data from one rider. Furthermore, by using different reference sequences and a suitable threshold, handsling classes can be defined. This way, it is possible to distinguish between, for example, high and low quality handslings during a training session.

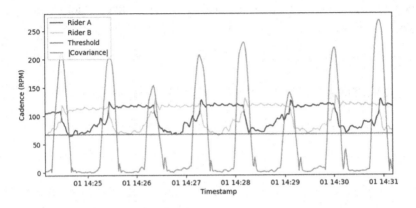

Fig. 4. Cadence values of both riders during a training session and the corresponding covariance and threshold used to detect handslings.

4   Handsling Performance Monitoring

Both performance and motion data sources can be used for in-depth analysis of the detected handslings. Whereas the results presented so far raise the opportunity to manually perform such an analysis, automatically generating performance statistics contributes to more efficiency and higher accuracy. Therefore, the last part of this study is dedicated to the search for insightful statistics on a madison handsling. Two statistics are presented in the form of rider performance use cases.

4.1   Inter-handsling Duration

Ideally, the average active duration of both riders in a rider pair is approximately equal. Nevertheless, during a training session or race, the duration among handslings might differ due to for example a sprint lap, where the goal is that one rider takes the majority of sprints, due to its sprinting abilities. Thus, race situations should be taken into account when comparing active durations of riders. The influence of a sprint lap is illustrated by handsling 8 in Fig. 5. Just before the sprint lap, Rider B accelerates, in order to save energy for the sprint and become active at one lap to go in the most ideal scenario. This leads to a long duration for Rider A as active rider.

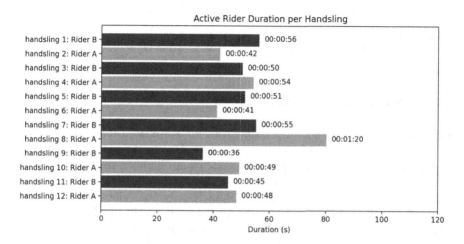

Fig. 5. Duration as active rider during a madison race simulation.

4.2 Power Statistics

Now, focus can be shifted to statistics based on power data. By calculating the average power of riders in a time range around the intersection timestamp t of cadence values, the exerted power during a handsling can be measured. This is shown in Table 1. The context (race dynamics) can also be derived from this Table - Handsling Active and Handsling Inactive represent the average power over the entire handsling and serve as a reference. Additionally, the average power over a few seconds before the handsling could be used as reference.

From the comparison in Table 1 it is clear that Rider C spends less power during the $[t - 2s, t + 2s]$ intervals, both as an active and inactive rider. Nevertheless, the higher values of Rider B and Rider D might originate from their more explosive rider type, meaning they can more easily reach higher peak power values with less effort. More important is the difference in power values as active rider, compared to being an inactive rider over the entire handsling. Here Rider C achieves similar power values, whereas the values for Rider B and Rider D significantly differ. When using the $[t - 5s, t]$ interval indicating the exerted power for the inactive rider just before the handsling, it becomes clear that only for Rider C, this exceeds the average power during the $[t - 2s, t + 2s]$ interval as inactive rider. This leads to the conclusion that Rider C exerts too much power just before the handsling, not optimally using the gradient of the track to gain speed. Once the handsling effectively takes place, the rider already gained sufficient speed, causing a less efficient transfer of speed from active to inactive rider.

Table 1. Comparison of average power for different handsling time intervals.

	Handsling Active	$[t-2s, t+2s]$ Active	Handsling Inactive	$[t-2s, t+2s]$ Inactive	$[t-5s, t]$ Inactive
Rider B	149 W	261 W	249 W	373 W	235 W
Rider C	192 W	199 W	174 W	201 W	271 W
Rider D	160 W	232 W	221 W	289 W	227 W

5   Conclusion and Future Work

In this paper, we proposed three approaches for automated madison handsling detection based on performance or motion data. Due to the nature of the madison discipline, variance and covariance metrics are highly suited for this task. Alternatively, the DTW distance between a reference and query sequence can be calculated, with the advantage that data of only one rider is required. Furthermore, use cases were employed to illustrate potential quality assessment statistics. Time between handslings can expose imbalanced active rider durations within a team, whereas power data illustrates how much effort a rider puts into the handsling at what moment in time.

When it comes to analysis of handsling quality, future work might focus on the assignment of an arm motion quality label or score, based on acceleration and gyroscope data. Initial experiments have shown that differences between a high and low quality handsling can be subtle. Thus, collecting data from various rider pairs with different levels of experience will be of utmost importance. Furthermore, other aspects of the madison discipline, e.g. optimal position before a sprint lap and influence of other riders on a handsling are promising topics for future research. Finally, the influence of handsling quality, position and timing on final outcome can probably also be studied in race situation in the future.

References

1. Kholkine, L., De Schepper, T., Verdonck, T., Latré, S.: A machine learning approach for road cycling race performance prediction. In: Brefeld, U., Davis, J., Van Haaren, J., Zimmermann, A. (eds.) MLSA 2020. CCIS, vol. 1324, pp. 103–112. Springer, Cham (2020). https://doi.org/10.1007/978-3-030-64912-8_9
2. Ofoghi, B., Zeleznikow, J., MacMahon, C., Dwyer, D.: A machine learning approach to predicting winning patterns in track cycling omnium. In: Bramer, M. (ed.) IFIP AI 2010. IAICT, vol. 331, pp. 67–76. Springer, Heidelberg (2010). https://doi.org/10.1007/978-3-642-15286-3_7
3. Sakoe, H., Chiba, S.: Dynamic programming algorithm optimization for spoken word recognition. IEEE Trans. Acoust. Speech Signal Process. **26**(1), 43–49 (1978)

4. Underwood, L., Jermy, M.: Determining optimal pacing strategy for the track cycling individual pursuit event with a fixed energy mathematical model. Sports Eng. **17**(4), 183–196 (2014). https://doi.org/10.1007/s12283-014-0153-3
5. Verstockt, S., et al.: Data-driven summarization of broadcasted cycling races by automatic team and rider recognition. In: icSPORTS 2020, the 8th International Conference on Sport Sciences Research and Technology Support, pp. 13–21 (2020)

Using Barycenters as Aggregate Representations of Repetition-Based Time-Series Exercise Data

Bahavathy Kathirgamanathan[1]([✉]), James Davenport[2,3], Brian Caulfield[2,3],
and Pádraig Cunningham[1]

[1] School of Computer Science, University College Dublin, Dublin, Ireland
bahavathy.kathirgamanathan@ucdconnect.ie
[2] School of Public Health, Physiotherapy and Sports Science,
University College Dublin, Dublin, Ireland
[3] Insight Centre for Data Analytics, University College Dublin, Dublin, Ireland

Abstract. This paper introduces the use of time-series barycenter averaging as a means of providing aggregate representations of repetition-based exercises. Time-series averaging is not straightforward as small misalignments can cause key features to be lost. Our evaluation focuses on the Forward Lunge exercise, an exercise that is used for strengthening, screening and rehabilitation. The forward lunge is a repetition-based movement so assessment entails comparing multiple repetitions across sessions. We show that time-series barycenters produced using Dynamic Time Warping are effective for this application. The barycenters preserve the key features in the component time-series and are effective as an aggregate representation for further analysis.

Keywords: Barycenter · Multiple-rep Exercise · Time-Series averaging

1 Introduction

The use of wearable sensors for the detection and evaluation of exercise has become widespread in recent years [6]. Evaluating exercise performance usually involves analysis of multiple repetitions of the same target movement profile [9]. The sensor data is typically high frequency and represents movement in three anatomical frames so each set of repetitions produces a significant amount of data.

In this paper we present a preliminary evaluation of the use of time-series barycenters (TSBs) to aggregate the multiple repetitions into a single 'average' signal. Averaging time-series is not straightforward as small shifts in the phase can cause key shared features to be *smeared out*. In this paper we consider time-series averaging incorporating Dynamic Time Warping (DTW) that stretches (warps) the time-series to find good alignments [11]. TSBs were first introduced to tackle clustering problems in time series research. Since then, TSBs have been

U. Brefeld et al. (Eds.): MLSA 2021, CCIS 1571, pp. 178–188, 2022.
https://doi.org/10.1007/978-3-031-02044-5_15

used mostly for data mining tasks such as data reduction to produce faster and more accurate classification [10]. TSBs have also been used as an averaging strategy in applications such as signature template matching where a mean template is calculated using a time series barycenter [7].

Our analysis compares the DTW based averaging approaches of DTW Barycenter averaging (DBA) and Soft-DTW Barycenter with the more commonly used Euclidean averaging technique in preserving the original features of the time series from the lunge exercises.

Functional exercises in general can be used to determine injury risk and can aid the clinician in recommending injury prevention strategies [3]. The Forward Lunge is a functional exercise that is representative of the lower limb function during activity and hence is commonly used in strength and conditioning, injury risk screening, and rehabilitation [8]. In most clinical settings, interpretation of the forward lunge remains subjective, depending on visual interpretation. Limitations associated with this is the poor level of intra/inter rater reliability and inability to assess multiple aspects simultaneously. 3D motion capture offers an in depth objective alternative but is expensive, time consuming, and restricted to a laboratory environment [8]. Wearable sensors such as Inertial Measurement Units (IMUs) offer a cost-effective and objective method to capture the movement during such exercises. However, this sensor data is time series in nature and due to the vastness of the data being outputted, can be difficult to visualize in a meaningful way. In this paper, we propose that the barycenter can act as an aggregate measure of the time series whilst also preserving the key features required to analyse the quality of the lunge.

The following section describes in detail the data used for evaluation and the concept of the time series barycenter and some of the different approaches that can be used to compute the barycenter. This is followed by an evaluation of the suitability of the different approaches in the representation of multi-rep lunges and the suitability to use barycenters for further data mining tasks.

2 Background

2.1 Multiple Rep Exercises

In sports science, it is common practice to perform repetitions of a functional movement exercise to gain insight into multiple components of that individual's movement pattern or strategy. The data used for this analysis is from a current study focusing on assessing the characteristics of the forward lunge and changes due to alterations in motor function using IMU's (under review). The data was collected using IMU sensors (Shimmer, Ireland) with sensors placed on the shanks, thighs, and the lumbar spine.

The data was collected from 25 participants performing forward lunges before and after an exercise bout, causing central and peripheral fatigue resulting in short term alteration to motor function. Three sets of five repetitions were performed both pre- and post-fatigue. Participants were fatigued through a modified 60-s wingate protocol using a cycle ergometer (Lode, Netherlands) [4]. The

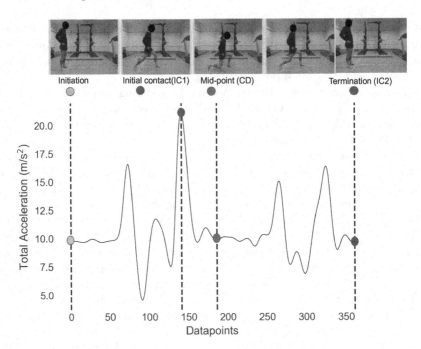

Fig. 1. Time series of forward lunge with corresponding image demonstrating key features used in identification of key lunge characteristics

lunges were performed bilaterally at time intervals 0, 10, and 20 min pre- and post-fatigue. For the analyses carried out in this paper, the signals from the sensor placed on the shanks were used.

The collected data is a set of time series capturing the duration of the lunge. Figure 1 shows a single time series with different stages of the lunge. Each of the features is associated with a functional event during the lunge and hence preserving these features is important in understanding performance. In particular, the initial contact (IC1) is the point where peak acceleration occurs and is a particular point of interest whilst analysing performance.

2.2   Time-Series Barycenter

The time series barycenter is an average measure of a collection of time series. Time series averaging strategies are generally classified as either local or global. Local averaging strategies use pairwise averaging through which a collection of series are iteratively averaged into one series. However, local averaging strategies are dependent on the order in which the series are averaged and hence changing the order could lead to different results. To tackle the problems associated with local averaging strategies, recent advances have looked at global averaging methods which aim to compute the average of the set of time series simultaneously. Two such global averaging strategies are the DTW Barycenter Averaging (DBA) proposed by Petitjean *et al.* [11] and Soft-DTW Barycenter proposed by Cuturi *et al.* [2].

Euclidean distance is generally considered the simplest distance between two series and is simply calculated by summing the point to point distances along the time series. However, Euclidean distance has many drawbacks, in particular when there is an offset in the time series or when we have variable length time series. Hence other similarity measures to deal with time series data have been proposed to improve the overall robustness [1]. One such similarity measure which will be focused on in this paper is Dynamic Time Warping (DTW) [13]. DTW allows for a mapping of the time series in a non-linear way and works to find the optimal alignment between both series. Euclidean mapping is generally a one-to-one mapping between two curves whereas DTW can be considered as a one-to-many mapping. This is illustrated in Fig. 2 where it can be seen that DTW aligns the series while Euclidean simply maps based on the time point.

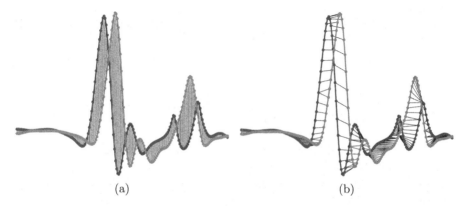

(a)   (b)

Fig. 2. a) Euclidean mapping and b) DTW mapping on part of a lunge exercise. These images were generated by modifying existing code for use with our data (https://github.com/e-alizadeh/medium/blob/master/notebooks/intro_to_dtw.ipynb).

DTW Barycenter averaging (DBA) and Soft-DTW barycenter are two averaging strategies that use the DTW metric and these are described in detail below:

DTW Barycenter Averaging (DBA) computes the optimal average sequence within a group of series in DTW space whereby the sum of squared DTW between the average sequence and the group of series considered is minimised [11]. So computing the DTW barycenter of a set of time series D is the optimisation problem outlined in Eq. 1.

$$\min_{\mu} \sum_{x \in D} DTW(\mu, x)^2 \qquad (1)$$

where x corresponds to a series belonging to the set D and μ is a candidate barycenter. In this optimisation, the DTW distance between each time series and a temporary average sequence (candidate barycenter) is calculated and the association between the coordinates of the average sequence and the time series are sought. This is then used to update the temporary average sequence until the optimal average sequence is found [14].

Soft-DTW barycenter computes the average sequence within a group of series whereby the weighted sum of the Soft-DTW distance between the average sequence and the group of series is minimised. The weights can be different for each sequence in the set but normalised to one [2]. The Soft-DTW approach is an extension of the DBA method where the min operator is replaced by the soft-min. This gives the advantage of being differentiable with respect to all of its inputs. Furthermore, where DTW alone only considers the optimal alignment, Soft-DTW considers all possible alignments. Soft-min can be computed as shown by Eq. 1 [16].

$$\text{softmin}_\gamma(a_1, ..., a_n) = -\gamma \log \sum_i e^{-a_i/\gamma} \tag{2}$$

γ acts as the smoothing parameter and hence as $\gamma \to 0$, the result gets closer to that of DTW.

3   Preliminary Evaluation

To evaluate the suitability of using barycenters to aggregate multi-rep exercise data, the ability of the barycenters to preserve key features and be representative of the entire set of the lunge data was analysed. Signals streamed from the wide range tri-axial accelerometer ($\pm 16g$) at a sampling rate of 102.5 Hz were used in this study. The total acceleration was derived as the magnitude of the acceleration independent of the direction as shown in Eq. 3.

$$a_{total} = \sqrt{a_x^2 + a_y^2 + a_z^2} \tag{3}$$

The signals were passed through a low-pass Butterworth filter with order of 6 and cut-off frequency 10 Hz to remove the high frequency noise and ensure that only the signals corresponding to the movement due to the lunge was considered. The series were all segmented prior to the analysis through an automated algorithm that searches for the key features in the lunge. The analysis used the entire time series from initiation to termination and hence all the lunges are aligned based on the initiation point. Hence any misalignments between sets of lunges will be minor and mostly due to varying tempos at which each lunge is performed. This is of importance as DTW is known to be sensitive to misalignments at the start or end of the time series. Although not within the scope of this paper, in cases where it is not possible to align the start point of the time series, psi-DTW which allows relaxation of endpoint can be considered [15]. The barycenters were all

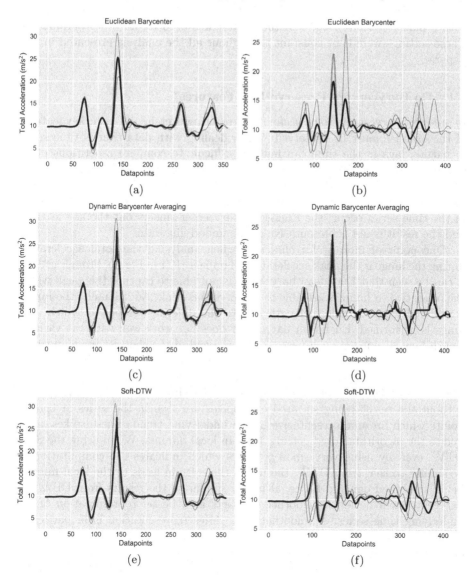

Fig. 3. Three repetitions of the lunge and the corresponding barycenter. Euclidean barycenter on a (a) well aligned set and (b) not well aligned set; DBA on (c) well aligned set and (d) not well aligned set; Soft-DTW barycenter on (e) well aligned set and (f) not well aligned set.

computed using the tslearn python package which provides machine learning tools for working with time series [16]. Soft-DTW barycenter, Euclidean averaging, and DBA were applied on the lunge data of 25 participants. The Soft-DTW was computed using a γ value of 10 and max iteration of 100. DBA was also computed with a max iteration of 100 and the default was used for all other parameters. These settings were kept constant throughout all the analysis presented in this paper.

3.1 Do Barycenters Preserve Key Features?

In order for barycenters to be useful in aggregating exercise data, the key features of the exercise must be preserved. When dealing with data that is time series in nature, lags in the time can make it difficult to compare repetitions of an exercise and hence difficult to get an aggregate measure. In Fig. 3(a, c, e) we can see that when the time series are all nicely aligned, all the methods do a reasonable job of capturing the underlying trend. However once misalignments in the time series occur, the Euclidean barycenter smears out the key features and the result is not representative of the underlying data.

One point of interest for clinicians when analysing the total acceleration during the lunge is the peak acceleration of impact (IC1 in Fig. 1). From Fig. 3(b), it can be seen that Euclidean barycenter is not able to capture this peak whilst the other two techniques are able to preserve this peak. Additionally, the lunges considered were variable in length due to the differing tempos at which each lunge is performed. Euclidean barycenter does not work well with the variable length lunges as it only computes up till the end of the shortest lunge meaning that any part of the lunges after this point is not considered. Both DTW methods are able to take the variable lengths into consideration in their computation.

Although, DBA is able to capture the underlying pattern of the time series without the result being smeared out, spikes are seen in the series at certain points which are unrepresentative of the underlying trend. These spikes occur due to the algorithms used getting stuck in local minima. When using the Soft-DTW, even by using very small γ values which indicates the computation to be similar to that from DTW, the use of the softmin leads to the local minima being smoothed out and hence, although similar to the results from DBA, the barycenter will be much smoother and acts as a better representation of the underlying time series. A smoother time series representation is in particular ideal for visualisation purposes and will be more meaningful for the physio or end user.

A comparison of the different methods indicates that the Soft-DTW provides the best visualisation of the underlying trends in the time series data of the lunge.

3.2 Using Barycenters to Represent Lunge Sets

Having an aggregate measure of a set of lunges, helps to visualise the data and facilitates comparisons across sets. The last three lunges of each set of five repetitions were used in this analysis. This is a common practice while working with multiple repetitions of data to avoid any learning effects there may be in the first two lunges.

To test the effectiveness of the barycenter measure at an individual level, the correlation between the peak acceleration obtained from each set of three lunges

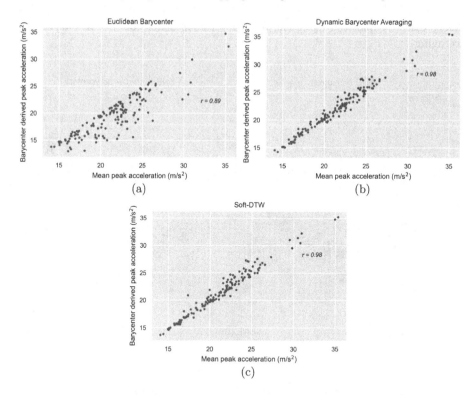

Fig. 4. Correlation plot between the mean peak acceleration from each three lunge set vs the peak acceleration from the corresponding barycenter for (a) Euclidean barycenter (b) DBA and (c) Soft-DTW barycenter

and its corresponding barycenter were analysed. The mean peak for the three lunges was computed simply by averaging the three peak accelerations. Figure 4 (b) and (c) show that using a DTW measure preserves the peak acceleration across the sets of lunges with both having a Pearson's correlation coefficient of 0.98. The Euclidean barycenter (Fig. 4 (c)) is also able to preserve some of the peaks very well whilst completely underestimating the peak for other sets of lunges and this can be attributed to how well the lunges are aligned to start with. As Soft-DTW shows the ability to preserve key features of the lunge and is representative of individual lunges sets, it is used as the choice of barycenter for all subsequent analysis.

3.3   Using Barycenters for Further Analysis

Data collected from multiple-rep exercises are often used for data mining tasks such as classification or clustering. Multiple-rep data can be noisy where one 'bad' repetition of the exercise can affect the quality of the data. Aggregating the data can reduce this noise and hence barycenters may help give better results for data mining tasks. This hypothesis is tested by comparing how well the classes can be separated using the full data versus using Soft-DTW barycenter averaging.

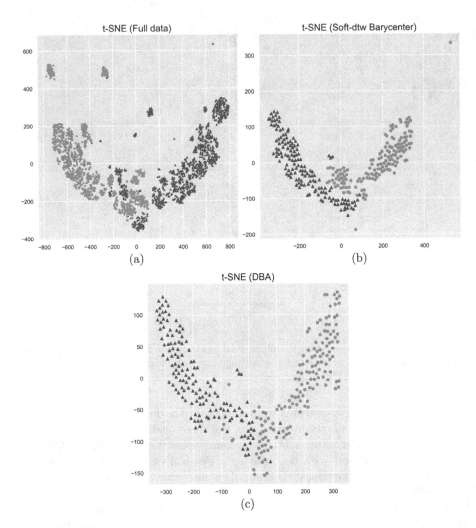

Fig. 5. t-SNE plotted for (a) full data and (b) Soft-DTW Barycenter where the two colours represent two classes

To visualise this capability to reduce noise, a t-distributed Stochastic Neighbour Embedding (t-SNE) [5] was used on the lunge data to reduce the 3D time series data into a 2D map. t-SNE is non-linear technique for dimensionality reduction and is generally used as a visualisation technique to represent high-dimensional datasets. For this analysis, the task of identifying left leg led vs right leg led lunges was considered. Figure 5 shows a t-SNE plot of the lunges with the two colours representing the different classes (Left leg vs Right leg). Each point in the plot represents a time series of the respective class. The Soft-DTW and DBA plots show the same data as in the full-data t-SNE plot but represented as aggregated barycenters. PCA initialization was used as it is known to be more globally stable than random initialization. It is clear that the DBA and Soft-DTW barycenters (Fig. 5b, c) provide a clearer separation between the two classes than is possible when working with the full data (Fig. 5a). This better separation will facilitate clustering. To test the goodness of the clusters of the two classes, the silhouette score was calculated [12]. The silhouette score measures the goodness of fit of clusters where the closer the score is to 1, the better separation there is between clusters and hence the classes should be more easily distinguishable. The full data from the t-SNE plot had a Silhouette score of 0.470 while the Soft-DTW barycenter had a Silhouette score of 0.492 and the DBA had a Silhouette score of 0.543. This suggests better separation when using the dtw techniques with DBA giving the best separation for this set of data.

4 Conclusions and Future Work

Preliminary evaluation shows the Soft-DTW barycenter to be an effective way of aggregating the time series from repetitions of an exercise into an 'averaged' series. The key features of multiple reps of the lunge were preserved in the Soft-DTW barycenters whereas the other approaches attempted did not perform as well in providing an accurate visualisation of the average. Particularly, the Soft-DTW approach performed well where there were phase shifts in the data. Furthermore, barycenter averaging shows potential for use in data mining tasks by allowing better separation between the classes.

The use of barycenters for the aggregation of time series can be useful in healthcare and sports studies where repeated trials are made as it helps to easily visualise the overall trend and better steer clinical decision making. This work can be extended for data reduction purposes, which could prove useful in clustering or classification tasks. Hence, as future work, an analysis of how classification/clustering performance is impacted by barycenter aggregation would be beneficial.

Acknowledgements. This work has emanated from research conducted with the financial support of Science Foundation Ireland under the Grant numbers 18/CRT/6183 and 12/RC/2289_P2. For the purpose of Open Access, the author has applied a CC BY public copyright license to any Author Accepted Manuscript version arising from this submission.

References

1. Cassisi, C., Montalto, P., Aliotta, M., Cannata, A., Pulvirenti, A.: Similarity measures and dimensionality reduction techniques for time series data mining (2012)
2. Cuturi, M., Blondel, M.: Soft-DTW: a differentiable loss function for time-series. In: 34th International Conference on Machine Learning, ICML 2017, vol. 2, pp. 1483–1505 (2017)

3. Garrison, M., Westrick, R., Johnson, M.R., Benenson, J.: Association between the functional movement screen and injury development in college athletes. Int. J. Sports Phys. Therapy **10**(1), 21 (2015)
4. Johnston, W., O'Reilly, M., Coughlan, G., Caulfield, B.: Inertial sensor technology can capture changes in dynamic balance control during the Y balance test. Digital Biomark. **1**(2), 106–117 (2018). https://doi.org/10.1159/000485470
5. Van der Maaten, L., Hinton, G.: Visualizing data using t-SNE. J. Mach. Learn. Res. **9**(11), 1–10 (2008)
6. Muro-De-La-Herran, A., Garcia-Zapirain, B., Mendez-Zorrilla, A.: Gait analysis methods: an overview of wearable and non-wearable systems, highlighting clinical applications. Sensors **14**(2), 3362–3394 (2014)
7. Okawa, M.: Template matching using time-series averaging and DTW with dependent warping for online signature verification. IEEE Access **7**, 81010–81019 (2019). https://doi.org/10.1109/ACCESS.2019.2923093
8. O'Reilly, M.A., Whelan, D.F., Ward, T.E., Delahunt, E., Caulfield, B.: Classification of lunge biomechanics with multiple and individual inertial measurement units. Sports Biomech. **16**(3), 342–360 (2017)
9. O'Reilly, M., Caulfield, B., Ward, T., Johnston, W., Doherty, C.: Wearable inertial sensor systems for lower limb exercise detection and evaluation: a systematic review. Sports Med. **48**(5), 1221–1246 (2018)
10. Petitjean, F., Forestier, G., Webb, G.I., Nicholson, A.E., Chen, Y., Keogh, E.: Dynamic time warping averaging of time series allows faster and more accurate classification. In: 2014 IEEE International Conference On Data Mining, pp. 470–479. IEEE (2014)
11. Petitjean, F., Ketterlin, A., Gançarski, P.: A global averaging method for dynamic time warping, with applications to clustering. Pattern Recogn. **44**(3), 678–693 (2011). https://doi.org/10.1016/j.patcog.2010.09.013
12. Rousseeuw, P.J.: Silhouettes: a graphical aid to the interpretation and validation of cluster analysis. J. Comput. Appl. Math. **20**, 53–65 (1987)
13. Sakoe, H., Chiba, S.: Dynamic programming algorithm optimization for spoken word recognition. IEEE Trans. Acoust. Speech Signal Process. **26**(1), 43–49 (1978). https://doi.org/10.1109/TASSP.1978.1163055
14. Shi, K., Qin, H., Sima, C., Li, S., Shen, L., Ma, Q.: Dynamic barycenter averaging kernel in RBF networks for time series classification. IEEE Access **7**, 47564–47576 (2019). https://doi.org/10.1109/ACCESS.2019.2910017
15. Silva, D.F., Batista, G.E.A.P.A., Keogh, E.: On the effect of endpoints on dynamic time warping. In: SIGKDD MiLeTS 2016, p. 10 (2016)
16. Tavenard, R., et al.: tslearn: a machine learning toolkit dedicated to time-series data (2017). https://github.com/rtavenar/tslearn

Non-physical Sports

Exceptional Gestalt Mining: Combining Magic Cards to Make Complex Coalitions Thrive

Wouter Duivesteijn[1](✉) and Thomas C. van Dijk[2]

[1] Technische Universiteit Eindhoven, Eindhoven, the Netherlands
`w.duivesteijn@tue.nl`
[2] Ruhr-Universität Bochum, Bochum, Germany
`thomas.vandijk@ruhr-uni-bochum.de`

Abstract. We propose Exceptional Gestalt Mining (EGM), a variant of Exceptional Model Mining that seeks subgroups of the dataset where a coalition becomes more than the sum of its parts. Suppose a dataset of games in which several roles exist within a team; the team can combine forces from any subset of roles, to achieve a common goal. EGM seeks subgroups for which games played employing a large role set have a higher win rate than games played employing any strict subset of that role set. We illustrate the knowledge EGM can uncover by deploying it on a dataset detailing *Magic: The Gathering* games: we find combinations of cards that jointly work better in multicolor decks than in decks employing fewer colors. We argue that EGM can be deployed on datasets from sports where several roles exist that directly interact in play, such as ice hockey.

Keywords: Local Pattern Mining · Magic: The Gathering · Team Composition · Gestalt · Subgroup Discovery · Exceptional Model Mining

1 Introduction

Magic: The Gathering (MTG, or *Magic* for short) is a turn-based collectible card game, where prior to playing the game proper, one builds a synergistic deck from a set of available cards; in the actual game of Magic, each player uses their own deck (which is typically constructed from the same set, but not necessarily the same sample from the set: some ways of deck construction involve chance or a drafting mechanic). The game was first released in 1993 as physical playing cards and has taken quite a flight since then: the initial stock of 10 million cards sold out within three months; a "Pro Tour" and several independent tournament circuits have existed since at least 1996. The game was patented in 1997 [13] and acquired by Hasbro in 1999 for 325 million dollars. After almost two decades and multiple versions of the much-maligned *Magic Online*, Magic only took off as a proper e-sport in 2018 with the release of *Magic Arena*.

U. Brefeld et al. (Eds.): MLSA 2021, CCIS 1571, pp. 191–204, 2022.
https://doi.org/10.1007/978-3-031-02044-5_16

Forest is a **land**   Jorn, God of Winter is a **spell**

Fig. 1. Two example Magic cards. On the left hand, a basic *land* that provides *mana* of a specific *color* (in this case: green). On the right hand, a *spell* that can be played when the mana cost is paid, some of which must be in specified colors (in this case: two mana of any color plus one green mana). In this example, the Forest can contribute to paying the cost for Jorn, God of Winter. This figure is unofficial Fan Content permitted under the Fan Content Policy. Not approved/endorsed by Wizards. Portions of the materials used are property of Wizards of the Coast. ©Wizards of the Coast LLC. (Color figure online)

1.1 Core Game Mechanics of Magic: The Gathering

A crucial feature of Magic's gameplay is the "mana system". Some of the cards are *lands* that produce mana of a certain *color*[1] (white, blue, black, red, or green). This mana is a resource used to play other cards called *spells*, which actually produce game effects as indicated on the card. This typically advances the game state in a manner that brings the player closer to their end goal. A game of Magic can be won in various ways, most prominently by reducing the opponent's life points from the starting total of 20 down to zero (or below) and by depleting the opponent's deck; other win conditions also exist, as specified by individual cards.

Of particular relevance to our analysis are the five *basic lands*, which are the main ways to acquire each color of mana. Most spells specify that part of their cost must be paid with mana of a specific color (or set of colors); a spell is said to be a certain color if it requires mana of that color. Figure 1 gives an example of a basic land and a spell that share a color; hence, the former can contribute to paying the cost required for playing the latter.

Beginning players often limit themselves to building a deck of cards using only a single color (for example: only forests and green spells). This is at least somewhat synergistic, since the cards of each color tend to lean into particular playing styles (with strengths and weaknesses) and the deck needs only one

---

[1] Most of our descriptions of the game are not completely accurate. With over 20 000 distinct cards there is an exception to almost any generalization. In this case: some lands can produce mana of multiple colors, or produce no mana at all. Our descriptions only serve to illustrate the context of the dataset.

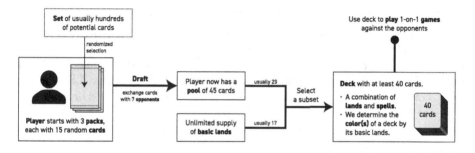

Fig. 2. Flowchart detailing the process of a Magic draft.

color of mana – and therefore only one type of basic land. Playing more than one color in the same deck allows the player to balance weaknesses with strengths and to combine powerful cards that happen to be in different colors. However, this introduces the risk of drawing mismatched lands and spells. The strategy behind color choice and selecting the optimal mix of lands (the "mana base") is deep and extensively discussed in the community. Here, we leave it at the observation that many decks play two colors. Even among professional players, a typical rule of thumb is that one is best served by limiting colors in a deck to two or three; exceptions of course exist.

In this paper, we analyze data from *draft* Magic, where the players open a booster pack containing a random selection of 15 cards from a particular set, select a card from the pack for their own pool, and pass the remainder of the pack to the next player. This process of selecting a card and passing on the others continues in a cycle until no cards remain, after which new packs are opened. In total, three packs are opened per player, and these three packs typically contain an identical distribution stemming from a certain collection of cards (called a *set*) such that gameplay can be expected to be thematically coherent. All players in a draft of Magic will see only a small subset of cards in the game: they will not have access to the same sample of cards and each will need to craft a coherent deck from whichever cards they managed to acquire through the drafting process. Independently of the draft packs, they may add any number of each of the five basic lands. See Fig. 2 for an overview of this process.

1.2   Gathered Data

For players who want to analyze their performance in online draft Magic, the people at 17lands.com – so-named after the conventional wisdom that playing 17 lands in a 40-card draft deck is optimal (although, again, exceptions apply) – have created an application that monitors the Magic Arena log files to track the state of the drafts performed and games played. The goal is not only to help players understand their own performance, but also to enable analytical insights from aggregated data. Some of these datasets are publicly available [20].

We analyze the Kaldheim (KHM) Traditional Draft dataset [19]. This is a single csv file containing game-level data. Every row describes a single game: its outcome (win/loss), some metadata on the players, the list of cards drafted by the player, and the list of cards in the player's deck. Existing analyses of this dataset focus on finding individual cards that affect the win rate: if it is in the deck, how is the win rate affected? Or: does it come at an increased or decreased win rate for the top-10% or bottom-10% players?

1.3   Main Contribution

In this paper we investigate the concept of *gestalt*: a whole that is bigger than the sum of its parts. We seek combinations of cards, that work better when they are in decks containing a bigger coalition of colors: we will deem the combination of cards interesting, if its performance in the multicolor combination is substantially better than its performance in subcoalitions of fewer colors.

Our main contribution is Exceptional Gestalt Mining, an instance of Exceptional Model Mining [12] that finds such exceptional combinations. This is also valuable for some major sports leagues, especially team sports where players have distinct roles or styles but do interact synergistically.

2   Related Entities

2.1   Related Work on Magic: The Gathering

Magic has already received some interest from the academic community [3], though not necessarily from an analytics perspective. Magic as a rule system is very complex – indeed, following the rules is Turing complete [6][2] and even checking whether particular game moves are legal is coNP-complete [4]. As a game with partial hidden information, its strategy is also challenging [5]. More tangentially, Magic and its community have been the subject of experimental studies on auction design [22] and marketing [23].

Outside of academia there is a large and active corpus of online strategy advice; as mentioned in the introduction, this ranges from folklore and anecdote to fairly advanced probability theory and more recently: data mining. Central to a lot of the discussion is the concept of *win percentage*: what fraction of games played against a (theoretical) field of opponents, including the distribution of player skill and their deck selection, do you expect to win? This is precisely the kind of data that is sampled by 17lands.com. In informal blog publications [7–9,24,25], they discuss wide-ranging themes revolving around this data, including the effect on win rate of a changed mulligan rule [8], simulations of draft strategies [9], winning deck archetypes in the Kaldheim set [24], and the limitations of win rate as a measure of success [25].

---

[2] Cards can react to in-game events with new effects of their own and the game rules define that if an unbreakable loop occurs, then the game is a draw; simulating a Turing machine with the available cards is nontrivial, but was finally achieved in 2019 after multiple steps of partial progress.

2.2 Related Work on Local Pattern Mining

Exceptional Gestalt Mining is a form of Local Pattern Mining (LPM), a sub-field of data mining exploring local structures in a dataset. The best-known LPM method is Frequent Itemset Mining and its cousin Association Rule Mining [1]. Here, all data is binary, and the focus lies on finding sets of products that co-occur frequently in transactions. Associations between these sets are sought; the process is unsupervised. Supervised Descriptive versions of LPM [18] exist. Subgroup Discovery (SD) [15,16,26] is such a version, seeking subgroups of the dataset where a designated target variable displays an unusual distribution. Emerging Pattern Mining [10] and Contrast Set Mining [2] employ different task formulations, which have been shown [18] to be unifiable with SD.

Exceptional Model Mining (EMM) [12,21] can be seen as a multi-target generalization of SD. Rather than a single target, EMM typically designates several columns as targets. Whereas SD assesses the interestingness of subgroups in terms of a difference in target distribution, EMM typically seeks a behavioral difference in some sort of interaction between the targets. For instance, one could seek an unusual correlation between two targets [21], allowing the identification of subgroups of the housing market where the lot size and sales price of a house are uncorrelated, while this correlation is positive on the entire dataset.

This last example illustrates an interesting design choice in EMM: in order to find subgroups displaying exceptional behavior, one must choose when behavior is exceptional; to do so, one must characterize what constitutes normal behavior. Naive approaches [12, Section 3.2.2] take behavior on the full dataset or the complement of the subgroup as a proxy for normality. This assumes that behavior on the entire dataset can be treated as a monolithic whole, which may not be realistic. A recent alternative [11] employs the Chinese Restaurant Process to model multiple kinds of normal behavior in the dataset; a subgroup is exceptional if its behavior matches none of the normal behaviors. Yet another alternative only compares a subgroup's behavior locally, with the behavior of a peer group [14, 17]. We take yet another approach, evaluating subgroups by seeking an *internal* behavioral bifurcation: a subgroup is interesting if it performs much better in a specific coalition of colors than it does in all subcoalitions; this evaluation is agnostic to behavior outside the subgroup.

2.3 Related Sports

So far we talked a lot about a card game and the potential for mining due to the availability of data. This paper, however, appears in the Proceedings of the 8th Workshop on Machine Learning and Data Mining for Sports Analytics. Besides arguing that Magic is a legitimate e-sport with professional players, we believe that there are fruitful parallels particularly to *team* sports. One way to make the analogy is as follows.

A deck consisting of Magic cards can be seen as the total set of players that a sports organization[3] has available to compete in matches in a season. Not all of these players participate in every individual team sports game, and similarly, not all cards in the deck are drawn during a particular game of Magic. A draft, like the one described for Magic, happens in all the big North American sports leagues (NBA, NFL, MLB, NHL), where organizations take turns to select new players from a limited pool; specific draft mechanics will be different across sports league from the ones in Magic, but the turn-based limited resources concept is shared. The colors of Magic – with distinct strengths and weaknesses that a deck can emphasize or counteract through combination – can be likened to strategic or tactical roles that players can have within the team. Some of these roles might have a tendency to synergize, such as "patient defense" with "counter attack" in Association Football, or the combination of red and white cards in so-called aggro decks; this does not mean that every red card works well with every white card, or that every patient defender plays well with every fast runner. Some players or combinations of players might perform especially well in teams that include a particular role other than their own (most interestingly when this not a general synergy between the roles, but in some way an exceptional synergy). A specific hockey center might score more shorthanded goals from assists of certain defenders on a specific penalty kill unit, than even-strength goals from open play on regular lines; a cheap green card that enables "mana fixing" might do particularly well when combined with red and white, even if green cards in general might not.

The concept we strive to find in this paper, a combination of Magic cards (or: players in a sports team) that works better in a particular multicolor coalition than in smaller subcoalitions, maps better to some sporting contexts than others. The analogy does not work well for the NFL, for example. In an American Football team, the offensive and defensive lines both work towards a common goal, but they never interact: these lines are never on the field at the same time. There may be some overlap between the offense or defense and some of the special teams, but by and large, gestalt cannot be expected between these lines. The analogy works much better for the NHL as seen by the example in the previous paragraph. In an Ice Hockey team, offensive and defensive lines each have their own major roles: offense should largely score goals, defense should largely avoid conceding goals. But these lines are on the field simultaneously, and the team cannot function well by focusing on a single strategy to the neglect of all others[4].

---

[3] Depending on what a specific sports league allows, this may include the current main squad, youth players, minor league affiliate team players, loan players, and players acquired in mid-season transfers.

[4] In fact, one standard hockey player performance metric, called $+/-$, acknowledges that good defenders enable a strong offense and good offensive lines contribute to a strong defense. The metric records the number of goals the team scores while you are on the ice, minus the number of goals the team concedes while you are on the ice. Hence, top-scoring centers or wingers who neglect their defensive duties can be found out by comparing their performance in terms of goals and assists with their performance in terms of $+/-$.

In some top NHL teams, offensive lines can be clustered into those that excel in offense itself, and those that excel in defensive support. Here, the synergy between offensive and defensive lines becomes of paramount importance: if an offensive line gels really well with a defensive line, their combination becomes much more than the sum of their parts. This is where exceptional gestalt can be found.

3   Exceptional Gestalt Mining

We assume a dataset Ω, which is a bag of N *games* of the form $g^j = (a_1^j, \ldots, a_k^j, R^j, \ell^j)$; the superscript index j refers to a specific game, and is omitted when unnecessary. Here, $a_1, \ldots, a_k$ are the *entities* in the data: binary columns indicating Magic cards, or sports players, that can form a part of an exceptional combination. The final column, ℓ, is the *outcome* of the game, which is binary: the game is either won or lost. Finally, we assume the existence of a set $\mathcal{R}$ of *roles* within the game: this can be the set of colors in an Magic game or the set of roles players take on a hockey team[5]. During every game g^j, a set $R^j \subseteq \mathcal{R}$ of roles is *deployed*.

Exceptional Gestalt Mining (EGM) falls under the framework [12] of Exceptional Model Mining (EMM), which seeks interpretable subsets of the dataset that behave exceptionally. A subgroup is defined as a conjunction of conditions on the entities (for instance: $a_7 = \text{false} \land a_{112} = \text{true}$), and this logical expression selects a subset of games from Ω. Informally, we call the conjunction the *description*, and the selected subset the corresponding *subgroup*, although we will conflate the two concepts if no confusion can result. Formally, we let a description D be a function $D : (a_1, \ldots, a_k) \to \{0, 1\}$, and the subgroup G_D corresponding to description D will be $G_D = \{ g^j \in \Omega \mid D(a_1^j, \ldots, a_k^j) = 1 \}$.

The beam search algorithm for EMM [12, Algorithm 1] traverses the space of candidate subgroups, evaluating their exceptionality along the way. That evaluation requires a *quality measure* φ, taking a description (or subgroup) as input and returning a value in $\mathbb{R}$, where conventionally higher is better. Philosophically, the quality measure must reflect how exceptional within-subgroup behavior is, when compared with behavior on a well-chosen reference group. This behavior can be a simple correlation coefficient or slope of a regression model, and the reference group could be the entire dataset. For EGM, however, we make different choices. The *win rate* of a subset $G \subseteq \Omega$ is $\varphi_{\text{winrate}}(G) = \frac{1}{|G|} \sum_{g^j \in G} \ell^j$. We could use this quality measure to find (combinations of) cards where the win rate is exceptionally high or low, but this would merely tell us what the best or worst cards in the pool are. Instead, we look at how win rate and roles interact.

---

[5] There may be multiple granularities on which roles make sense. For instance, in a hockey team, one can specify $\mathcal{R} = \{\text{defender, goalkeeper, forward}\}$ or $\mathcal{R} = \{\text{center, defender, goalkeeper, left winger, right winger}\}$. In Exceptional Gestalt Mining, we need to pick one set of roles, and stick with it.

3.1   Measuring Exceptional Gestalt

It is quite likely that a given combination of cards, when used as a description, defines a subset of games featuring more than a single distinct role set. We explore this spectrum of role sets, and the distribution of win rates across that spectrum. Given a subgroup G_D, define its *Role Set Set* (RSS) to be

$$RSS(G_D) = \left\{ \, R^j \mid g^j \in G_D \, \right\}$$

and its *Conditional Win Rate* (CWR) *given role* R as:

$$\varphi_{\text{cwr}}(G_D, R) = \frac{\displaystyle\sum_{g^j \in G_D \text{ s.t. } R^j = R} \ell^j}{\left| \left\{ \, g^j \in \Omega \,\middle|\, D(a_1^j, \ldots, a_k^j) = 1 \,\wedge\, R^j = R \, \right\} \right|}$$

The *gestalt* quality measure can now be defined:

$$\varphi_{\text{gestalt}}(G_D) = \max_{R_i \in RSS(G_D)} \left(\varphi_{\text{cwr}}(G_D, R_i) - \max_{\substack{R_j \in RSS(G_D) \\ R_j \subset R_i}} \varphi_{\text{cwr}}(G_D, R_j) \right) \quad (1)$$

Hence, we seek subgroups for which the CWR given a role set R_i is larger than its CWR given the best possible strict role subset $R_j \subset R_i$. The subgroup for which this distance is largest, is the subgroup with the most exceptional gestalt.

3.2   Why Does This Make Sense, Intuitively Speaking?

If a card r requires mana of a specific color, say, red, it will only function in decks that can produce red mana. If another card b requires black mana, most decks featuring r and b will contain both Mountains and Swamps (the red and black basic lands). For this combination of two cards, we expect the RSS to consist of supersets of {red, black}. It is possible that the combination of r and b works even better when combined with playing styles that are typically associated with a third color, e.g. blue. In this case, there is not necessarily a *specific* blue card u that interacts well with r and b (though a positive association with most good blue cards is likely present). However, one can expect that the combination of r and b has a higher CWR in decks with role set {red, black, blue} than its CWR in decks with role set {red, black}. In fact, even more colors may be necessary to unleash the full potential of the card combination. This sort of added value is the gestalt for which EGM is designed.

4   Experimental Setup

The Kaldheim Traditional Game Dataset [19] encompasses 182 401 rows, each detailing a single game. The dataset logs match information from the point of view of one of the two players in the game, namely the player who has installed the 17 Lands plugin. Hence, in each row there is a player and an opponent, which the dataset does not treat symmetrically. We use the 321 columns detailing which of the available cards are in the deck of the player (the opposing deck is unknown). In the original dataset – and the game – a card can occur more than once in a deck. We convert these columns to binary conditions: does it appear in the deck at all? These columns form the *entities* $a_1, \ldots, a_{321}$ in EGM. The binary column indicating if the player won the game is the outcome ℓ in EGM.

To perform EGM, we need to know what colors are present in the player's deck. We infer this by aggregating over the card information columns representing that color's basic lands (including snow-covered variants): if the deck contains *Forest*, we say the color *green* plays a role in this deck. Applying this for all basic lands and colors, we obtain the set of deployed roles R for this game.

Our EGM implementation is built on an existing EMM implementation [11]. Source code can be found at our companion website[6]. We parameterize the underlying beam search algorithm for EMM ([12, Algorithm 1]) by setting the beam width $w = 100$, the search depth $d = 3$, and the number of reported subgroups $q = 100$; these settings are in line with existing work. In order to prevent the discovery of spurious subgroups, we skip any terms R_i and R_j in either maximum of Equation (1) if the support for that G_D combined with that role set is below 200.

5   Experimental Results

First and foremost, notice that $\varphi_{\text{winrate}}(\Omega) = 0.54$. Since every MTG game has a winner and a loser, the win rate in the general population must necessarily be 0.5. However, the players in our dataset opted to install the 17 Lands plugin to track their statistics, and it stands to reason that this sample of players skews away from the most casual players, which in turn likely skews the win rate upwards.

For each experiment that follows, we report the top-five distinct subgroups found with Exceptional Gestalt Mining. More results can be found for all these experiments on our companion website (see footnote 6). Here we report distinct subgroups; if a subgroup of the form A ∧ B performs best, the subgroup B ∧ A typically ranks second. Such duplicates are filtered out of the results reported here.

5.1   Main Results

Table 1 lists the top-five distinct subgroups found with Exceptional Gestalt Mining. The top subgroup combines two cards. Raise the Draugr is a black card that resurrects creatures that died earlier in battle. Glittering Frost is a green card that allows a land to generate additional mana of any color. Decks in which these cards jointly appear almost surely have black and green in their role set; the result in the table indicates that these cards perform best in an extended

---

[6] http://wwwis.win.tue.nl/~wouter/Gestalt/.

Table 1. Top-5 distinct subgroups found with Exceptional Gestalt Mining.

# Description	φ_{gestalt}	Best Role Set R_i (CWR(R_i))	Second Best R_j (CWR(R_j))
1. Raise the Draugr ∧ Glittering Frost	0.2002	WUBG (64.5)	WBG (43.5)
2. Jorn, God of Winter ∧ Snow-Covered Forest ∧ Sculptor of Winter	0.1902	WUBRG (73.7)	UBRG (54.6)
3. Jorn, God of Winter ∧ Glittering frost	0.1872	WUBRG (72.7)	UBG (54.0)
4. Sulfurous Mire ∧ Masked Vandal	0.1821	WUBRG (63.9)	WBRG (45.7)
5. Inga, Rune Eyes ∧ Behold the Multiverse ∧ Berg Strider	0.1800	UBR (65.8)	UB (47.8)

role set with white and blue (the latter is abbreviated as U, since B is black); the conditional win rate of this card duo in WUBG decks is 20 percentage points higher than its CWR in any strict subset of this color set. It is not obvious how these two cards synergize specifically with each other, but a more general interpretation is possible. Glittering Frost makes any color of mana, thereby enabling large role sets. However, due to the specifics of Magic gameplay, Glittering Frost is best suited for long, drawn-out games – which is exactly the kind of game where Raise the Draugr is effective.

The second subgroup combines three cards with explicit internal synergy. Jorn, God of Winter is a green snow creature card; when it attacks, all snow permanents are untapped (i.e.: become available for further use in the same turn). Snow-Covered Forest is a source of green mana that would be untapped by Jorn attacking. Sculptor of Winter is a green snow creature that can untap a snow land, which could be the Snow-Covered Forest; since it is a snow creature itself, it gets untapped by Jorn attacking, which allows it to untap a further snow land. All these cards are green, which does not make it immediately apparent why they would be prime candidates for the all-color role set that EGM finds for them. However, all three cards interact with snow, which is a recurring theme throughout cards of all colors in the Kaldheim set, and they make snow-related mana sources and cards more flexible in use. We postulate that these cards make it feasible to unleash the full potential of decks encompassing powerful cards of all colors: without these cards, it would be difficult to juggle mana sources of all colors; with these cards, this is less of a problem. As a consequence, the CWR of this trio of cards in all-color decks is 19.02 percentage points higher than its CWR for any strict subset of colors.

Table 2. Top-5 distinct subgroups found with Exceptional Gestalt Mining while limiting evaluation to role sets involving a maximal number of roles.

(a) Evaluation limited to roles sets with at most four roles.

# Description	φ_{gestalt}	R_i
1. Raise the Draugr ∧ Glittering Frost	0.2002	WUBG
2. Inga, Rune Eyes ∧ Berg Strider ∧ Behold the Multiverse	0.1800	UBR
3. Disdainful Stroke ∧ Bind the Monster	0.1754	WUBG
4. Shimmerdrift Vale ∧ Narfi, Betrayer King ∧ Snow-Covered Island	0.1705	UBR
5. Shimmerdrift Vale ∧ Jarl of the Forsaken ∧ Snow-Covered Swamp	0.1701	UBGR

(b) Evaluation limited to roles sets with at most three roles.

# Description	φ_{gestalt}	R_i
1. Inga, Rune Eyes ∧ Berg Strider ∧ Behold the Multiverse	0.1800	UBR
2. Shimmerdrift Vale ∧ Narfi, Betrayer King ∧ Snow-Covered Island	0.1705	UBR
3. Behold the Multiverse ∧ Bind the Monster ∧ Ice Tunnel	0.1664	UBR
4. Inga, Rune Eyes ∧ Behold the Multiverse ∧ Snow-Covered Island	0.1648	UBR
5. Disdainful Stroke ∧ Augury Raven ∧ Snow-Covered Island	0.1645	UBR

(c) Evaluation limited to roles sets with at most two roles.

# Description	φ_{gestalt}	R_i
1. Tuskeri Firewalker ∧ Axgard Cavalry	0.0483	UR
2. Tuskeri Firewalker	0.0420	UR
3. Breakneck Berserker ∧ Axgard Cavalry	0.0417	WR
4. Battlefield Raptor	0.0339	WG
5. Run Amok	0.0326	WR

We observe a theme in the top results. They do not necessarily involve cards that display multicolor synergies among themselves. Instead, they are often sets of coherently-behaving cards that allow for more color flexibility (either explicitly by making mana of different colors or by stalling for time, so more lands may be drawn), thus allowing a deck to make the most of multicolor synergies in the wider card set.

5.2 Results When Limiting the Number of Roles

In order to perhaps find more specific results, we change our experiments as follows: in the evaluation of exceptionality with φ_{gestalt}, we only allow role sets R_i to take part that consist of at most r roles. Games with bigger role sets still contribute to the support of a subgroup, but they take no part in CWR computations. Results when limiting the evaluation in this manner can be found in Table 2, for $r \in \{4, 3, 2\}$.

We observe that all top-5 subgroups for $r = 3$ (and indeed, 69 of the top-100) have UBR (blue-black-red) as the superior role set. For all those subgroups, UB is the second-best role set and has a losing record, even though UB in general (outside the subgroup) has good win percentage. That is, of the decks playing these specific cards, the ones with role set UBR have high win rate, but the ones with role set UB have win rate under 0.5 (and other role sets are even worse or have insufficient support).

6   Conclusions

We introduce Exceptional Gestalt Mining (EGM) as a form of Exceptional Model Mining, seeking subgroups whose combination delivers more than just the sum of their parts. EGM is applicable on datasets of games that are either won or lost, where a set of entities can play part in the game or not, and where a set of *roles* exist in the dataset of which a subset is deployed during the game. In such a dataset, EGM finds subgroups of entities whose win rate when a larger coalition of roles is deployed, is substantially higher than its win rate when each strict subset of that role coalition is deployed. Hence, these subgroups display an exceptional level of gestalt.

On a dataset of the Kaldheim Traditional Draft, an online game setting of the collectible card game *Magic: The Gathering*, EGM finds card combinations having a higher win rate in large multicolor decks than in decks of subsets of that color coalition. For instance, in Table 1 we see that the combination of *Jorn, God of Winter*, *Snow-Covered Forest*, and *Sculptor of Winter* has a win rate 19 percentage points higher in decks of all five colors than in decks of fewer colors. All these cards are green; they could function fine in a monocolor green deck. However, their combination makes the deck more versatile, which enables easier combination of forces of multiple colors in a single deck. This is the sort of gestalt that EGM can detect in a dataset.

We argue that EGM is directly deployable on data from major sports leagues, such as the NHL. In its current form, EGM requires a game to have a binary outcome, and a clearly defined subset of the team entities that contributed to the win or loss. A complete NHL game seems incompatible with this setting: players are subbed on or off the rink at will, and a game has a score as outcome (which can be converted to a win/loss binary outcome, but is richer than that); it is not immediately apparent which players contributed to the win or loss. However, the gap can be bridged by decomposing an NHL game into individual scoring plays; a goal scored corresponds to a win for the players currently on the ice, while a goal conceded corresponds to a loss. Hence, Exceptional Gestalt Mining can find synergy between NHL players on specific lines, measured in terms that are related to the standard hockey $+/-$ player performance metric. In future work, we plan to deploy EGM as is on such data.

Additionally, we intend to make intelligent use of more information that is present in the Kaldheim dataset (or can be derived from it), but which currently goes untouched. For instance, we know for each game which roles were observed from the deck of the opponent (possibly a subset of all colors in their deck); it stands to reason that certain coalitions have stronger gestalt when opposed by certain colors than when opposed by others. We also know how many turns each game took (gestalt in faster/slower decks[7]), and in what win rate bracket the player resides (gestalt for experienced/novice players); incorporating such information in EGM may uncover further interesting subgroups.

References

1. Agrawal, R., Srikant, R.: Fast algorithms for mining association rules in large databases. In: Proceedings of VLDB, pp. 487–499 (1994)
2. Bay, S.D., Pazzani, M.J.: Detecting group differences: mining contrast sets. Data Min. Knowl. Discov. **5**(3), 213–246 (2001)
3. Bosch, R.A.: Optimal card-collecting strategies for magic: the gathering. College Math. J. **31**(1), 15–21 (2000)
4. Chatterjee, K., Ibsen-Jensen, R.: The complexity of deciding legality of a single step of magic: the gathering. In: Proceedings of European Conference on AI (2016)
5. Cowling, P.I., Ward, C.D., Powley, E.J.: Ensemble determinization in Monte Carlo tree search for the imperfect information card game magic: the gathering. IEEE Trans. Comp. Int. AI Games **4**(4), 241–257 (2012)
6. Churchill, A., Biderman, S., Herrick, A.: Magic: The Gathering is Turing Complete (2019). arXiv preprint: arXiv:1904.09828 [cs.AI]
7. Conroy, R.: Do the Bots Send Signals? 01 July 2019. https://www.17lands.com/blog/bot_signals. Accessed 16 June 2021
8. Conroy, R.: Impact of the London Mulligan, 23 October 2019. https://www.17lands.com/blog/london_mulligan. Accessed 16 June 2021
9. Conroy, R.: Simulated Draft Strategies, 28 July 2020. https://www.17lands.com/blog/simulating_draft_strategies. Accessed 16 June 2021
10. Dong, G., Li, J.: Efficient mining of emerging patterns: discovering trends and differences. In: Proceedings of KDD, pp. 43–52 (1999)
11. Du, X., Pei, Y., Duivesteijn, W., Pechenizkiy, M.: Exceptional spatio-temporal behavior mining through Bayesian non-parametric modeling. Data Mining Knowl. Disc. **34**(5), 1267–1290 (2020). https://doi.org/10.1007/s10618-020-00674-z
12. Duivesteijn, W., Feelders, A.J., Knobbe, A.: Exceptional model mining - supervised descriptive local pattern mining with complex target concepts. Data Mining Knowl. Discov. **30**(1), 47–98 (2016)
13. Garfield, R.C.: Trading card game method of play. United States Patent US5662332A, United States Patent and Trademark Office, 02 September 1997
14. Giacometti, A., Soulet, A.: Dense neighborhood pattern sampling in numerical data. In: Proceedings of SDM, pp. 756–764 (2018)
15. Herrera, F., Carmona, C.J., González, P., del Jesus, M.: An overview on subgroup discovery: foundations and applications. Knowl. Inf. Syst. **29**(3), 495–525 (2011)
16. Klösgen, W.: Explora: a multipattern and multistrategy discovery assistant. Advances in Knowledge Discovery and Data Mining, pp. 249–271 (1996)
17. Konijn, R.M., Duivesteijn, W., Kowalczyk, W., Knobbe, A.J.: Discovering local subgroups, with an application to fraud detection. Proc. PAKDD **1**, 1–12 (2013)
18. Kralj Novak, P., Lavrac, N., Webb, G.I.: Supervised descriptive rule discovery: a unifying survey of contrast set, emerging pattern and subgroup mining. J. Mach. Learn. Res. **10**, 377–403 (2009)

---

[7] Compare the discussion of the Raise the Draugr/Glittering Frost in Sect. 5.1.

19. 17 Lands: KHM Traditional Draft Game Data, 04 April 2021. https://17lands-public.s3.amazonaws.com/analysis_data/game-data.KHM.TradDraft.tar.gz. Accessed 17 June 2021
20. 17 Lands: Public Datasets. https://www.17lands.com/public_datasets. Accessed 17 June 2021
21. Leman, D., Feelders, A., Knobbe, A.: Exceptional Model Mining. In: Daelemans, W., Goethals, B., Morik, K. (eds.) ECML PKDD 2008. LNCS (LNAI), vol. 5212, pp. 1–16. Springer, Heidelberg (2008). https://doi.org/10.1007/978-3-540-87481-2_1
22. Lucking-Reiley, D.: Using field experiments to test equivalence between auction formats: magic on the internet. Am. Econ. Rev. **89**(5), 1063–1080 (1999)
23. Martin, B.A.S.: Using the imagination: consumer evoking and thematizing of the fantastic imaginary. J. Consum. Res. **31**(June), 136–149 (2004)
24. Sierkovitz: 5000 Words for Snow, 18 February 2021. https://www.17lands.com/blog/khm_snow_decks. Accessed 16 June 2021
25. Sierkovitz: Servant, not Master, 27 April 2021. Available online at https://www.17lands.com/blog/using_wr_data. Accessed 16 June 2021
26. Wrobel, S.: An Algorithm for multi-relational discovery of subgroups. In: Proceedings of PKDD, pp. 78–87 (1997)

Author Index

Printed in the United States
by Baker & Taylor Publisher Services